REHABILITATION COUNSELING
Theory and Practice

REHABILITATION COUNSELING
Theory and Practice

Edited by

Brian Bolton, Ph. D.

Associate Professor and Coordinator of Rehabilitation Education,
Arkansas Rehabilitation Research and Training Center,
University of Arkansas

and

Marceline E. Jaques, Ph. D.

Professor and Director of the Rehabilitation Counseling Program,
Department of Counseling Psychology,
State University of New York at Buffalo

University Park Press

Baltimore

UNIVERSITY PARK PRESS
International Publishers in Science, Medicine, and Education
233 E. Redwood Street
Baltimore, Maryland 21202

Typeset by The Composing Room of Michigan Inc.
Manufactured in the United States of America by Maple Press Company.

Library of Congress Cataloging in Publication Data

Main entry under title:

Rehabilitation counseling.

Selection of articles drawn from the first 20 volumes of Rehabilitation counseling bulletin.
Includes bibliographical references and index.
1. Rehabilitation counseling — Addresses, essays, lectures. 2. Rehabilitation research — Addresses, essays, lectures. 3. Rehabilitation counseling — Study and teaching — Addresses, essays, lectures.
I. Bolton, Brian F. II. Jaques, Marceline Elaine, 1920—   III. Rehabilitation counseling bulletin.
HD7255.5.R39   362.8'5   77-18287
ISBN 0-8391-1199-1

CONTENTS

Section V **Rehabilitation Counselor Education**

DEDICATION

On behalf of the rehabilitation counseling profession, the editors are pleased to dedicate this volume, which commemorates twenty years of publication of the *Rehabilitation Counseling Bulletin,* to the first twenty presidents of the American Rehabilitation Counseling Association. Their untiring efforts and purposeful leadership are responsible in good part for the existence of an outstanding professional organization and a highly respected academic journal.

1958–1959	Salvatore G. DiMichael
1959–1960	William M. Usdane
1960–1961	Abraham Jacobs (Deceased)
1961–1962	Lloyd H. Lofquist
1962–1963	Cecil H. Patterson
1963–1964	William Gellman
1964–1965	Daniel Sinick
1965–1966	John F. McGowan
1966–1967	John E. Muthard
1967–1968	Marceline E. Jaques
1968–1969	Martin H. Acker
1969–1970	Leonard A. Miller
1970–1971	Gregory A. Miller
1971–1972	Richard W. Thoreson
1972–1973	George E. Ayers
1973–1974	Lawrence B. Feinberg
1974–1975	George N. Wright
1975–1976	Thomas L. Porter
1976–1977	Raymond A. Ehrle
1977–1978	Bob G. Johnson

CONTRIBUTORS

William A. Anthony Associate Professor, Department of Rehabilitation Counseling, Boston University

Ben N. Ard, Jr. Professor of Counseling, San Francisco State College

C. D. Auvenshine Director, Rehabilitation Counseling Program, University of Kentucky

Lois Bendix Psychotherapist, Chestnut Hill Psychotherapy Associates, Chestnut Hill, Massachusetts

Jerold D. Bozarth Professor and Chairman, Department of Counseling and Human Development Services, University of Georgia

Duane Brown Professor and Coordinator, Counseling Psychology Program, University of North Carolina

Robert R. Carkhuff Chairman, Board of Directors, Carkhuff Institute of Human Technology, Amherst, Massachusetts

Robert P. Clark School Psychologist, Greensboro, North Carolina

Corrine S. Cope Professor, Department of Counseling and Personnel Services, University of Missouri-Columbia

Arnold B. Coven Assistant Professor of Rehabilitation Counseling, Wayne State University

John Fenoglio Assistant Deputy Commissioner of General Programs, Texas Rehabilitation Commission

William I. Gardner Professor, Department of Studies in Behavioral Disabilities and Rehabilitation Research and Training Center in Mental Retardation, University of Wisconsin-Madison

Suzanne M. Gaughen Assistant Professor, Department of Counselor Education, California State University at Sacramento

Robert J. Grantham Assistant Professor of Community Psychiatry, State University of New York at Buffalo

Dwight R. Kauppi Associate Professor of Rehabilitation Counseling, State University of New York at Buffalo

Shlomo P. Kravetz Senior Lecturer, Department of Psychology, Bar Ilan University, Ramat Gan, Israel

Joseph T. Kunce Professor, Department of Counseling and Personnel Services, University of Missouri-Columbia

Daniel C. McAlees Director, Research and Training Center, University of Wisconsin-Stout

Greta Mack Registrar, Arkansas State University

Robert Masson Professor of Rehabilitation Counseling, West Virginia University

Douglas E. Miller Assistant Professor, Counseling Center, Michigan State University

Stephen T. Murphy Assistant Professor of Rehabilitation Counseling, Syracuse University

John E. Muthard Head, Rehabilitation Research Institute, University of Florida

Heather Nicholas Formerly Research Assistant, West Virginia Rehabilitation Research and Training Center, West Virginia University

James C. Parks Director and Professor, Institute for Human Development, Northern Arizona University

C. H. Patterson Professor of Educational Psychology, Emeritus, University of Illinois at Champaign-Urbana

Kathleen M. Patterson Counselor, First Step ADA Center, Nashville, Tennessee

B. Douglas Rice Assistant Professor, Arkansas Rehabilitation Research and Training Center, University of Arkansas at Fayetteville

Richard Roessler Associate Professor, Arkansas Rehabilitation Research and Training Center, University of Arkansas at Fayetteville

Stanford E. Rubin Associate Professor, Arkansas Rehabilitation Research and Training Center, University of Arkansas at Fayetteville

Herbert Rusalem Co-Director, The Learning Capacities Research Project, Glen Ridge, New Jersey

Paul R. Salomone Professor of Rehabilitation Counseling, Syracuse University

Horace Sawyer Research Associate, Rehabilitation Institute, Southern Illinois University at Carbondale

Brockman Schumacher Professor and Coordinator, Rehabilitation Counselor Training Program, Southern Illinois University at Carbondale

Robert B. Slaney Assistant Professor, Department of Psychology, University of Akron

Peter Slowkowski Instructor-Trainer, New England Volunteer Employment Service Team, Waltham, Massachusetts

John M. Stamm Anchorage, Alaska

Joseph M. Steger Assistant Professor of Rehabilitation Counseling, State University of New York at Buffalo

J. Blair Stone Professor of Educational Psychology, University of Utah

Kenneth R. Thomas Associate Professor and Chairman, Department of Studies in Behavioral Disabilities, University of Wisconsin-Madison

Howard E. A. Tinsley Associate Professor, Department of Psychology, Southern Illinois University at Carbondale

Robert J. Wagner Psychologist, Buffalo Psychiatric Center, Buffalo, New York

Martha Lentz Walker Associate Professor and Coordinator, Rehabilitation Counseling Program, Kent State University

Richard T. Walls Professor of Educational Psychology and Rehabilitation, West Virginia Rehabilitation Research and Training Center, West Virginia University

Marlene S. Winter Professor, Department of Psychology, Carlow College, Pittsburgh, Pennsylvania

EDITORS

Brian Bolton, Associate Editor of the *Rehabilitation Counseling Bulletin,* is Associate Professor and Coordinator of Rehabilitation Education at the Arkansas Rehabilitation Research and Training Center, University of Arkansas at Fayetteville. He is author or editor of five textbooks in rehabilitation counseling, author or co-author of 150 publications and presentations in rehabilitation and related areas, past president of the Southwestern Multivariate Society, Fellow of the American Psychological Association, and has received seven ARCA Research Awards, including the 1975 National Award.

Marceline E. Jaques, Editor of the *Rehabilitation Counseling Bulletin,* is Professor and Director of the Rehabilitation Counseling Program at the State University of New York at Buffalo. She is past president of the American Rehabilitation Counseling Association and The Council of Rehabilitation Counsel Educators, and a Fellow of the American Psychological Association. She has written extensively in the rehabilitation counseling literature and has received both an ARCA Research Award and a Distinguished Service Award.

PREFACE

With the June 1977 issue, the *Rehabilitation Counseling Bulletin* completed twenty years of publication. To commemorate this publication milestone, we selected 33 outstanding articles from the first twenty volumes and made arrangements with University Park Press to publish them as a book of readings. As the title suggests, all 33 articles are focused on rehabilitation counseling; published articles concerned predominantly with the client, attitudes toward disability, research methodology, etc., were not considered for inclusion. Thus, *Rehabilitation Counseling: Theory and Practice* contains especially noteworthy articles that pertain to the work roles and professional training of rehabilitation counselors.

Volume 1, Number 1, of the *Bulletin of Rehabilitation Counseling* was published in March, 1958, under the editorship of Lloyd H. Lofquist, starting with a format devoted to news and materials of interest to professional workers in the field of rehabilitation. Beginning with Volume 3, September, 1960, a new format included both professional manuscripts and news, and that date marked the first use of the name *Rehabilitation Counseling Bulletin*, with Daniel Sinick as editor. In total, *Rehabilitation Counseling Bulletin (RCB)* has had seven editors. These include, besides Lloyd Lofquist, Daniel Sinick, and the current editor, Marceline E. Jaques, the following persons: Bernard Somers, Martin Acker, Frank Touchstone, and Jane Ayer. Fourteen assistant or associate editors have also been involved in developing *RCB* during this period.

In additon to commemorating twenty years of service by the *RCB* to the rehabilitation counseling profession, we believe that this volume will serve as a textbook for several rehabilitation education courses and various inservice training seminars, and as supplementary reading in many rehabilitation-related professional courses. The selected articles cover the entire spectrum of rehabilitation counselor functioning, from professional issues to educational preparation. We have organized the articles into five sections that parallel standard divisions within rehabilitation counseling courses in order to make the book most useful for educational purposes. In addition to the 33 *RCB* articles, we have included the 1974 revision of the ARCA policy statement on the preparation of rehabilitation counselors, which was heretofore unpublished and available only in mimeographed form.

With the one exception just noted, all articles in *Rehabilitation Counseling: Theory and Practice* are reprinted with the permission of the American Personnel and Guidance Association, which is the copyright holder, and the authors. The original *RCB* citations are included in the footnotes on the first page of each of the articles. We wish to express our sincere thanks to the authors of the articles, who are all listed in the Contributors section with their current affiliations, and to Paul Brookes, Executive Editor of University Park Press, for undertaking this project. Special thanks are given to Helen Foulke, Patty George, and Nell Spencer for assembling the index.

The American Rehabilitation Counseling Association (ARCA) has officially endorsed the book, which, incidentally, was undertaken on an entirely nonprofit basis on the part of the editors and contributors. We hope that we have represented the best interest of ARCA, the *RCB,* and the rehabilitation counseling profession.

Brian Bolton
Marceline E. Jaques

Section I

REHABILITATION COUNSELING
Professional Issues

1 Editorial Introduction

This section provides exclusively a historical perspective on the emerging profession of rehabilitation counseling. The six articles comprising the section are presented in chronological order: the first four are concerned with the problem of professional identity, while the last two address issues of continuing professionalization. In the first article, Patterson outlines four trends that he observed in 1961: an increasing specialization of services, an increasing variety of situations in which rehabilitation counselors work, the professionalization of rehabilitation counseling, and the recognition of the common interests of special education and vocational rehabilitation.

In the second paper, Rusalem chides rehabilitation counselor educators for relying too much on courses taught in psychology, social work, education, etc., rather than developing their own self-contained programs. (The counter-argument, in favor of "borrowing" from other departments and disciplines, is based on the premise that rehabilitation counseling is, in fact, an interdisciplinary profession. Despite the protestations of Rusalem and others, rehabilitation counseling programs have remained much more broad-based than have many other helping professions, e.g., social work, psychiatric nursing, etc.)

In the next article Stone describes the basic differences between rehabilitation counseling and other forms of counseling for the purpose of "defining what has proven to be a rather ambiguous discipline." He locates the uniqueness of rehabilitation counseling in three areas: the degree of maladjustment that characterizes the clientele, the extent of responsibility assumed by the rehabilitation counselor, and the focused expectations of the client. In particular, rehabilitation clients are seriously impaired, clients expect that rehabilitation counseling will lead to job placement, and the rehabilitation counselor is responsible for providing assistance ranging from therapeutic counseling to community adjustment.

Next, Patterson considers the advantages and disadvantages of specialization within rehabilitation counseling. He argues that specialization may legitimately be construed to mean the development of knowledge of and understanding of clients who have specific disabilities. However, he rejects the concept of specialization of rehabilitation counselor function, maintaining that rehabilitation counseling has a general purpose: to deal with the psychological problems of clients. (It is interesting to note that at the time this article was written, there was apparently only one specialized rehabilitation counseling training program. Now there are several, e.g., rehabilitation of deaf clients, job placement, psychiatric rehabilitation, vocational evaluation, administration, etc.)

In conjunction with their now-classic study of the roles and functions of rehabilitation counselors, which is summarized in Section IV, Muthard and

Salomone asked 70 leaders in rehabilitation to describe what they believed would be the major tasks of rehabilitation counseling in 1980. After the presentation of the leaders' projections, these authors discuss the consequences of some of the anticipated changes. The changes include a continued emphasis on work and life adjustment services, greater use of the team approach and interdisciplinary services (see the articles by Wagner, and Roessler and Mack in Section III), and the expansion of undergraduate programs.

The final article in this section consists of brief descriptions, in question and answer format, of two procedures that complete the formal establishment of rehabilitation counseling as an independent profession: 1) certification, which is the examination and approval of the individual counselor as a professional practitioner, and 2) accreditation, which pertains to the assessment of rehabilitation education programs. Both processes are concerned with standardized evaluation and the ultimate improvement of professional practice in rehabilitation.

The six articles in this section well document the development of rehabiltation counseling from stepchild of the counseling and guidance movement to an independently recognized speciality within the helping professions. Although the roles and functions of the rehabilitation counselor have become increasingly differentiated from other types of counseling practice, rehabilitation counseling continues to be an interdisciplinary profession with a broadbased foundation for education and practice.

2 Trends in Vocational Rehabilitation Counseling

C. H. Patterson

In a rapidly growing or changing field, trends are often difficult to discern. We can never be sure whether what we see is actually there, or whether we have projected it into the situation. What I see may not be what others see. Moreover, even if we can agree on what we see, there may be varying interpretations of the facts.

The rapid expansion of rehabilitation services makes it difficult to pick out trends, to tell what is significant or insignificant, essence or accident. Certain facts are clear—more clients will be served and served earlier in the rehabilitation process, services will be extended to the more severely disabled and to special disability groups to a greater extent, especially the emotionally disturbed, the mentally deficient and the aged. But will this expansion be limited to the approaches we now use—will it be more of the same, or will there be changes in the methods and techniques, and in the settings in which services are rendered? I think there is some evidence that the latter is occurring. I can only touch briefly on several of what are to me significant trends in the current expansion of vocational rehabilitation counseling services.

In any expanding and developing field, one of the characteristic developments is an increasing specialization of services. This, then, is the first trend on which I would like to comment. In a broad and complex field, when expansion takes place, there is a tendency to break the job down into parts, for more efficient performance of the needed services. This is usually resisted by those in the field; it is being resisted by some rehabilitation counselors today. Counselors want to feel that they are not limited in the services which they provide to a client. They feel a responsibility to try to meet all the client's needs, to handle the case from beginning to end, from case finding to placement and follow-up. There are no doubt some advantages to such a plan.

But with the increasing knowledge about each phase of the process of vocational rehabilitation, no one person can hope to be highly skilled or competent in every aspect, or with every type of client. To attempt to be so results in a jack-of-all-trades and master of none. Professionalization means specialization. Such specialization will be of two kinds. First, there will be specialization within the rehabilitation process.

Presented at the Annual Conference, Region V, National Rehabilitation Association, Detroit, Michigan, May 16, 1961. The three articles by Dr. Patterson reprinted in this volume are also included in his book *Rehabilitation Counseling: Collected Papers*, Stipes Pub. Co., 1969.

Reprinted by permission from the December 1961 *Rehabilitation Counseling Bulletin*, pp. 59–67.

Counselors will tend to do more counseling, and less clerical work, less public relations work, less social work, less placement. Or, to some extent, the professional aspects of the vocational rehabilitation process will be broken up, with counselors specializing in the various parts of the process, such as intake and eligibility and feasibility determination (which has become a separate function already in California), evaluation or psychological testing, counseling per se, placement, supervision of training or during follow-up, social casework or therapeutic counseling. Secondly, counselors will specialize in the clients they serve, becoming experts in particular disability areas. This trend will be and is being resisted, but it seems to me to be inevitable. Every field of work has gone through this process in becoming professionalized. Social work clearly illustrates this, first in defining its particular place and function, in the total array of services given to individuals, and in specialization according to the type of client served.

An objection to such specialization has been that the client is a whole person, and cannot be broken up in providing services. It is true that every client *is* a complex social organism. But it is the very complexity which makes it impossible for one person to serve all his needs. We have already accepted this in the major divisions of the total rehabilitation process, that is, in the separation of the functions of medical or physical rehabilitation, or therapy, and vocational rehabilitation. Within the medical rehabilitation process there is also further specialization. Although

there are those who say it would be desirable for the doctor to carry out the total process, this is not only unrealistic, but actually undesirable where, as must be the case, the doctor cannot be both a medical specialist and a rehabilitation counselor at the same time. If rehabilitation counseling is, or is to become, a profession, it must specialize, it must be something more than a routine clerical or administrative process of coordinating services, which the doctor or anyone untrained in counseling could do if he had the time. Doctors do not feel that they have to perform all the services in the medical area, even, but utilize ancillary professions and technicians. If seems to me that the medical profession is developing a better appreciation of the complexity and professional nature of rehabilitation counseling, and we should continue to foster this attitude of respect by limiting ourselves to the providing of professional services.

A second trend in vocational rehabilitation is the increasing variety of situations in which counselors are working. There is growing recognition that every institution or hospital should have rehabilitation counseling services. And more and more it it is being accepted that these services should be on an itinerant or visiting basis, but provided by the institution itself, by counselors who are staff members of the institution. Counselors are thus working in new settings, institutional or otherwise. This means that the counselor must adapt to new situations, new kinds of personnel. There is a need to define, or redefine, duties and functions in these situations, and for working out problems of overlap in services among community organizations which have sprung up and grown "like Topsey," with no planning or coordination.

With counselors working in varied settings, the nature of their services, their duties and functions, will change. There is thus perhaps a trend away from rigid definitions of what a rehabilitation counselor is and should do. While this might seem like an undesirable trend, it is tied in with another trend. This again is a trend which is perhaps controversial, which is perhaps being resisted, but which I believe is inevitable. This is the trend to define and to train rehabilitation counselors as generic counselors, to use as a social work term. We cannot expect to train rehabilitation counselors for the specific situations in which they will work. We do not have the time to train them for all possible situations. We can only give them the basic training required in all the varied situations. And this training—and here again I might be biased and therefore mistaken—is basically psychological. The future need in rehabilitation counseling, it seems to me, is for psychologically trained counselors. Rehabilitation counseling is not a unique, entirely different or new field of work—a separate profession. It is part of the profession of counseling. Rehabilitation counselors are psychological counselors working with physically and mentally handicapped clients. Their uniqueness is small, compared to what they have in common with other psychological counselors. It is, therefore, in my opinion desirable for pro-

fessionalization of the field, and a present trend, for rehabilitation counselors to be identified, and to identify themselves, with a general field of psychological counseling. By doing so they will best achieve the professionalization which is necessary if they are to function adequately in the type of work which appears to be developing in the field of vocational rehabilitation.

There is a third trend, related to the two already mentioned, but which deserves separate consideration. This is the professionalization of rehabilitation counseling. There are several evidences of progress in professionalization. These may be discussed in terms of the criteria of a profession as listed by Wrenn and Darley (4).

1. First is the performance of a socially needed function. There is now no question of the need for rehabilitation counseling. Society has, through its government agencies, given us a mandate to fulfill this need.

2. The definition of job titles and functions. The title rehabilitation counselor is now established and generally accepted. There is a DOT code number for the position. While there may still be lack of unanimity about all the functions of a rehabilitation counselor, it is becoming increasingly accepted that his major and most professional function is counseling. "Any emerging profession must justify its claim to certain unique skills which other professions and the general public do not have access to" (2). The one thing which the rehabilitation counselor does that other workers in rehabilitation do not do, and cannot do because of its professional

nature, is counseling. The building of the rehabilitation counselor's job around the counseling function is thus fostering the professionalization of his functions.

3. A third criterion is the existence of a body of knowledge and skills. While some would feel that this body of knowledge and skills of the rehabilitation counselor consists in knowledge of disabilities and special skills in working with the disabled, and thus would claim that rehabilitation counseling differs from counseling in general, or is unique in this respect, this would seem to be a mistaken approach to professionalization. Other workers in rehabilitation share this knowledge and these skills, so that the rehabilitation counselor is not unique among them in this respect. Rather, as indicated above, the rehabilitation counselor is unique in rehabilitation in the possession of knowledge and skill in counseling. The sharing of this with other counselors, rather than weakening his professional position, strengthens it, since he can share the gains in professionalization of counseling as a whole.

4. A fourth characteristic of a profession is the application of standards of selection and training. Here also there is evidence of progress. Selection constitutes a problem, as it does in all professions, and I have dealt with this in detail elsewhere (3). In the area of training, we now have established graduate programs. There is general agreement on the basic content of the training. The problem for the future is similar to that of other professional training programs—the incorporation into a time-limited program of as much

desirable content as possible. We must recognize that it is impossible to include everything that. is desirable, or everything that everyone thinks is relevant or desirable.

5. A fifth characteristic of a profession is the self-imposition of standards of admission to practice and of professional performance. In this area we are just beginning. But there are groups at work on the development of professional standards. The existence of an accepted training program provides a base for admission requirements.

6. A sixth characteristic of a profession is the development of professional consciousness and professional groups. This is something that perhaps must precede most of the other characteristics of a profession. There is no question but that there is now a strong professional consciousness among rehabilitation counselors. The establishment and rapid growth of the Rehabilitation Counseling Division of NRA and the Division of Rehabilitation Counseling of APGA are sufficient evidence of this consciousness.

7. Seventh is the development of a code of ethics. This also is an area in which, although no final product has been achieved, there is much activity. A code of ethics was adopted by the APGA in Denver in March, 1961, which provides a basis for a general code for counselors, including rehabilitation counselors. The Rehabilitation Counseling Division of NRA has a committee working on a code of ethics specifically for rehabilitation counselors.

8. Finally, a profession ultimately acquires legal recognition by certification

or licensing of practitioners. It is too early to expect such progress in this area, but there has been some thought given to achieving this goal. One state (Oklahoma) already has a certification procedure (1).

There is thus considerable evidence that rehabilitation counseling is achieving the characteristics of a profession, and this progress represents a current trend and an area of future development.

I have time for perhaps one more development. This is a very recent one. It is the recognition of the common interests of special education and vocational rehabilitation. This has been manifested perhaps more by special education than by rehabilitation counseling. The Council for Exceptional Children has had programs on vocational rehabilitation at its annual conventions for the past two years. There is beginning to develop, I think, a reciprocal interest on the part of rehabilitation counseling.

On the one hand, vocational rehabilitation may be conceived of as the ultimate goal of special education. Education is not a goal in itself; it is education toward or for something. While a vocation is not the only goal of education, it is one of the goals, and special educators should be aware of this goal and informed about the process of vocational rehabilitation which follows the educative process in which they are directly involved.

On the other hand, rehabilitation counselors need to be aware of the basic importance of special education as the foundation upon which they build in their vocational counseling and training programs for the disabled. Without the support of an adequate educational program which has enabled the disabled individual to progress and develop educationally to the limits of his potential, the job of vocational rehabilitation is more difficult. One of the problems in the rehabilitation of adults, a problem recognized in the recent White House Conference on Children and Youth, is that of the young disabled adult whose education has not been adequate, but who now is beyond school age, which complicates the remedying of his educational deficiencies.

Now there is no sharp age line between education and vocational rehabilitation. Vocational development begins early in the life of the child, and progresses and is interwoven with his education. Thus one does not limit his concern to education until the age of 16, and then begin the process of vocational rehabilitation. I have suggested that the special educator needs to be oriented towards vocational rehabilitation. The rehabilitation counselor also needs to be educationally oriented. The inadequacy of counseling services to disabled pupils was another area upon which the White House Conference focused. We need more counseling services for the disabled youth in special schools and in our regular schools. While counseling services for the nondisabled pupil are inadequate, they are more inadequate for the disabled pupil.

It is too early to tell just what the relationship of special education and rehabilitation counseling should be. At the working level there certainly should be cooperation and joint activities and efforts, just as rehabilitation counselors work together with various other contributing professions to total rehabilitation. At the training level, I am not sure what is the best way of expressing and implementing our common interests. The curricula are basically different, but there should be some common areas. I am not sure, however, whether there need be or should be any administrative relationship other than that between any two training programs at the graduate level.

These, briefly, are some of the current developments or trends in rehabilitation counseling. I am sure there are others, perhaps even more significant. Another prophet would no doubt select something else for emphasis. But I can do only what any individual can do, that is, to call them as I see them.

REFERENCES

1. Balyeat, F. A. Investing in growth. Rehab. Couns. Bull., 1961, 4:59–63.
2. Mueller, Kate H. Criteria for evaluating professional status. Personnel Guid. J., 1959, 37:410–417.
3. Patterson, C. H. The selection of rehabilitation counseling students. Paper read at APGA Annual Convention, Denver, Colorado, March 29, 1961.
4. Wrenn, C. G., & Darley, J. G. An appraisal of the professional status of personnel work. In E. G. Williamson (Ed.) Trends in student personnel work. Minneapolis: University of Minnesota Press, 1949.

3 Rehabilitation Counseling–The End of the Borrowing Phase?

Herbert Rusalem

Each profession develops in its own idiosyncratic way. Some, like medicine, law, and the clergy, are so old that their beginnings are shrouded in myths. Others are so new that their first few steps toward maturity are still painfully evident. Rehabilitation counseling is a case in point.

Within the lifetime of some of the readers of this journal, this field first emerged, delivered from the womb of P.L. 565 by eminent midwifes, tenderly caring for the fragile infant not yet endowed with an identity. Since then, debates, discussions, and declamations have surrounded the offspring, all designed to give it character and purpose. This is not the time or the place to add to the controversy centering about the nature and need for rehabilitation counseling. With more than thirty institutions of higher education providing training in the field and with the concept of the rehabilitation counselor embedded firmly in rehabilitation legislation and procedure, the act of birth has been completed and is irreversible.

Confronted by this fait accompli, those interested in rehabilitation counseling now have the task of strengthening and nurturing it. One area of current concern is that of content. Virtually every definition of a profession indicates that a field of work earns the designation, in part, when it develops its own unique body of knowledge. Indeed, as one traces the growth of various professions, one of their benchmarks is a body of knowledge and skill that gradually takes shape and characterizes the profession. In the beginning, a new profession borrows liberally from neighbor disciplines, even seeking entrance for its trainees into selected courses offered by the elder brothers. Such a phenomenon can be observed in an emerging field called therapeutic recreation which, in certain institutions, borrows almost half of its training from a school of social work. But, this cannot long endure. Sooner or later, a new field creates its own content or is swallowed up by another profession.

Rehabilitation counseling has grown up in the balmy climate of interdisciplinary borrowing. Lacking a substantial body of knowledge and skill of its own, it has basked in the reflected glow of a dozen other professions. Contrast the rehabilitation counseling curriculum and its tendency to assign its students to medicine, social work, psychology, education, etc. with the firm, well-organized in-group training provided by each of these other profes-

Reprinted by permission from the September 1962 *Rehabilitation Counseling Bulletin*, pp. 30–34.

sions. The student in social work spends his training period firmly rooted under the social work umbrella. It is inconceivable that social workers would agree to have group work trainees spend a half or even a quarter of their training period in recreation, rehabilitation, or other fields. Can you visualize a school of medicine encouraging its students to take a considerable number of courses in other non-medical institutions?

It may be argued that rehabilitation counseling is demonstrating a newer and stronger training pattern; that in borrowing training experiences from other disciplines, we are setting an example of breadth and interdisciplinary awareness. Is this the case or is it merely that we are trying to rationalize our current inability to build a body of content unique to our own field?

The situation varies with different rehabilitation counseling curricula. In some cases, in a master's degree program of some fifty semester hours, the student may take only five or six courses that are clearly recognizable as rehabilitation counseling courses. The others represent administrative arrangements to admit rehabilitation counseling students into courses devised expressly to train graduate students for other professions. In other rehabilitation counseling curricula, the proportion of rehabilitation counseling material is higher, but even in these programs, sizeable segments of the curriculum consist of experiences in courses devised for other professional groups.

An important example (and only one of a number that could be cited) is that of a course in social work, required by many universities in their rehabilitation counselor training programs. Often, this provision seems to have good validity and happily fulfils external pressures toward the "interdisciplinary ideal." But, the rehabilitation counselor is not a social worker. Hopefully, he belongs to a profession that is unique, differing from social work in knowledge, approach, method, and emphasis. Social work shares certain common understandings of human behavior and principles of counseling with many other professions, but this is no argument that these other professions should receive training in a social work course. Indeed, social work has, over the years, borrowed concepts and techniques from vocational rehabilitation but has not prescribed rehabilitation courses for its students.

The argument is often offered that through taking a course in social work or some other discipline, rehabilitation counseling trainees begin to understand a sister profession better and learn to work with its members more effectively. This hypothesis is still unproven. I don't have to enter my neighbor's house and share his food to work well alongside of him. Effective interdisciplinary teamwork seems more related to the encouragement given it by community and agency leaders and to the individual's personality needs than to an intimate induction into the skills practiced by another profession.

I am concerned with the attitudes of rehabilitation counseling trainees, the public image of rehabilitation counseling, and the question of whether we are really a profession. Rehabilitation counseling students who undertake a curriculum that is studded with unrelated courses, many of them borrowed from other departments, schools, and professions, have identity problems. A school teacher has a firm professional image, reinforced, in part, by state certification requirements and a teacher education curriculum almost totally composed of sequences of experiences within a school of education. On the other hand, the rehabilitation counseling student may wander through the thickets of medicine, psychology, social work, teaching, and others. When he completes the program, is he a product of a well-organized curriculum embodying a "discipline," or a victim of a set of disparate experiences borrowed from good neighbors?

Do our practices in using the courses offered by other disciplines add to their respect for us? Experience indicates that they tend to have some of the same questions about rehabilitation counseling what many of us do. If there is insufficient content within our own field with which to construct a curriculum, they ask, are we truly a profession? For example, in one training program in which negotiations were conducted with a school of social work to open one or more of its courses to rehabilitation counseling students, the executive officer of the school of social work wondered what could be gained by training incomplete social workers with a dangerously limited knowledge of the field. He indicated that social work courses were designed to train social workers and, as such, had a viewpoint and an approach distinctive to social work. The only concession he would make was to set up a new course called Social Work for Rehabilitation Counselors to which only rehabilitation counseling students are admitted and which has a semiprofessional emphasis on principles which could be adequately taught by skilled rehabilitation counseling trainers.

In a long experience working with, and training rehabilitation counselors, I have become convinced that we have the makings of a profession. As in the case of other emerging professions, we have had to borrow liberally from other fields to close a gap, that, at best, is only tentative. There should be little difficulty today in identifying the desired rehabilitation counseling content in a training program and teaching that content rather than the content of some other profession. If we need training in interdisciplinary teamwork, there may be alternatives to sitting in on the classes of other professions. For example, some institutions are developing interdisciplinary seminars open to students training for a variety of health professions in which understanding and bases of cooperation may be cultivated.

Have we been deluded by the ideal of interdisciplinary relationships to the point of "watering down" our own profession and our own training programs? I have watched some training institutions scramble around like mad to line up cooperation with other university departments to fulfill the pressures put upon them by fund-granting agencies. Is there inherent goodness in this procedure? Does it insure a stronger rehabilitation counseling program? Or does it impoverish the new profession and underscore its immaturity?

4 Counseling and Rehabilitation Counseling
Differences in Emphasis

J. Blair Stone

Despite many attempts in recent years to define the field of rehabilitation counseling, there continues to be a great deal of controversy over what rehabilitation counseling is or should be. There are those who see the rehabilitation counselor as a professional counselor who simply happens to work in a rehabilitation setting. Thus Patterson (1957) states:

> Counseling is broader than rehabilitation, and its basic principles are the same whether one is counseling children, adolescents, high school students, delinquents, college freshmen, displaced persons, those with marital problems, the emotionally disturbed, or the physically handicapped.

There are also those who see the rehabilitation counselor not as a counselor at all, but as a coordinator of rehabilitation services and a jack-of-all-trades. Clements (1957), in discussing how the rehabilitation counselor sees himself, says,

> In himself and his fellow counselor, he (the rehabilitation counselor) sees a combination of parent, doctor, psychologist, teacher, policeman, public relations expert, personnel manager, placement specialist, and jack-of-all-trades.

Finally, there is a third group which sees rehabilitation counseling as a separate professional entity but which is having difficulty in defining that entity. The present article is an attempt to describe the basic differences between rehabilitation counseling and other forms of counseling in the hope that such a description may help this latter group in defining what has proven to be a rather ambiguous discipline. Briefly, it is the position of this writer that rehabilitation counseling is a counseling profession, but just as there are differences between the psychotherapist and the vocational counselor, there are also important differences between the rehabilitation counselor and counselors in other settings. Before beginning a discussion of these differences, it is necessary to mention one problem in describing the work of the rehabilitation counselor.

Many who have been preoccupied with describing the profession of rehabilitation counseling have concluded that such an attempt is impossible due to the variety of settings in which the rehabilitation counselor finds himself. It must be granted that setting plays an important part in the day-to-day work of the rehabilitation counselor as it does with any professional counselor. Such considerations as case load, degree of supervision, amount of clerical work,

Reprinted by permission from the June 1966 *Rehabilitation Counseling Bulletin,* pp. 127–133.

and physical facilities have a great effect on how the rehabilitation counselor does his job. However, I would submit that, so long as the rehabilitation counselor's basic job is working with the physically or mentally disabled, his role remains essentially the same regardless of setting. The discussion which follows is meant to apply to rehabilitation counseling in all of its settings.

DIFFERENCES

Differences in the Nature of the Client

Some of the most basic differences between the work of the rehabilitation counselor and that of other counselors arise from differences in the nature of the client with whom each works. In discussing the relationship of counseling psychology to psychotherapy, Merrill states, "The major concern of the counselor is with the normal individual in a setting of normal activity."

This deviates sharply from the rehabilitation counselor's concern with individuals suffering from problems of physical and/or mental disability often leading to serious maladjustment. Such persons can hardly be called "normal" and life in a setting of "normal activity" is frequently almost impossible for such persons. In fact, if the client is able to function in a setting of normal activity, he is probably not eligible for rehabilitation services.

Merrill further points out that, since the counselor works with normal individuals in a setting of normal activity, he relies heavily on normative data to assist him in his counseling procedures. The rehabilitation counselor is interested in determining how well his client may compete in society. Therefore, it is helpful to compare his client with the normal population whenever this is possible. However, as Cottle (1958) has said, the rehabilitation counselor cannot rely on normative data in much of his work because his clients are not normal. There is a need to develop normative data for specific disability groups and sub-groups on all kinds of standardized measures. Unfortunately, this kind of work has not progressed very far in the rehabilitation field.

As would be expected from those who work with "normal" individuals, much of the work done by counselors is based on theories of individual differences and developmental theory (Merrill). While the rehabilitation counselor bases much of his work on such theories, it must be emphasized once again that he is not dealing with "normal" individuals. Thus, his work is based heavily on the psychology of disability which, at this stage of its development, is largely personality theory. This distinction is not meant to indicate that the rehabilitation counselor should be a psychotherapist, for his knowledge of personality theory is likely to be limited to the special case of psychology of disability. It can be argued, however, that the training of rehabilitation counselors should place more emphasis on theories of personality.

There is one final difference in the nature of the client that affects the duties of the rehabilitation counselor. This involves the problem of communication. Cottle (1958) has pointed out that communication, which is the basis of counseling interviews, is often more difficult in rehabilitation counseling. This is because disability often directly affects the ability to communicate (the deaf, the blind, the aphasic, etc.). Not only is communication a problem for the rehabilitation counselor, but it is a rapidly changing problem depending on the nature and extent of the client's disability.

Differences in Counselor Responsibility

Merrill points out that the counselor typically stresses an informational and educational approach in his work with normal individuals. This, according to Merrill, is in contrast to the psychotherapist who stresses remedial and curative treatment since he deals with abnormals. The rehabilitation counselor is also best equipped to work on an informational and educational level. The difference between the rehabilitation counselor and other counselors in this regard is in the degree of responsibility that the rehabilitation counselor must assume for the client who needs remedial and curative therapy. When the counselor finds a client who is so seriously ill or maladjusted that he requires remedial help beyond the counselor's competencies, his response is to refer this client to a person or agency who can provide such help. Such action typically ends the responsibility of the counselor toward the client. The rehabilitation counselor, as has been stated, is required to deal with individuals who are not normal and who often require remedial and curative therapy. When this is the case,

the response of the rehabilitation counselor, like that of other counselors, is to refer the client to the proper therapist. This, however, does not terminate the rehabilitation counselor's responsibility for the client. The basic reason why the rehabilitation counselor must accept responsibility for his client, even though the client's needs are beyond the realm of the rehabilitation counselor's competencies, is that in almost all rehabilitation settings the ultimate goal of the rehabilitation counselor is the successful employment of his client. The rehabilitation counselor is, therefore, responsible for his client until the goal of successful employment has been achieved. Not only does the rehabilitation counselor have continuing responsibility for his client, but because of this responsibility he also remains the client's focal point for help until the goal of employment has been achieved. Thus, the rehabilitation counselor remains responsible for his client due to the nature of the rehabilitation goal.

In order to deal with this most difficult problem, the rehabilitation counselor must become more familiar than counselors in other settings with community organization and community relationships if he is to make meaningful referrals and cooperate with these referral sources in the rehabilitation of *his* client. He may also need a better understanding of the remedial and curative aspects of therapy with non-normal individuals than is true of counselors in other settings.

The responsibility the rehabilitation counselor has for the vocational placement of his client deserves special mention. While counselors in other settings may also concern themselves with the placement of some of their clients, it is only in rehabilitation counseling that successful placement becomes the criterion of successful counseling. Thus, the rehabilitation counselor must not only develop competencies in counseling and community organization; he must also develop some of the competencies of the placement specialist.

Differences in Client Expectations

Diller (1959) reports an interesting study involving an analysis of the stated goals of 120 adult males in a medically oriented rehabilitation center. While the findings of this study cannot be generalized to other rehabilitation settings, I believe the findings are suggestive of the type of client expectations which may be encountered by the rehabilitation counselor in almost any setting. Diller found:

> Almost every patient expressed a wish for a return to physical normality or a desire to acquire motor skills. Almost one-half of the group expressed a wish for help in regard to a vocational problem. Less than ten per cent expressed a wish for freedom from worry or tension as a primary goal.

These findings would seem to imply a rather clear-cut expectation on the part of the client that his rehabilitation counselor will provide rather specific services leading to: (1) amelioration of his disability and/or (2) placement on a job. Under these conditions, any attempt on the part of the rehabilitation counselor to deal with problems of personality or adjustment may be perceived by the client as a threat to his goals rather than assistance in achieving them.

In other counseling settings, the client typically has certain felt needs that attract him to a counselor, but these needs are usually more vague and difficult to define than the needs associated with disability. Furthermore, the client is unsure as to how the counselor will meet his needs. In rehabilitation, the client's needs are so overwhelmingly associated with his particular disability that he can perceive assistance as something that will deal directly with that disability and perhaps the associated economic discomfort which the disability may be causing. In this situation, ambiguity, one of the most useful characteristics of the counseling relationship, is missing.

When a client comes to a counselor, he is usually unsure as to what to expect, and thus the counselor can introduce as much ambiguity into the situation as he desires. The counselor does this by the degree to which he defines the topic he considers it appropriate for the client to discuss, by the degree of closeness he exhibits toward the client, and by the determination of goals toward which he and the client will work (Bordin, 1955). The counselor does not necessarily define the above feature of the counseling interview verbally but by his actions and general demeanor as well. Thus, at least initially, it is the counselor who structures the counseling interview and determines the degree of ambiguity he wishes. Ambiguity is important to the counseling relationship because, as Bordin points out,

> From the client's reactions to the ambiguity of the situation, we can

draw inferences about the general nature of his defenses, and from the content and sequence of his responses we can obtain some understanding of his conflicts and the types of relationships with people which embody them.... by being ambiguous, the therapist provides a background against which the client's irrational feelings will be more clearly etched and therefore more readily brought to awareness.

The degree of ambiguity that the client can tolerate is determined in large measure by the anxiety level of the client. If the level of anxiety is excessive, ambiguity simply feeds that anxiety and all the client's energy is directed toward defense. In rehabilitation counseling the client typically is extremely anxious. Furthermore, the client has already defined the topic he wishes to consider in the counseling relationship and the goals toward which he wishes to move. Any departure on the part of the rehabilitation counselor from the topic and goals the client wishes to consider serves only to increase anxiety.

SUMMARY

The foregoing material is an attempt to describe differences in emphasis between rehabilitation counseling and other forms of psychological counseling. These differences involve primarily:

1. differences in the nature of the client
2. differences in counselor responsibility including, especially, the function of placement
3. differences in client expectations and perceptions of the counselor's role.

More specifically, it is the author's thesis that rehabilitation counselors deal with persons who cannot be considered "normal persons in settings of normal activity." As a result, they cannot rely as much as most counselors do on normative data but instead must either ignore much normative data or develop their own. Communications problems are also much more likely to occur in the work of the rehabilitation counselor than is true in other fields of counseling. In addition, there is the possibility that rehabilitation counselors should receive more training in personality theory as the basis for their work.

In terms of counselor responsibility, it appears that the rehabilitation counselor is usually responsible for his client up to and including successful job placement, regardless of the severity of his client's problems and the nature of the therapy required. The rehabilitation counselor must thus become expert in the field of community services and community organization. Since placement is usually the goal of the rehabilitation counselor's work, he must develop skills in this area exceeding those of counselors in most other settings.

The rehabilitation counselor faces a special problem in that he is likely to be perceived by his clients as a person who will provide specific services. These services are typically perceived in terms of amelioration of disability and job placement. Thus, the client's perceptions along with his high level of anxiety may eliminate from the rehabilitation counseling relationship one of the most useful tools of counseling—ambiguity.

REFERENCES

Bordin, Edward S. Psychological counseling. New York: Appleton-Century-Crofts, 1955.

Clements, Stanley W. The counselor as he sees himself. J. Rehabilit., 1957, 23(3), p. 5.

Cottle, William C. Special problems of the rehabilitation counselor. J. Counsel. Psychol., 1958, 5, 295–299.

Diller, Leonard. Psychological theory in rehabilitation counseling. J. Counsel. Psychol. 1959, 6, p. 189.

Merrill, Reed M. The relationship of counseling psychology to psychotherapy. Unpublished paper. Department of Educational Psychology, University of Utah, Salt Lake City.

Patterson, C. H. Counselor or coordinator? J. Rehabilit., 1957, 23(3), p. 13.

5 Specialization in Rehabilitation Counseling

C. H. Patterson

We live in an age of specialization. The development of new specialities seems to be continuing in all areas of our lives. In the face of increasing specialization, each of us becomes a layman in more and more aspects of life and knowledge, with increased feelings of inadequacy accompanying increased respect for experts.

To anyone who becomes aware of what is happening in science and the professions, it becomes clear that specialization is inevitable. Knowledge increases at a geometrical rate. Francis Bacon, it is said, knew about all that was to be known in his day. Today this is beyond the capabilities of a single mind. We are facing problems of information storage and are turning to machines to help us. A whole new specialty of information storage and retrieval is being developed, consisting of people who know no subject matter in the traditional sense but who know how to store and retrieve subject matter information.

Rehabilitation itself is a specialty in the general area of medical, social, and psychological services. In the medical field, physiatry or physical medicine is a recent specialty. In the field of counseling, rehabilitation counseling at a professional level is a recent development within the field.

Specialization is a natural development in a situation where there are large numbers of clients who form clearly definable subgroups, or where complex professional functions can be easily or logically subdivided. Thus we have specialties in medicine related to differences among patients, such as age, and differences in the nature of the disease or disorder. There are also specialties in terms of functions, such as surgery, radiology, etc.

Since specialization is inevitable, our problem is one of utilizing its advantages while minimizing its disadvantages. This involves the determination of rate of specialization, avoiding overspecialization, or specialization for which we are not ready, or that is not warranted by the state of our knowledge. In some cases specialization may provide more advantages than disadvantages, but may be too costly to develop and adopt.

ADVANTAGES

In rehabilitation counseling we are seeing the beginning of both kinds of specialization. In terms of function,

From a paper presented at the Conference on Vocational Rehabilitation Counselor Specialization: Cause and Effects, sponsored by the Georgia Division of Vocational Rehabilitation, Atlanta, Georgia, April 29–30, 1965.

Reprinted by permission from the June 1967 *Rehabilitation Counseling Bulletin,* pp. 147–154.

there is the beginning of specialization in the function of placement. Specialization has proceeded farther in terms of kinds of clients, or disability areas, since this has developed naturally. Counselors have become interested in clients with a particular disability. They begin to become sensitive to special problems related to the disability, and special needs of the clients. They become more knowledgeable about the disability, more aware of the individual differences among those having the same disability. They learn more about ways of working toward rehabilitating such clients. They become experts in the area. Other counselors consult them about clients having the same disability. Or, they refer some of their more difficult clients to the experts. Eventually, most, if not all, cases with the particular disability are assigned to the counselor who is recognized as an expert. In short, he has become a specialist.

This process indicates one of the advantages from the point of view of the counselor. It is an advantage that has not been sufficiently recognized. Specialization allows an individual to find and engage in an occupation or profession that is more closely suited to his interests, aptitudes and abilities, and personality than would be possible without specialization. It allows for the exercise of his unique characteristics and pattern of traits. It thus makes possible a greater degree of satisfaction in his work.

The other side of this advantage to the counselor is an advantage to society and to clients. Specialization capitalizes upon individual differences,

and makes possible the maximum use of the talents and abilities of the individual for the good of society. The individual who is more satisfied with his job does a better job. The individual utilizing special talents is a better professional or practitioner. The specialist, therefore, renders better service not only because he is better trained or prepared to do so, but because he is better fitted to do so in terms of his interests, aptitudes, and abilities.

The advantages of specialization seem to be recognized, even by those who resist specialization. Counselors who are opposed to the development of specialization would strongly resist being limited to the services of a general practitioner if they were seriously ill, or for their own clients. They want the services of specialists when they seem to be indicated.

Thus, specialization is not only inevitable, it is desirable. However, there are problems, or disadvantages, that accompany specialization. Whether all of these are necessary or inevitable is a question. Some of them probably are not inevitable, but can be avoided.

DISADVANTAGES

The major disadvantage associated with specialization is the breaking of the individual into parts. The client may be seen and dealt with as a problem, as a disease, or a disability, rather than a total person. Now it is true that specialization requires focusing upon an aspect of the whole person. This is necessary, and specialization would not be possible without it; this is a price we must pay for specialization. But this concentration upon an aspect of an individual need not mean the complete neglect of other aspects or of the individual as whole. In fact, the specialist must view the disease or disability as a part of a whole if he is to understand or treat it adequately.

In counseling there is a danger in a problem orientation to clients. The counselor who focuses upon a particular problem, be it educational, vocational, social, marital, or what, is not able to deal adequately with the client. This has been the problem with traditional vocational counseling, which has isolated the vocational aspects from the rest of life. Vocational problems were dealt with apart from emotions, and were attacked in a logical manner by providing information and attempting to reason with the client. Many counselors, among them rehabilitation counselors, still use this approach with clients. Fortunately, it is being recognized that vocational or occupational choices involve feelings and emotions, as do all choices. If he is to function adequately, the vocational counselor must be more than one who knows tests and measurements, and occupational information and opportunities. He must be able to recognize, understand and therapeutically handle affect and feelings. The vocational counselor must be a psychological counselor, in other words.

It may appear that I am saying there is no place for specialization in counseling. To an extent this is the case, for in a broad sense there is no specialization of function. All counselors have the same general function: to deal with psychological problems of clients. Counselors may specialize in clients with certain kinds of problems, but they are all psychological problems or the client would be seeing another professional person.

Thus counseling is fundamentally the same, regardless of the particular problem or the kind of client. Nevertheless, there are some differences related to particular kinds of clients. These differences do not relate so much to the counseling relationship as to the ability of the counselor to develop and continue an appropriate relationship with the client on the basis of understanding the client and his problems and his needs.

It seems, therefore, that by the very nature of counseling, the individual must be dealt with as a whole if counseling is actually to occur. While a client might be dealt with piecemeal, as by providing certain material services such as a prosthesis, if counseling is to occur then he must be dealt with as a whole. If counseling is to be successful, then the counselor must understand the client as a unique individual. Specialization with a particular kind of client enables the counselor to know the common problems and needs of such clients, and to recognize individual differences among them rather than lumping them together as a homogeneous group. He is then better able to understand and thus to help such clients.

Specialization in rehabilitation counseling is thus in terms of developing a knowledge and understanding of clients possessing specific disabilities, as a basis for working more effectively with such clients. It does not involve the utilization of any new, unique, or highly specialized techniques of counseling, although it may include the use of specialized resources, facilities, or personnel for their rehabilitation.

PROBLEMS OF SPECIALIZATION

There are certain practical problems of specialization that are often raised. One of these is related to the concern for the individual as a person. The use of specialists usually involves referrals, and this means that the client must work with a greater number of individuals. There are those who contend that it is undesirable for the client to have to relate to many different persons. But life is a process of relating to different people. It is not the matter of referral that is bad; it is the way in which the referral is made, the way in which the client is treated by the different people who work with him. Clients do not object to being referred to specialists if they understand what is going on. Too often the client is treated as an object rather than an individual, and is shuffled back and forth from specialist to specialist. It is not the use of specialists that creates the difficulty, but the way in which they are used. The procedure of referral too often assumes that the client does not need to know what is happening to him, that he would not understand anyway, and that he should not know the nature or results of special examinations or studies. The difficulty lies in the acceptance of these assumptions and their influences on referral,

rather than anything inherent in referral and the use of specialists.

Thus it should not be a problem for a counselor who first comes in contact with a client who has a disability that is dealt with by a special counselor to make a referral to that counselor. Rather than impairing the attitude toward and the relationship of the client with the agency, it should lead to a better attitude and relationship, since the client will appreciate being provided the services of a specialist. Perhaps some of this referral from one counselor to another might be reduced by centralized case finding, eligibility determination, and assignment of clients to the appropriate counselor.

There is of course a problem in providing specialized counseling services in rural or sparsely settled areas. The question might be raised as to whether such clients are denied specialized medical services. They usually are not, though there may be a tendency to less readily obtain such specialized services. Usually it is accepted that the client can travel to the specialist. However, where counseling is concerned, the reverse seems to be the practice, both in terms of efficiency in the use of the counselor's time and the professional nature of the counseling relationship. This is not to deny the value, in some cases, of a visit to the client's home, or the inclusion of his family in any plans, but why cannot the client travel to the counselor? A regional office arrangement, which is the organization of the Veterans Administration, would permit having specialized counselors serving a geographical area, perhaps around a fairly populous city or town.

These problems with regard to specialized counselors do not seem insurmountable, once it is recognized as desirable to use them. These problems do not exist, of course, where the counselor is a part of the staff of an institution that serves clients with a particular disability.

PREPARATION FOR SPECIALIZATION

Perhaps the most difficult problem at present is the matter of adequate preparation for functioning as a specialized counselor. Most of the counselors now functioning as specialists have not had extensive special preparation for their work as part of a regular counselor education program. Any specialized preparation they have had probably has been obtained in special workshops or short courses, for there are no long-term rehabilitation counselor education programs that are preparing specialists. All the rehabilitation counselor education programs of which I know are preparing general counselors.

Now, if it takes two academic years to prepare a general counselor, it must take longer to prepare a special counselor. The fundamentals of counseling are the same, regardless of the client, whether he is disabled or not, or the nature of his disability. Therefore, it is not reasonable or possible as one counselor has suggested (Harper, 1965), to concentrate upon training for work with a specific disability and to accomplish this in the same period of time. The specialist requires additional preparation beyond that of the general counselor if he is to function any more adequately with a specific disability group than a general counselor. And it should be primarily on the basis of special skill derived from special training that differential pay is justified. To be sure, it is possible to learn from experience, or through on-the-job training, but this cannot continue to be an adequate basis for a profession. Where and how, then, is the counselor to obtain such specialized training.

It is of course possible for a student to obtain some background in a special disability area during his general preparation in rehabilitation counseling. All students get some exposure, in lectures and reading, to the nature and problems of the major disability areas. In addition, a student can probably make a special study of an area as a project or term paper. Then in his field training, placement may be in an agency or institution specializing in a specific disability.

However, the general training program in rehabilitation counseling does not provide sufficient background in a specialized field to prepare specialized counselors. I believe it would be undesirable to attempt specialization in the regular program. Courses dealing with special disabilities would crowd out basic courses in psychology and counseling, resulting in inadequate preparation in counseling. There would be the danger that rehabilitation counseling would become separated from the basic field of counseling and become splintered into a group of specialties, with the special counselors being inadequately grounded in counseling.

Many counselor educators believe that the preparation of rehabilitation counselors involves basic preparation in counseling, with students in rehabilitation taking many of their courses with school counselors and those preparing for work in other institutions or agencies, such as the state employment service. This is the position of the American Personnel and Guidance Association (1964) in its statement on the preparation of counselors, which applies to all counselors in all settings. This statement is to be supplemented by statements applying to the preparation of counselors for specific settings, such as rehabilitation. The period for this basic preparation is two academic years.

It is apparent, therefore, that specialized training must be in addition to the present two years of graduate preparation for rehabilitation counselors. If undergraduate programs could be planned better, there might be room for more specialization than at present in the two-year program, although I doubt that much could be done.

The line that such preparation could take is illustrated by what I believe is the only program for the preparation of specialists that currently exists. This is the program for the preparation of counselors in the area of the deaf, located at the University of Illinois and supported by a VRA grant. This program prepares not only rehabilitation counselors, but teachers of the deaf, researchers, college teachers, and administrators. The preparation for counselors for the deaf consists of a one-year program for students who have completed the general rehabilitation counseling program.

The addition of a year or more for the preparation of specialists to the current two years required for the preparation of general counselors has implications for salary levels. It is only reasonable to expect that additional specialized preparation will require a higher salary scale.

SUMMARY

In summary, we may say, with some confidence, that specialization is inevitable, in rehabilitation counseling as in all other professional fields. It is of course possible that specialization can proceed too rapidly, that is, before there is sufficient knowledge and skill to warrant specialists and programs for preparing specialists. It is also probable that specialization may be warranted in only a few disability areas, which present special problems, such as the blind, the deaf and hard of hearing, the mentally retarded, and the emotionally disturbed.

If specialization is inevitable, then we should prepare for it by considering the nature of the special preparation that is desirable. It is contended that such special preparation must be built upon the present two-year program for the preparation of rehabilitation counselors. Specialists are still counselors, and cannot skip over the basic preparation necessary to become counselors. Specialization requires preparation above and beyond the regular preparation for general counseling. Such preparation should consist of specialized study of the nature of a particular disability, and the needs and problems of clients with such a disability, so that the counselor will better understand his clients and be better able to assist them in their rehabilitation.

Specialization seems to be becoming generally accepted. However, programs for the preparation of specialists do not now exist. We must move forward from the workshop and short-term study programs for the preparation of general rehabilitation counselors.

REFERENCES

American Personnel and Guidance Association. The counselor: professional preparation and role. (A statement of policy.) Personnel and Guidance Journal, 1964, 42:536–541.

Harper, R. B. Professional dilemma? NRCA News, 1965, 7(2): 3.

6 The Future Roles of the Rehabilitation Counselor

John E. Muthard
and Paul R. Salomone

Futurists are persons with the temerity to speculate on the future. We do not aspire to such status. Instead, we wish to report the predictions of rehabilitation leaders about the work of the rehabilitation counselor in 1980. In addition to summarizing the expectations of rehabilitation leaders, we will offer some of our own speculations.

As part of a study of roles and functions (Muthard & Salomone 1969), we asked a group of 70 individuals, who were rehabilitation leaders in 1966, to systematically describe the major tasks of the rehabilitation counselor in the future and to comment upon the goals which would guide them in 1980. For this study, leaders in rehabilitation included persons in the following positions or settings:

1. Directors or program administrators of rehabilitation centers and facilities (*n*—12)
2. Rehabilitation counselor educators (*n*—13)
3. State DVR directors and directors of commissions for the blind, and Vocational Rehabilitation Administration personnel at the national and regional levels (*n*—25)

They were asked to anticipate new settings in which the counselor would work, the kinds of clients he would serve, and the types of services he would provide. These rehabilitation leaders included occasional high-flying futurists, but for the most part they stepped into the future with one foot still in the past.

COUNSELOR TASKS

The rehabilitation leaders' responses to the Abbreviated Rehabilitation Counselor Task Inventory consisted of 40 statements of counselor activities in counseling, vocational and social diagnosis, psychological testing, arrangement and coordination of rehabilitation services, placement and follow-up, and collaboration with other rehabilitation workers. The task inventory data showed that rehabilitation facility administrators, counselor educators, and state and federal administrators did not differ in their projections of the extent to which future counselors would perform various job functions. The results also indicated that the rehabilitation leaders did not think the level of involvement in specific job tasks for rehabilitation counselors would change to any great extent. Rehabilitation leaders expected counselors to become more active in building client work motiva-

This article is adopted from a speech presented at the American Rehabilitation Counseling Association's Annual Meeting in Chicago, March 27, 1972.

Reprinted by permission from the December 1972 *Rehabilitation Counseling Bulletin,* pp. 71–79.

tion, group counseling, placement and follow-up, and collaboration with other rehabilitation workers. Counselors were expected to be less involved in psychological test administration and medical information decision making.

GOALS

The responses of the rehabilitation leaders to four open-ended questions were more provocative, although more difficult to summarize. We noted several themes in reactions to the question, "How will his goals be different from those of present day counselors?" One theme was the anticipated broadening of the counselor's responsibilities to include concern for the total development of the client and his family and the provision of extensive follow-up services. However, several thought the counselor would relinquish responsibility for placing the client in a job and expected that task to be taken over by nonprofessional specialists. Such views are exemplified by statements such as: "He will deal more with social, cultural, and environmental handicapping factors" and "Not only [will he] work with the client but also with the family constellation. Those goals will involve total adjustment of the client. . . ."

A second theme with respect to goals was broadening services so individuals who—because of age, disability, or other circumstances—were not employable could get help to cope with their problems. For example, "[The counselor's] rehabilitation objectives will not be confined to vocational reinstatement but will be whatever is needed by the client for effective functioning. Among his important goals will be prevention."

Leaders in this group differed in the degree to which they saw vocational adjustment for clients as the future counselor's primary goal. Some expected this goal to be emphasized even more. A small minority expected the counselor to turn away from the vocational emphasis. However, most rehabilitation leaders thought there would be a broadening of the goals counselors would set with their clients rather than a de-emphasis of vocational goals.

Rehabilitation leaders working within the state/federal program in nearly all instances saw a continuation of concern for helping the client become employable. About half of the group saw little change in goals, but expected some change in emphasis: "Although the major emphasis will continue to be on vocational goals, we will recognize and give increasing concern to the fact that many of our clients will not be full-time workers." "The goals should be the same; the difference will be the methods of achieving them." "Goals will be concerned with assisting the client to develop and maintain his highest potential of self-sufficiency and social contribution, with or without remunerative work as we now conceive of it."

SETTINGS

Many rehabilitation leaders outside the state/federal program predicted that the rehabilitation counselor would enter correctional settings, community hospitals, and other community based programs to a much larger extent than in the past. A few saw the counselor as being more frequently based in school settings.

Few of the rehabilitation leaders mentioned the extent to which the worker in the new settings would participate in the state vocational rehabilitation system. However, the pattern of extending vocational rehabilitation services seems to have held for many programs which have been established in prisons, correctional centers, mental health community centers, and mental hospitals. In a similar vein, the state/federal leaders thought the rehabilitation counselor would be found more often in community settings such as schools, prisons, rehabilitation facilities, and the like. Leaders in state/federal programs also frequently mentioned the counselor working in the community with public welfare clientele. One response which reflects this expectation was that the counselor will work in comprehensive service centers "where all the needs of all the indigent, disadvantaged, and disabled are met." Another similar response indicated that counselors would work "possibly to a much greater degree in institutions dealing with people in trouble— prisons, half-way houses, mental hospitals, correctional schools, and the like."

CLIENTS

Rehabilitation leaders were unanimous in anticipating that the 1980 counselor would work with a broader range of clients and particularly with the disadvantaged. It was also expected that there would be less restriction on the establishment of client eligibility and that the counselor would work with clients who are not only physically handicapped but may have other kinds of adjustment problems. Typical of such responses is one state director's forecast that counselors would work with "all persons needing specialized help in securing and retaining suitable positions in the community." Another state director expected that counselors will ultimately serve the "educationally, socially, and economically disadvantaged (disabled), as well as those traditionally defined as handicapped." A substantial minority expected "that the client would be the person who is not productive, but who has a potential for productivity after training."

SERVICES

In predicting possible changes in the range of services the counselor would provide, most state/federal professionals mentioned a broad range of services or more complex services. More emphasis was expected upon conventional activities such as job placement, follow-up services, and supportive counseling after placement, as well as the novel (for vocational rehabilitation in 1967) provision for family services. As one regional office representative put it, "More services will be provided in the context of family needs rather than individual needs."

Another major theme with several state directors in the group was the expectation that there would be less concern with physical restoration and a greater variety of educational, social, and vocational services. A few state directors anticipated that technological developments in orthotics and prosthetics would lead to dramatic changes in the extent and quality of physical restorations.

Rehabilitation leaders in the private and university sector often mentioned the probability of greater specialization by the counselor, with increased emphasis upon the counseling or vocational adjustment role. They also thought there would be more emphasis on client psychological adjustments: "Thus, [I expect] more counseling, comprehensive evaluations, training, placement, and especially more effective follow-up services."

Although many persons in both leader groups expected that 1980 would see a notable change in the range and breadth of services, it is noteworthy that about half of the group anticipated relatively little change in the pattern of counseling services. The same leaders tended to see services being improved through specialization or through refocusing the counselor's efforts upon critical aspects of the rehabilitation process, rather than through major changes in counseling procedures or in the delivery of case services.

PROFESSIONAL DEVELOPMENTS

In reacting to an open-ended question asking for supplemental comments, one of the more provocative comments was provided by a specialist in rehabilitation and occupational medicine who said:

Our current and pending legislation demands strong, aggressive coun-

selors to get programs going. We need a greater public image of the counselor. He must be a person who, all of his life, planned to be a counselor and must not be a medical drop-out or a lower IQ health activities aspirant. We need sharp, bright, non-passive leaders who can hold their heads up with the rest of the team.

To the same question a prominent rehabilitation educator stated:

The professional organizations of the rehabilitation counselor [need] to exercise leadership in establishing his identity and strengthening his confidence. Interorganizational rivalries (especially ARCA vs. NRCA) must be brought to an end soon.

To some degree that particular plea has proven prophetic since the two rehabilitation counseling associations have undertaken a series of joint professional activities.

More dramatically, one facility administrator expected that vocational rehabilitation agencies would no longer exist:

All services, except medical, would be provided by the Labor Department in manpower centers. They will use multidisciplinary staff—the rehabilitation counselor as he now exists will be no more, since specialized staff can do a much better job—the days of the generalists are numbered.

Although the Department of Labor manpower programs and Community Service Administration case service programs have assumed an increasing rehabilitation aura and orientation, the likelihood that there will be no place for the competent rehabilitation counselor still appears rather remote. It seems that rehabilitation counselors, especially those with an MA level education, have proven capable of adapting to new programs and undertaking more complex and responsible jobs than their counterparts in public welfare and employment service offices. One sign of this phenomenon is the number of well-qualified rehabilitation counselors who attain administrative positions in new programs, while interviewers and caseworkers may be found migrating to the rehabilitation agencies. To some extent, these comments may seem chauvinistic, but they point to the viability of the individualized rehabilitation approach and the lasting value of basic rehabilitation counselor education programs.

THE FUTURE OF REHABILITATION COUNSELORS

In the immediate future, rehabilitation counselors, educators, and administrators will need to cope with three major developments: (a) the reordering of national priorities and goals; (b) the impact of the current manpower shortage on rehabilitation services and present steps being taken to alleviate this insufficiency; and (c) the trend toward greater accountability of counselors and agencies. Although the extrapolation from past events to future trends in social service programs may be hazardous, the first development is already upon us. The current emphasis on vocational rehabilitation services to reduce dependency of individuals who are receiving public assistance will be a major determinant of the type of clients seen and the type of services provided by counselors. The increasing concern among legislators and the executive branch of government for the plight of

the aged may also have long-run implications for counselors.

When these priorities are linked with the present national concern for delivering health services to all people and with the debates about welfare reform and income maintenance, it seems that the future rehabilitation counselor will be working with an even broader and larger clientele than he currently serves.

As a consequence of the increased demand for services to facilitate the work and life adjustment of the disadvantaged, we anticipate that there will be a continuing strong demand for individuals capable of providing work and life adjustment services.

It is not only the current legislative discussions which suggest the need for an expansion of rehabilitation services, but also the rising expectations for viable programs in the health and income maintenance areas and the changing social philosophy which they seem to reflect. The changing social climate has had a strong impact on the present national administration. Responding to a public mandate, a conservative administration has reacted by proposing a welfare reform bill which lays the groundwork, however inadequate, for income maintenance. The fact that the present administration has proposed programs in many social service areas reflects a belief that the American people think these services are desirable and are willing to pay for them.

As we see it, the consequences of this increased concern for ameliorating the plight of our disadvantaged citizens will be a marked increase in the demand for rehabilitation-type services, as well as some changes in the administrative arrangements for delivering such services. It seems likely that by 1980 many of the independent and dispersed agencies which provide fragmented services to the disadvantaged will be functioning within a state/federal system that will unify the services in a more efficient manner. Within this framework, program coordination and integration will be established at a level that is now impossible because of interfering regulation, petty rivalries, and the cost in time and energy imposed by physical distance between agencies. Within such multi-service centers, the professionals and other workers involved will collaborate in small teams to meet the needs of particular clients. They will request the services of specialists who may be a part of the organization or who are available on a consultation basis.

Such programs will likely require professional individuals of different types and varying levels of competence. The widespread introduction of these programs will result in a move away from the rehabilitation or social work generalists so that individuals with competencies in vocational and psychological counseling will spend more time with clients who need such services and spend relatively little time providing the coordinating and expediting services. In the multiservice center, the main needs of clients will determine which team member would have primary responsibility for assisting the client. Such an arrangement will probably increase the need for individuals prepared at the baccalaureate level to function effectively as social service and rehabilitation specialists. These specialists will not need to have exten-

sive preparation in conducting intensive counseling interviews, but will instead be expected to have a broad knowledge of the individual, the community services, and the basic skills involved in providing a helping relationship.

Similarly, the work of the integrated program will provide an opportunity for individuals who have high school or junior college level preparation to function as placement specialists and expediters of rehabilitation and social services. At the bottom of the career ladder, we envision the academically unqualified individual working with special client groups as an outreach person. He might serve as a bridge between the minority group client and the social service team. In addition, if a minority group member, he will be a consultant to his colleagues on the special problems and needs of the group of his origin.

Thus, one consequence of the anticipated development and change of national priorities is the likely increase in educational programs at the bachelor's degree level designed to meet the manpower needs of the rehabilitation and social services. Although this may be distressing to some rehabilitation counselor educators, it is our view that such a development will serve to strengthen and clarify the roles and functions of the professionally qualified rehabilitation counselor. It may also lead to better counseling for clients and greater work satisfaction for counselors. Such a change may also strengthen the graduate programs by providing a relevant undergraduate background for individuals having an interest in and commitment to rehabilitation or social services.

Furthermore, with an undergraduate program as a base for graduate study, educators will be better able to prepare counselors to perform the vocational-psychological counselor role. With such an undergraduate background the vocational components of counselors' preparation can also be strengthened. Counselors can develop an increased capability to assist clients with occupational exploration, vocational decision making, and vocational adjustment. With junior college programs preparing individuals to be human relations aides, a reality which exists in many communities now, it would be essential to establish a workable career ladder which will enable supportive personnel with the interest, commitment, and talent to progress in the rehabilitation field.

As we look to the future work of rehabilitation counselors, it seems likely that our profession must begin to assess the extent to which those who profess rehabilitation counseling as a profession are abreast of the best present procedures. It seems likely that we will not be satisfied with lifetime qualification for counselors, but that we may, within the decade, elect to require our peers to show through proficiency examinations or continuing education a knowledge of and competence in applying the best current practices.

Clearly, the next decade will be a time of change and challenge. From their long history of useful service and continued growth, it seems reasonable to expect that rehabilitation counselors will cope with the new realities and accept the challenges to grow and improve their capabilities. Leadership to promote positive community change and a strong advocacy for client rights will be among the rehabilitation counselor's privileges and responsibilities. We look for a hopeful and exciting future in rehabilitation for the rehabilitation counselor.

REFERENCE

Muthard, J. E., & Salomone, P. R. The role and functions of rehabilitation counselors. Rehabilitation Counseling Bulletin, 1969, 13:81–168.

7 Toward a New Professionalism
Certification and Accreditation

Daniel C. McAlees
and Brockman Schumacher

CERTIFICATION *Daniel C. McAlees*

What Is Certification in Rehabilitation Counseling?

The primary purpose of certification is to establish professional standards whereby disabled individuals, related professionals, agency administrators, and the general public can evaluate the qualifications of persons practicing rehabilitation counseling. Certification has as its primary impetus the provision of assurances that professionals engaged in rehabilitation counseling will meet acceptable standards of quality in practice. Such standards are considered to be in the clients' best interests.

How Did Certification Develop, and How Is It Organized in Rehabilitation?

The certification program is a direct outgrowth of the concern of the two professional associations—American Rehabilitation Counseling Association (ARCA) and National Rehabilitation Counseling Association (NRCA)—to establish standards and consequently stabilize the field of rehabilitation counseling and to provide a baseline for future professional growth. These two associations appointed a joint committee on certification which became an independent incorporated Commission on Rehabilitation Counselor Certification. The Commission consists of five appointees from ARCA, five appointees from NRCA, and one each from the Council of Rehabilitation Education, Council of State Administrators of Vocational Rehabilitation, International Association of Rehabilitation Facilities, National Association of Non-White Rehabilitation Workers, Council of Rehabilitation Counselor Educators, and a representative from a national consumer organization.

Who Is Eligible for Certification?

Professional rehabilitation counselor certification may be established by:
Graduation with a master's degree from an accredited rehabilitation counseling training program, which includes a supervised internship and one year of acceptable experience in rehabilitation counseling;
Attainment of a master's degree in rehabilitation counseling, not including a supervised internship, or a master's degree in a related area (as defined by the Commission) along with two years experience in rehabilitation counseling;
Attainment of a master's degree equivalency level by (a) graduation with a

Reprinted by permission from the March 1975 *Rehabilitation Counseling Bulletin*, pp. 160–165.

bachelor's degree in rehabilitation, along with four years of acceptable experience in rehabilitation counseling or (b) graduation with a bachelor's degree, along with five years of acceptable experience in rehabilitation counseling.

"Grandfathering" those members who meet the above criteria will be carried out until July 1975. Membership in ARCA, NRCA, and/or an allied professional association will be a prerequisite for "grandfathering." After July 1975, all persons who qualify for certification will be required to demonstrate competence in the following content areas on a certification examination: (a) rehabilitation philosophy, history, and structure; (b) medical aspects of disability; (c) psychosocial aspects of disability; (d) occupational information and the world of work; (e) counseling theory and techniques; (f) community organization and resources; (g) placement processes and job development; (h) the psychology of personal and vocational adjustment; (i) evaluation and assessment; (j) the ability to use research findings and professional publications.

What Are Specific Features of the Certification Program?

The main features include (a) a commission broadly representative of the entire field of rehabilitation; (b) participation in the development of a certification examination by all present members of the profession who apply for grandfathering; (c) the use of supervisor and peer evaluations to supplement examination data; and most im-

portantly, (d) the establishment of minimum standards for practice as a rehabilitation counselor.

What Is Grandfathering?

Those persons currently working in the profession who meet the minimum educational, experiential, and professional affiliation standards outlined above will not be required to demonstrate competence on a certification examination. They will be required, however, to take the examination for field review purposes.

How Do I Apply for Certification?

All inquiries regarding certification and requests for application forms should be directed to the Commission on Rehabilitation Counselor Certification, 520 North Michigan Avenue, Suite 1504, Chicago, Illinois 60611; telephone—(312) 644-4329.

Please Discuss the Examination— What Is It? How Do I Prepare for It? and Where Do I take It?

The examination is a practice-based examination; therefore, it is not necessary for an individual to do a great deal of studying prior to the examination. In fact, intensive study may not help a person pass this kind of examination. Items included in the examination put a higher premium on the application of knowledge in managing clients rather than on isolated bits of factual information.

The first field review was held on 19 July 1974 at 40 sites, and the second on 15 October 1974 at 21 sites. The third field review will be held 22 March 1975. The primary site for this field review will be New York City in conjunction with the annual ARCA-APGA meeting.

Two additional field reviews have been scheduled: one on 18 July 1975 (deadline for applications, 1 April 1975) and one on 12 October 1975 (deadline for applications 1 July 1975). Sites for these field reviews will be selected based on the location of the applicants. Any geographical or organizational entity of rehabilitation counselors may determine the most appropriate site for administering the field review within their area. When twenty or more counselors can be brought together under the conditions set by the Commission for the field review, the Commission will administer the examination at the site requested. A checklist detailing criteria for site selection is available on request. If you would like to arrange for a site in your area, please contact the Commission office.

The field review will be available in a Spanish translation, and the Commission will provide equal access and opportunity to participate to all disabled counselors who apply.

What Will Certification Cost Me?

The total fee for certification during the grandfather period is $45. Fifteen dollars of this total fee should be sent with the completed application. When approved, you will be assigned to a field review site and requested to send the remaining $30 of this fee. These fees reflect the total cost for certification and no additional fees will be assessed for annual renewal of the certification certificate.

What Will Be the Effects of Certification on Rehabilitation Counseling as a Profession?

The intent is not to certify that any individual is suitable for employment or attempt to impose personnel requirements upon any agency; the intent is to establish a national professional scale which any interested group, agency, or individual may use as a measure. It would be hoped that voluntary cooperation by a majority of rehabilitation counselors would, over time, exercise an increasing influence on the field and ultimately guide legislation, personnel practices, and training programs. Aside from establishing a good measure of professional qualifications for the counselor, certification will further the public interest and the confidence of other professions and clients.

To date, more than 5,000 rehabilitation counseling professionals have made application to participate in the certification program, an overwhelming and revealing response. It is evident that rehabilitation counselors are encouraging, through certification, a higher level of performance and qualifications that will benefit both the public and the profession.

ACCREDITATION
Brockman Schumacher

What Is Accreditation?

Since the United States has no federal ministry of education, the responsibility to ensure quality training programs for practicing professionals rests with individual states, educational institutions, and professional organizations. Thus, accreditation is concerned with the quality of educational programs in certain institutions and professions. This process entails nongovernmental self-evaluation of training within a professional discipline. It serves to identify acceptable levels of training so as to maintain high standards and to establish goals for self-improvement in professional education.

Is There any Relationship Between Accreditation and Certification?

Although both accreditation and certification are assessment processes, there is no formal or procedural relationship between the two. However, both these processes are concerned with evaluation and improvement of professional practice and, therefore, they are parallel in nature. Constant dialogue concerning issues, criteria, objectives, and goals is necessary to deal with ongoing, crucial matters associated with a profession.

How Did Accreditation Develop in Rehabilitation Counseling?

In 1970, leadership from the American Rehabilitation Counseling Association (ARCA), the National Rehabilitation Counseling Association (NRCA), the Council of Rehabilitation Counselor Educators and Council of State Administrators of Vocational Rehabilitation, and the International Association of Rehabilitation Facilities recommended establishing a planning committee to address itself to the issues of accreditation. This planning committee became

incorporated and developed strategies for the accreditation process. These strategies included procedures, instruments, and standards, which received approval of the National Commission on Accrediting.

Presently the Council on Rehabilitation Education (CORE) is composed of two representatives from each of the participating professional rehabilitation organization. CORE's major responsibility now is the implementation of the accreditation process, program assistance, and development.

What Are the Features of the CORE Approach to Accreditation?

The major emphasis of CORE's approach to accreditation is on program development and improvement, rather than mere formal approval. During the pilot phase of developing the accreditation process, site visits were used as a basis for evaluation. These have now been replaced by a systematic, research-based collection of data on a particular training program, although site visits may be used as supplemental sources of data when needed. The data include both a review of the training program itself and employer evaluation of the program's graduates. The accreditation process also stresses continued reevaluation of its methods, criteria, and standards.

How Does a Training Program Become Accredited?

A training program must meet initial eligibility criteria and be evaluated and approved by CORE's Commission on Standards and Accreditation.

What Is Expected from a Program Undergoing the Accreditation Process?

The faculty is expected to carefully complete a Program Evaluation Self-Report Schedule, which reviews curriculum, faculty, and students. Cooperation in supplying further information or collecting more data for the Commission is essential. Successful implementation of specific recommendations for improving a program's standards is also expected.

What Advantages Are There to a Program's Being Accredited?

The major advantages in accreditation are to ensure self-evaluation and to assist in the improvement of preparation programs for rehabilitation counselors. The achievement and maintenance of quality in preparation programs accrue special advantages to consumers—applicants, students, graduates, employers, and the general public. Publication of a program's mission and status among other programs in the country lead to the knowledge of its standing in relation to accepted professional criteria of preparation in rehabilitation counseling.

What Does It Cost?

A fee of five hundred dollars is charged for the accreditation year or initial participation in the process. In order to sustain accreditation, the program must continue contact with the Commission yearly. A fee of two hundred dollars is charged for this continued support.

The individual program must bear the cost of accreditation and any additional expenses, if a site visit is necessary. In the case of providing assistance in program development, CORE has a separate fee schedule.

How Often Does a Program Need to be Reevaluated?

Reevaluation for continued accreditation must occur every five years. In some instances, special conditions will be set which might make accreditation more frequent.

What Is the Value of Accreditation to the Profession of Rehabilitation Counseling?

The basic purpose of accreditation is to ensure quality education of rehabilitation counselors, thereby promoting the effective delivery of vocational rehabilitation services to persons with handicaps. The accreditation procedure will promote program self-improvement as a regular system. Accreditation will assist in placing rehabilitation counseling on a par with other professional desciplines. Finally, and most importantly, such procedures ensure a level of excellence in professional training with the ultimate goal of improving service delivery to rehabilitation clients.

Section II

REHABILITATION
COUNSELING
Individual Approaches

8 Editorial Introduction

The articles in this section and the one that follows are concerned with various techniques and procedures used by the rehabilitation counselor. The division into individual approaches and system approaches parallels the longstanding distinction in the rehabilitation counseling literature between "counselor" and "coordinator" roles. Many counselor educators believe that the central activity of the rehabilitation practitioner should be one-to-one counseling with disabled clients, while others maintain that the primary role of the rehabilitation counselor is that of a coordinator of diverse services. What was once a highly debated issue has more or less been resolved with the recognition of the fact that counseling and case management are both important job functions of the rehabilitation counselor.

The first and second articles in this section pertain to counseling with special populations. Patterson discusses the unique circumstances surrounding the disabled college student. After outlining three areas of counseling—admissions counseling, educational-vocational counseling, and therapeutic counseling—he poses five questions of special interest to counselors who may work with severely disabled college students. Although this paper was written 15 years ago and many of the architectural and attitudinal barriers faced by this group have been alleviated, the basic problems discussed by Patterson are much the same now as they were then.

Gardener and Stamm begin by reviewing the research literature on traditional counseling relationships with mentally retarded young adults and conclude that counseling and psychotherapy with this population "remains a vague, ill-defined, and suspect form of behavior intervention." They argue that a learning theory approach to counseling with mentally retarded clients, while requiring a different role for the counselor, has been demonstrated to be successful in changing behavior. The extension of the learning paradigm to systematic work with groups is discussed in the article by Walls and Nicholas in the next section.

Kravetz and Thomas also adopt a learning approach in their article addressing a specific client problem: the inability to make vocational decisions. They outline a counseling strategy based on the principles of verbal operant counditioning. This presentation illustrates how a relatively straightforward procedure can be used to deal with a complex problem that is not uncommon among rehabilitation clients. Readers may find a challenging conceptual exercise in attempting to apply the general principles discussed by Kravetz and Thomas to other types of counseling problems.

The next article, by Brown and Parks, examines the role of nonverbal behavior in the counseling relationship and thus serves to complement the preceding article, which deals with verbal interview behavior. The authors hypothesize that by becoming aware of their own as well as their clients' nonverbal behaviors—eye contact, gestures, and use of personal space—rehabilitation counselors can work more effectively with their clients. Following brief reviews of the research literature, implications for the rehabilitation counselor are discussed.

The final two articles in this section each outline a highly popular counseling theory and discuss its potential application in rehabilitation counseling. First, Ard gives an overview of rational therapy and illustrates how the rehabilitation counselor might employ this procedure. Rational therapy, as the name implies, focuses on the cognitive aspects of the client's problems; the counselor helps the client identify and discard irrational ideas and self-defeating values. Because of rational therapy's seeming disregard for clients' feelings, this article provoked several reactions, (e.g., the article by Miller and Porter, 1969). Coven describes the fundamentals of the theory of Gestalt therapy and relates this approach to rehabilitation counseling philosophy and practice. In contrast to simple, direct techniques utilized in rational therapy, the Gestalt approach is diffuse and all-encompassing. It provides an existential framework in which the counselor can help the client move toward self-sufficiency and self-fulfillment.

REFERENCE

Miller, L., and Porter, T. 1969. Reactions to Ard's "Rational therapy in rehabilitation counseling." Rehab. Couns. Bull. 12: 130–135.

9 Counseling the Severely Handicapped College Student

C. H. Patterson

The number of physically handicapped applicants for college education is rapidly increasing. Fouracre in his foreword and Rusalem in his monograph (3) note that this increase is the natural result of the spectacular growth of special education in the public schools in the past decade. Rusalem estimates that the number of handicapped applicants and students runs into the tens of thousands. Many of these, of course, have minor handicaps or limitations. But an increasing number is severely handicapped. And the range of handicaps represented includes all those which occur, with the exceptions of mental deficiency or mental retardation and the disabilities associated with and limited to old age.

In the past, many of the severely disabled have resigned themselves to accepting the closing of college doors to them and have not applied for admission. Others have been discouraged from applying by well meaning counselors who felt that there was no point in obtaining college or professional education only to face unemployment because of their disability—a practice advocated by Cruickshank (1). I have indicated elsewhere (2, pp. 277-278) that this is an unacceptable point of view. We cannot suggest or expect that counselors or college admission officials take this attitude. The severely handicapped are now pounding on the college doors, and these doors must be opened to them on the same basis as to the nonhandicapped.

ADMISSIONS COUNSELING

The selection of students through the admissions process is an activity in which staff members trained in counseling should be involved. The background of such staff members should include training and experience in working with the disabled. While it could be maintained that staff members trained in counseling should be involved in the admission process with all students, there are several reasons why it is necessary in the case of severely disabled students.

While mass screening of nondisabled applicants on the basis of standard criteria applied to data contained in the application is possible without doing great injustice to many of the appli-

Presented September 1, 1962, at the American Psychological Association Convention, St. Louis, Missouri.

Reprinted by permission from the December 1962 *Rehabilitation Counseling Bulletin,* pp. 58–69.

cants, the severely disabled must be dealt with on an individual basis if they are to be fairly evaluated.

Many of these applicants have an atypical educational background. They may not have attended public schools consistently, but may have attended special schools or hospital schools, or have had home instruction. Grades obtained in such situations may not be equivalent to those on the records of able-bodied applicants. One must know this background, if only to recognize that little if any confidence can be placed in grades as a measure of achievement.

This means that more emphasis must be placed upon other measures, such as objective tests. Such test results may not be available from the public schools, either because the applicant did not attend, or if he did, because he may not have been able to take the standard tests used in the school. This means that the administration of tests, usually on an individual basis, adapted to the particular disability, may be necessary. Often, however, test results may be available from another source. Many disabled applicants are sponsored and supported by State Divisions of Vocational Rehabilitation. These applicants will have test results available. But the particular tests will vary, depending upon the residence of the applicant, since no standard batteries are used. Moreover, the results of such tests will need to be evaluated. It should be apparent that evaluation of academic potential may be a difficult task and requires a person who is thoroughly trained in tests and measurements.

In addition, individual attitudes, motivation, and personality factors may be more significant in the case of the severely disabled applicant. These factors are to some extent included in achievement as indicated by grade point average in the case of able-bodied applicants, but less so in the case of a severely disabled applicant. Therefore, it is necessary to evaluate these factors on an individual basis. While sources such as personality inventories and recommendations by former teachers *may* be helpful, the individual interview by a trained interviewer must be relied upon as the major source for the evaluation of motivation and other personality factors.

The evaluation of the physical capacities of the applicant also is essential. This requires a staff member who is knowledgeable in the area of disability, who can understand and interpret medical records and evaluations. And while such records are necessary and useful, they are not always sufficient. They should be supplemented by the interview. Medical consultation and examinations may be required to supplement the records and the interview. The emphasis here is upon the physical capacity to adapt to the college environment, not upon the etiology and treatment of the disability. However, admissions officials must be alert to recognize the applicant who has not had adequate or complete medical treatment, whose physical capacities could be improved by further treatment, either prior to admission, if necessary, or following admission while in attendance at college.

The scarcity of physicians who are specialists in physical medicine or physiatry, and the lack of information concerning new developments in this field by general practitioners, means that one should look carefully at each applicant, rather than accepting a general medical report. It is true that applicants who are clients of State Divisions of Vocational Rehabilitation are likely to have had adequate evaluation and treatment. But there are still some applicants whose condition, while presumed to be stationary, may be improved by additional treatment. This suggests that a college which has any number of disabled applicants should have a staff physician, or at least a consultant, who is a specialist in physical medicine.

Along with the appraisal of the physical capacity of the applicant, there must be consideration of the physical demands of the environment. Rusalem suggests that every college should make a survey of the physical plant, so that the physical demands of the environment will be known. Often the physical demands will vary among different curricula, so that it is necessary to know the specific demands of the curriculum the applicant plans to enter. Some departments may be housed in, and hold all its classes in, a building which is inaccessible to wheelchair students.

The applicant and the college environment can then be compared to determine if they are compatible. Some college environments may be suitable for students with some limitations but not to students with others. In some cases the environment may be adapted by a slight modification, or a greater modification which can easily be made. It would be unreasonable to expect a college to make major changes for a single student. We must accept the fact that some applicants may be unable to meet the requirements of any college, and unfortunately not be able to acquire a college education. Sometimes the physical capacities of the applicant can be modified or increased by treatment or training, or a limitation can be removed by a prosthesis or other special aid.

The process which has been briefly summarized has been referred to as admissions counseling. I have refrained from using the word counseling, however, or the word counselor, but instead have referred to interviewing and to a staff member trained in tests and measurements and counseling.

The admissions process is mainly one of selecting rather than counseling. Its major emphasis is upon evaluation as a basis for accepting or rejecting an applicant. But while this is not counseling, the process should be permeated by a counseling attitude and may include some counseling. Rusalem recommends a "counseling interview" following notification of the applicant of the admissions decision. This I would agree is desirable, but I am not sure that a rejected applicant, or even an accepted one, would be able to become a client following the evaluation process. But I do feel that, although the process and the interview following the decision may not be therapy, it should and can be handled therapeutically, which is what I think Rusalem means, and only a person trained in counseling can be expected to be able to do this adequately. However, Rusalem does suggest that such an interview with an accepted applicant "has the value of reinforcing the counseling relationship so that it may be most effectively used by the accepted applicant in his later college experience" (3, pp. 77–78). But the evaluative attitude and process, no matter how well handled, may prevent the accepted applicant from seeing the admissions person as a counselor, if by counselor we mean one who avoids evaluation and a judgmental attitude. This suggests that the counselor who works with accepted applicants who become students should not be involved in the admissions process.

EDUCATIONAL-VOCATIONAL COUNSELING

The fact that the physical demands of curricula may vary, indicates that educational-vocational counseling may be a part of the admissions process. Of course, as in the case of able-bodied students, the disabled student will probably enter a general curriculum for the first two years, and select a major later. For the applicant who is interested in a professional curriculum which requires some specialization during the first two years of college, the physical demands of such a curriculum must be considered. Even when specialization comes after the first two years, it is desirable to consider the long range plans of the applicant during the admissions process.

Applicants who are sponsored by a State Vocational Rehabilitation Division usually have had extensive vocational counseling, since a specific vocational plan with a vocational objective is required before support is given. Such plans should be reviewed during admission.

It is therefore apparent that the severely disabled applicant is under pressure to think of education in vocational terms. The admissions procedure thus must include provisions for vocational counseling where it is indicated, or where some vocational choice must be arrived at before a decision on admission can be reached. Those who feel that there is no conflict between evaluation and educational-vocational counseling, or that such counseling involves evaluation, may feel that the same staff member who evaluates the applicant can engage in educational-vocational counseling with him. However, I have indicated elsewhere (2) that in my opinion educational-vocational counseling should be and can be free of evaluation by the counselor. Thus, I would question the desirability, if not the possibility, of the same staff member evaluating the applicant and engaging in educational-vocational counseling with him.

As I have indicated above, many disabled applicants will be sponsored by State Vocational Rehabilitation Divisions, and thus may already have had vocational counseling. The admissions staff will have the records of such counseling for review. It may be, of course, that during the admissions process occasion may arise to modify or change these plans. In such cases, of course, any such change will need to be approved by the State Division.

In addition, disabled students, like other students, may need and want educational-vocational counseling following admission. Counselors who are trained and experienced in vocational rehabilitation should be available to provide this service. Rehabilitation counselors, in addition to the qualifications of the vocational counselor who works with the able-bodied client, are familiar with the nature and limitations of physical disabilities. For those students supported by State Divisions of Vocational Rehabilitation, such continued counseling is provided by this agency. Most colleges and universities also provide educational-vocational counseling for their students. It may be more convenient for the student to work with a college counselor rather than the State Division counselor. In any event, it should be apparent that in these cases the college and the State agency must work together and agree on procedures and responsibilities for services to the disabled student. At the University of Illinois, a staff member of the State Division of Vocational Rehabilitation is assigned to the Student Rehabilitation Center. However, he does not necessarily work with all students who may have educational-vocational problems, although in cases where a change in the vocational goal is involved, his approval as a representative of the State Division is necessary.

A procedure practiced at Illinois would appear to warrant favorable consideration. In the spring of each year, all disabled students who entered the University that year, participate in a testing program, which serves as an opportunity for the student and the University to reevaluate educational and vocational objectives. It is possible that the interests and goals of disabled students may change more frequently and more radically than those of able-bodied students following exposure to the college environment. Many of them have led rather sheltered, protected, or isolated lives prior to the college experience. Some of them have not been aware of vocational opportunities which may be opening up to the disabled. And in some cases the opportunities available become more varied as a result of new-found aptitudes and abilities, and changes in physical capacities.

A word might be said about the unrealistic vocational choices, or over-aspirations of the disabled. The disabled are no different from the able-bodied in this respect. And their treatment should be no different. They should not be over-protected, or prevented from experiencing failure in reality testing. A disabled student should be allowed to attempt an apparently unrealistic curriculum or course or activity if he insists, as long as it is medically feasible and administratively possible.

THERAPEUTIC COUNSELING

In addition to educational-vocational counseling, disabled students, as do others, often need counseling in the area of personal problems. As Rusalem notes, "The principles of counseling disabled students are the same principles which govern all counseling. Human personality and the techniques of working with it are not changed in a qualitative sense by the presence of a physical disability.'' The personal problems of the disabled are essentially the same as those of the able-bodied. It is possible that the incidence of problems is greater, but this could be accounted for in terms of the reality problems imposed by the environment and the attitudes of others toward the disabled. Two areas in which problems may be more frequent and more severe are in the achievement of independence and in heterosexual relationships. In the former area, the extremes of dependence on the one hand and excessive drives for independence on the other, may constitute problems. But they are essentially no different in nature from similar problems of the able-bodied. In the area of boy-girl relationships, the same situation exists. The disabled may be limited or restricted in their contacts and dating activities. Beatrice Wright (4, pp. 189–193) cites autobiographical accounts of frustrating boy-girl relationships of the disabled during adolescence, but she comments that such trying experiences are common to adolescents in general. I have counseled disabled college students who have experienced the agonies of unrequited love, infatuations, rejections, and limited contacts and relationships with the opposite sex which were in no way different from similar experiences of the nondisabled. It is true, however, that the severely disabled may be justifiably concerned about their chances for marriage, and, as in the case of one of my clients may have a difficult time distinguishing between failure in heterosexual relationships because of the restrictions imposed by the disability and other attitudes toward it, and failure related to personal attitudes and relationships with others.

It is of course necessary that the counselor have knowledge of the disability of his clients. Rusalem, noting that ''some counseling orientations minimize the use of background information,'' states that ''in working with a disabled student, such information is vital to the understanding of the student's problem for a number of reasons'' (3, pp. 106–107). He is of course referring to the client-centered orientation, which I represent. While I have indicated above that information about the disability is essential for evaluation for admission, and in vocational counseling, I do not feel that detailed medical information is necessary in counseling on personal problems. In fact, in my practice I make it a point not to become familiar with the nature of the client's disability from his file. The essential aspects of the disability for understanding the client in counseling are available first from observation and interaction with the client, and secondly from the client's communication of them from his point of view. These are the important facts for the counseling relationship which is concerned with the client's attitudes and feelings, rather than with the medical details of the disability.

SOME QUESTIONS

Rather than summarizing, I would like to close with a few questions which I think should be faced by those who are concerned with counseling the disabled college student.

The first one concerns the problem of requiring that disabled applicants make a vocational choice prior to or on admission. Applicants who are sponsored are required to reach a vocational decision, acceptable to the Division of Vocational Rehabilitation, before obtaining support for their education. Presumably these students are concerned about their vocational futures and desire vocational counseling. But other applicants may not be concerned, or may wish to postpone consideration of this problem until later, and may not wish counseling. The college, on the other hand, may need to determine whether the applicant can meet the physical demands of a particular curriculum, or to determine the suitability of a particular choice of curriculum or major. While a college may deal with this problem as one of selection, it would appear to be more desirable that it be based upon or include vocational counseling. But can vocational counseling be made a required part of the admission procedure for all disabled students?

The second problem is similar, and can be simply stated. There are some who feel that all disabled students need counseling, and that therefore they should all be routinely scheduled for counseling appointments or interviews, if only as a regular checkup procedure. While this may seem like a desirable procedure, I wonder if we should follow this practice of attempting to impose counseling on all disabled students. We don't feel it necessary for able-bodied students. I wonder if we can't depend on those students who

have problems to seek counseling when they need it, and to concede them the right not to seek it even if they seem to need it, as we do other students. Isn't one of our goals with the disabled, as with others, to encourage independence and self-reliance? Another aspect of this forced counseling or interviewing is its reflection of a tendency to invade the privacy of disabled students in a way which is not done in the case of the able-bodied. I know that some will say that we must do this if we are to help them. But on the other hand, we should respect the right of a person to decline or refuse help if he so desires. Of course, if the student is failing to meet requirements, he can be called in to discuss this, and be offered help.

The third question has to do with the distinction between evaluation and counseling which was made earlier. Rather than having the counselor who will work with accepted students be involved in the admissions process, as Rusalem proposes, would it not be better to separate these functions so that they are performed by different individuals? I am aware that in a small institution with few disabled students this may be difficult to do, but the question concerns its desirability.

A fourth problem has to do with the function of the counselor in leading the disabled student to accept his disability and its limitations. Considerable emphasis has been placed upon the desirability and importance of this. One might well question this, and raise a question regarding the possibility of overdoing this matter of acceptance of limitations. I am concerned with the insistence of some that the counselor actively engage in specific attempts to force a client to accept his limitations. This, I think, is not consistent with what many of us consider a function or purpose of counseling. Of course, the counselor will be concerned with this if the client presents it as a problem, and will work with the client toward helping him face the reality of his limitations if he desires to do so.

Finally, there is the problem of the organization of services to the disabled. On the one hand, the disabled applicant and student may be handled separately from other students. While some might regard this as segregation (a term used by Rusalem), it can be justified with severely disabled students on the basis of the special problems and needs which they present, which require trained and experienced personnel. Where large numbers of disabled students are accepted, it becomes more easily possible and efficient to handle them separately. This is the procedure at the University of Illinois.

On the other hand, there are those who feel that disabled applicants and students should not be differentiated from others in admissions and personnel services, but "integrated" into the regular procedures. While this may ap-

pear to be desirable, it is not usually practical in the case of the severely disabled, who cannot be handled by the routines established for able-bodied students.

The extent to which all services are differentiated or integrated depends upon the nature of the services and the facilities of the college. But the question involved is one which all colleges must face in their programs for disabled students.

REFERENCES

1. Cruickshank, W. M. The exceptional child in the elementary and secondary schools. *In* Cruickshank, W. M., & Johnson, G. O. (Eds.) Psychology of exceptional children and youth. Englewood Cliffs, N. J.:Prentice-Hall, 1955.
2. Patterson, C. H. Counseling and guidance in schools: A first course. New York: Harper, 1962.
3. Rusalem, H. Guiding the physically handicapped college student. New York: Bureau of Publications, Teachers College, Columbia University, 1962.
4. Wright, Beatrice A. Physical disability—A psychological approach. New York: Harper, 1960.

10 Counseling the Mentally Retarded

A Behavioral Approach

William I. Gardner
and John M. Stamm

In 1967 *Mental Retardation* published a statement that raised serious reservations about the use of traditional counseling and psychotherapy in work with the mentally retarded (Gardner, 1967). A year later Halpern (1968), in reply to this article, defended the traditional approach. The present article briefly examines the traditional treatment position as espoused by Halpern and presents a conceptual and methodological alternative to this approach.

Traditional counseling and therapy techniques rely heavily upon one-to-one verbally oriented techniques. General intellectual level, general verbal skills, and more specific skills relating to verbal control over other classes of behavior appear to be critical in order for treatment to be effective. Krasner (1965) suggested that psychotherapy is a verbal modification process between two people in which one (the more knowing therapist or counselor) seeks to change the verbal behavior of another (the less knowing client). Moreover, Krasner suggested that "*if* changes in verbal behavior have consequences for change in other kinds of behaviors, the systematic modification of verbalization is itself a treatment" (p. 230).

It is assumed that changes in verbal behaviors will result in changes in behaviors that the verbal content represents. As an example, if psychotherapy results in changes in verbal behavior from "I do not like to work and will not cooperate with my supervisor" to "I like to work and will cooperate with my supervisor because I can get along better if I do so," it is assumed that there will in fact be a change in work and work-related behaviors. The verbal behavior will gain control over and give direction to other overt (nonverbal) behaviors in other settings. However, with respect to the retarded who is experiencing significant behavior adjustment problems, this assumption appears tenuous.

The present writers take the position that one of the significant psychological (functional) deficits that characterizes the mentally retarded adolescent and young adult who present personal and social behavior difficulties is the lack of adequate verbal control of nonverbal behaviors. Stimulus events other than the person's own verbal behavior provide the major discriminative or control influence over classes of behavior. In many instances, the control or functional relationship

Reprinted by permission from the September 1971 *Rehabilitation Counseling Bulletin*, pp. 46–57.

has not developed between verbal behaviors and other classes of behaviors represented by the verbal content. That is, the retardate can be encouraged to say, "I will do that" or "I should not do that," but frequently he does not reflect these verbally expressed intentions in overt behavior.

In other instances such relationships between verbal cues and other classes of behavior are distorted or may have even lost their control function. The retarded frequently do not behave in a rational fashion or do not have "self-control" over their behaviors, i.e., they are unable to direct appropriate behaviors or to make a rational decision in a choice or conflict situation because they do not have the appropriate verbal mediational responses which have strong or sufficient stimulus control over other classes of their behaviors. Moreover, the retarded exhibit a deficiency of appropriate intraverbal or mediational responses necessary for organization, storage, and retrieval of information and the establishment of situationally appropriate overt behavior. Thus they fail to act "rationally," "logically," or "intelligently" on the basis of environmental contingencies.

A treatment approach that aims merely at development of insight or at an expanded system of verbal behaviors does not insure systematic change in other behavior areas. What the retarded client says or may be taught to say may or *may not* be related to other classes of behavior. The treatment strategy must go further and promote discriminative cues for other classes of behavior as these other behaviors occur in natural

settings. This development can best be achieved by reinforcing the occurrence of verbal behaviors that immediately precede or occur concomitantly with other behaviors—an accomplishment seldom present in traditional counseling.

Doubros (1966) studied the effects of deliberate and systematic manipulation of the verbal behavior of two retarded clients as a therapeutic technique. Therapy sessions "often became exercises in memorization of critical, appropriate verbal patterns" (p. 230), upon which selective reinforcement was contingent in order to provide verbal cues that would gain discriminative control of overt behavior outside the therapy environment. However, no attempt was made to insure that the newly learned verbal responses were actually made and reinforced in critical social and interpersonal situations. This study, labeled by its writer as an example of behavior therapy, differs little from traditional approaches in that it merely attempted to shape new verbal responses in an isolated artificial office setting.

Brodsky (1967) described a study designed to assess both the changes in verbal behavior as a function of changes in nonverbal behavior as well as changes in nonverbal behavior as a function of changes in verbal behavior in two retarded males with low rates of social behaviors. Both had high rates of verbal behavior, but they rarely initiated or engaged in sustained social contacts. Treatment consisted of providing one with token reinforcement for social interaction in a laboratory setting and the other with reinforcement for social statements (e.g., "I like to play with Jane") during standardized clinic sessions. Results indicated that the person reinforced for social behavior in the laboratory behaved more socially in a natural social situation, whereas the client receiving reinforcement for social statements showed no increase in overt social behavior in the natural environment. Further, reinforcement of social behavior led to increased prosocial verbal behavior. The results, although limited by the small sample, failed to support the assumed relationship between verbal and nonverbal behavior change. Also, it suggests that it may be more efficacious to bypass verbally oriented therapy and *re-program directly in the appropriate social environment*. Again, it would appear that verbal behaviors, if these are to function as discriminative cues for other classes of behaviors, should accompany these other behaviors as they occur in the natural environment. Contingent reinforcement of the verbal behavior-other behavior sequence would strengthen the control relationship between the two.

The results of verbal learning research with the retarded (e.g., Borokowski & Johnson, 1968; Penny, Seim, & Peters, 1968) further qualify the use of verbally oriented therapy with the retarded. This research indicates that the retarded, when confronted with paired-associate verbal learning tasks, do not spontaneously generate effective verbal mediators, nor, when provided, use them appropriately in associating stimulus and response items. This suggests that their

intraverbal behaviors (thinking or verbal associations) are relatively ineffective. That is, appropriate associations are absent or distorted. To the degree that this it true, the acquisition of "insight" (e.g., verbal understanding or description of co-relationships between behavior histories and contemporaneous events), which is deemed crucial in psychotherapy, is limited, and the possible control of verbal behavior over classes of nonverbal behavior is greatly reduced. More studies are needed that systematically investigate the degree to which verbal response classes of the retarded may be differentially conditioned and the degree to which these response classes, acquired independently of a discriminative association with other nonverbal behaviors, may in turn exercise control over nonverbal behavior. Until more data are available, the assumption that the retarded have good verbal control over nonverbal behaviors remains only a hypothesis needing empirical verification.

Little systematic data are presently available that assess the relative usefulness and effectiveness of psychotherapeutic procedures with the retarded. Sternlicht (1966) concluded a lengthy review of individual and group psychotherapy procedures with the retarded by noting that " . . . therapeutic work in this field, however, still lacks sufficient theoretical and empirical basis. A major shortcoming in this area is efficient research dealing with *outcomes* of psychotherapeutic treatment" (p. 349). Moreover, he states ". . . the review of research in this area pointed out the need for greater clarification of terms" (p. 349). On the basis of

Sternlicht's conclusions and the failure to find suitable research to support the efficacy of personal counseling and psychotherapy with the retarded, it may be concluded that neither salient psychotherapeutic *process* nor *outcome* variables have been delineated or independently manipulated in order to determine their relative usefulness with the mentally retarded. As Baumeister noted, "To put it bluntly, maybe the typical psychologist has developed no unique and effective skills relevant to the *modification* and *control* of retarded behavior" (1967, p. 5). Carkhuff and Berenson (1967) suggested a possible cause for this:

> Counselors and clinicians have, for too long, settled for apparent insight as the criterion for success, with little or no concern for the behavior of the patient outside of, or following therapy. Perhaps most significant, the complexity of our abstractions, and their vague implications for therapeutic treatment are so far removed from behavior and life that assessing efficacy takes the form of crude judgments based upon modification of hypothetical dynamics. The dynamic, living, breathing person is lost in labels [p. 87].

Prior to a description of characteristics of a behavioristic approach to the modification of behavior of the mentally retarded, an example will serve to illustrate some of the major deficiencies of the traditional psychotherapy or counseling approach. In a recent article, Jones (1969) described his attempt to "... establish the utility and efficiency with which counseling can be done with the mentally retarded" (p. 19). However, Jones provided not even a hint of objective data concerning the effects of his counseling efforts on the behavior of the retarded client. Although he initially identified excessive fantasy behavior as an area of concern, he concluded that "... exposure to a concerned therapist on an intensive schedule enhanced the establishment of trust and a feeling of acceptance on the part of the client, two vital factors in establishment of rapport ... " (p. 21), and "If ... goals include treatment of apathy, establishment of drive objects and motivation and building of ego strength, it is felt that intensive counseling programs can make meaningful contributions to these ends" (p. 21).

Jones did not present any conceptual or empirical relationships between excessive fantasy behavior and any of these other "personality" constructs. Apparently, he assumed some degree of functional relationship among these, but its nature was not identified. He made no mention of the specific therapy techniques used, the specific behavioral effects of therapy, nor of the evaluation procedures used to assess therapeutic effects. Although Jones spoke of extensive diagnostic testing, there was no conceptual or procedural framework provided for translating the testing data into treatment strategies. As a result of these and related deficiencies, it is not at all surprising that counseling and psychotherapy with the retarded remain a vague, ill-defined, and suspect form of behavior intervention.

BEHAVIOR APPROACH TO COUNSELING

It appears that a functionally integrated analytic approach to the conceptualization of behavior development and behavior control (treatment) is needed rather than reformulations of theories, principles, and practices which are largely ineffective. A minimal number of theoretical statements, operationally defined and subject to empirical verification, accounting for acquisition of both deviant and nondeviant behaviors with unambiguously derivable treatment procedures, is required. A natural science approach (Bijou, 1966) to the acquisition and control of human behavior offers an effective, efficient, and meticulous basis for behavior theory and clinical practice. This is particularly true, it is believed, with respect to the counseling and guidance of the retarded.

The broad area of learning theory, particularly operant and respondent learning (Ferster & Perrott, 1968; Skinner, 1953), has provided the basis for the applied analysis of behavior (Baer, Wolf, & Risley, 1968) and related clinical treatment techniques. The applied or functional analysis of behavior is based upon analytic behavioral application of

> ... sometimes tentative principles of behavior to the improvement of specific behaviors, and simultaneously evaluating whether or not any changes noted are indeed attributable to the process of application—and if so, to what parts of the process. In short, analytic behavioral application is self-examining, self-evaluating, discovery oriented ... [Baer, Wolf, & Risley, 1968, p. 91].

The major focus of this behavior approach is upon getting an individual to do something efficiently as a function of the manipulation of the events controlling his behavior. Thus, the clinician or therapist "studies what the subject can be brought to do rather than what he can be brought to say, unless, of course, a verbal response is the behavior of interest. Accordingly, a subject's verbal description of his own nonverbal behavior usually would not be accepted as a measure of his actual behavior unless it were independently substantiated" (Baer, Wolf, & Risley, 1968, p. 93).

Unlike the traditional or disease model approach to behavioral treatment, the learning theory approach is technological, analytic, and provides conceptual clarity and relevance of treatment to behavior principles. It is technological in that the techniques and procedures for effecting specific behavior change are completely delineated. Thus, none of the terms *play therapy, psychotherapy, self-awareness, insight,* or *social reinforcement* are technological descriptions. However, the statement that "the *S* was given token reinforcers, redeemable for back-up reinforcer every hour, on a variable ratio schedule, for making eye contact with the counselor during therapy" is technological. Technological sufficiency permits unambiguous understanding and precise replicability.

A technological approach to behavior change, moreover, requires reliable quantification of the behavior under consideration in order to provide succinct, objective, and unambiguous definition of these behavior(s) and the relative change in their rate, intensity, and/or topography as a function of the treatment procedures. Reliable observation of specific behavior is possible outside of the laboratory or clinic and in the natural environment (e.g., Neuringer & Michael, 1970; Tharp & Wetzel, 1969; Ulrich, Stachnik, & Mabry, 1970). Reliable, objective observation provides the basis for direct measurement and change of specific nonadaptive behavior.

The learning theory approach is analytic in that the clinician has achieved an analysis or an explanation of behavior in the degree to which he exercises control over it. As Bijou (1966) noted:

> Many of the conventional approaches to counseling aim to get into and as near as possible to the *presumed* internal processes and conditions of the individual so that *hypothetical* causes may be modified. The behavioral science approach aims to get into and as near as possible to the *actual* situation in which the problem behavior may be modified [p. 34].

All behaviors, both those labeled adaptive and maladaptive, are assumed to be learned and are conceptually a function of the same variables which are, or which potentially may be, manipulative. There is no concept of the unconscious nor of a pathology underlying the "symptomatic" behavior (Ullman & Krasner, 1965). Behavior is a symptom of nothing. It may be controlled by or serve to control other behaviors, but these functions must be demonstrated. The behaviors dealt with are observable, and more importantly, quantifiable. Also, their manipulation is possible through the analysis of their reinforcement history and present environmental contingencies.

The learning model requires that specific problem behaviors be dealt with. As Bijou (1966) observed:

> It is *not* advantageous to try to reorganize, in one fell swoop, the "whole personality" or even attempt to modify some hypothetical part of the personality such as the "sense of ego-identity." If such global objectives do in fact refer to changes in behavior, then the units selected to be changed are much too large to manage well [p. 34].

Moreover, as Carkhuff and Berenson (1967) have suggested, there is less chance of explaining away failures in terms of client resistance, or lack of readiness for therapy when treatment focuses on specific problem behaviors.

The learning theory approach provides conceptual clarity to counseling theory and behavior change. Unlike the psychodynamic orientation, theoretical statements are subject to operational definition and empirical verification. The techniques of behavior control are related to the principles and concepts of learning theory. The clarity and explicitness thus permitted facilitate the systematic development of clinical techniques rather than a grab-bag of counseling and therapeutic tricks.

The behavior modification or learning approach, however, may create problems for counselors trained in the psychodynamic tradition in that it requires him to assume a new role:

> Instead of conceiving of the counselor as a reflector of feelings, or an explorer of resources, or a habit changer, or a remediator of self-concepts and values, or a releaser of repressions, we might come to think of him as a behavioral engineer—one whose function it is to arrange and rearrange the environment in order to bring about desired changes in behavior [Bijou, 1966, p. 44].

This role would include, as Gardner (1967) suggested, functioning as a consultant-educator to day care and rehabilitation facilities for the retarded and as a specialist in arranging optimal learning experiences in the "real" world. Moreover, it may be more efficient, and of less expense in terms of professional time and money, to function mainly as a trainer of those who have natural contact with the retarded, e.g., teacher, attendant, nurse, parent, and others. Tharp and Wetzel (1969) provide well-documented evidence that such "mediators" can exert a positive effect when trained to function in a contingency management environment. Zeilberger, Sampen, and Sloane (1968), as another example, successfully demonstrated that the frequency of "disobedience" behaviors can be decreased and "obedience" increased in the home by arrangement of differential reinforcement contingencies by parents. Adequately trained paraprofessional personnel, who interact with the individual continuously in his real world, may be more efficient and effective in changing behavior than a "qualified" psychologist or counselor who interacts with him only occasionally in an artificial world of office or playroom.

The psychodynamic orientation has not provided the integral relationship between theory and clinical practices in vocational counseling with the retarded. Particularly, the goals of counseling and therapy have been poorly defined. Additionally, specific techniques are ill defined and only vaguely related to theory; the therapist is still confronted with the question:

"Just what *do* I do in order to change the behavior of the client?" In contrast, learning orientation stresses the statement of goals in behavioral terms. As Krumboltz (1966) points out, "Stating goals of counseling in terms of observable behavior will prove more useful than stating goals in terms of inferred mental states as 'selfacceptance'" (p. 153), and he feels these goals should be differentially and specifically determined for each client. For example, if a therapy goal were one of developing a "healthier" or more "positive" identification as a worker, the counselor would need to: (a) specify the behaviors taken as evidence of a poor indentification as a worker; (b) specify the conditions under which these behaviors occur; (c) establish the functional consequences controlling these behaviors; and (d) determine their rate of occurrence. Moreover, the responsible clinician will need to state behaviorally the therapy objective, delineating: (a) who will act; (b) when and under what conditions they will act; (c) the specific behaviors to be dealt with and how they will be influenced; and (d) the criterion for assessing the relative success or failure of the treatment.

Although requiring the counselor to acquire a new or different professional role and thus creating a certain amount of cognitive dissonance, the learning theory approach contributes much to him. Some of the contributions, as noted by Carkhuff and Berenson (1967) are: (a) he is provided with a system of well-defined procedures; (b) there is a high level relationship between treatment goals and techniques of behavior change; (c) there is more effective involvement in behavior change beyond the therapy hour; (d) he quite naturally looks for ways of making transitions from therapy to real life; (e) the theory dispells the concern for transference/counter-transference neurosis; (f) it requires that more attention be paid to nonverbal cues effecting behavior change; and (g) it provides an opportunity for not only eliminating maladaptive behavior but also for establishing adaptive ones.

Perhaps the most important contribution of the behavior modification or learning model is that it has proved effective with populations, particularly the mentally retarded, who were formerly excluded from dynamically oriented counseling programs, or for whom the procedures were ineffective. There is a growing body of clinical research literature which demonstrates empirically and objectively the usefulness of an applied learning approach to the treatment of the adaptive behavior problems of the mentally retarded (e.g., Birnbrauer, Wolf, Kidder, & Tague, 1965; Chaffin, 1969; Lent, 1968; Zimmerman, Stuckey, Garlick, & Miller, 1969).

More systematic applied behavior research obviously is needed to determine the parameters of behavior control techniques most effective in facilitating behavior change with the mentally retarded. Questions raised by Halpern (1968, p. 50) are relevant in this respect: "Which technique works best, under what circumstances, and with whom?" While the questions are appropriate, the conceptual and procedural orientations assumed by traditional counseling and psychotherapy models have been and remain inappropriate. More specifically, it appears pertinent to ask such questions as: What are the antecedent stimulus conditions which are most effective in controlling behavior? What is the nature of the behavior to be changed in frequency, intensity, or amount? What are the reinforcement or consequent events currently maintaining the behavior? And, what are the effective reinforcement contingencies or schedules for shaping and maintaining more adaptive behaviors? The learning theory orientation provides both conceptual and operational guidelines for answering these questions.

REFERENCES

Baer, D. M., Wolf, M., & Risley, T. R. Some current dimensions of applied behavioral analysis. Journal of Applied Behavior Analysis, 1968, 1(1):91–97.

Bijou, S. W. Implications of behavioral science for counseling and guidance. In J. D. Krumboltz (Ed.), Revolution in counseling. Boston: Houghton, Mifflin, 1966.

Birnbrauer, J. S., Wolf, M. M., Kidder, J. D., & Tague, C. E. Classroom behavior of retarded pupils with token reinforcement. Journal of Experimental Child Psychology, 1965, 2:219–235.

Borokowski, J. G., & Johnson, L. O. Mediation and the paired-associate learning of normals and retardates. American Journal of Mental Deficiency, 1968, 72(4):610–613.

Brodsky, G. The relation between verbal and non-verbal behavior change. Behavior Research and Therapy, 1967, 5:183–191.

Carkhuff, R. R., & Berenson, B. G. Beyond counseling and therapy. New York: Holt, Rinehart and Winston, 1967.

Chaffin, J. D. Production rate as a variable in the job success or failure of educable mentally retarded adolescents. Exceptional Children, 1969, 35(7):533–538.

Doubros, S. G. Behavior therapy with high level, institutionalized retarded children. Exceptional Children, 1966, 3(34):229–233.

Ferster, C. B., & Perrott, M. C. Behavior principles. New York: Appleton-Century-Crofts, 1968.

Gardner, W. I. What should be the psychologist's role? Mental Retardation, 1967, 5(6):29–31.

Halpern, A. A. Why not psychotherapy? Mental Retardation, 1968, 6(6):48–50.

Jones, J. G. The case of Mary. Mental Retardation, 1969, 7:19–21.

Krasner, L. Verbal conditioning and psychotherapy. In L. Krasner and L. P. Ullman (Eds.), Research in behavior modification. New York: Holt, Rinehart and Winston, 1965.

Krumboltz, J. D. Behavioral goals in counseling. Journal of Counseling Psychology, 1966, 2(13):153–159.

Lent, J. R. Mimosa Cottage: Experiment in hope. Psychology Today, 1968, 2:51–58.

Neuringer, C., & Michael, J. C. Behavior modification in clinical psychology. New York: Appleton-Century-Crofts, 1970.

Penny, K. R., Seim, R., & Peters, R. The mediational deficiency of mentally retarded children: I. The establishment of retardate's mediational deficiency. American Journal of Mental Deficiency, 1968, 77(4):626–630.

Skinner, B. F. Science and human behavior. New York: The Free Press, 1953.

Sternlicht, M. Psychotherapeutic procedures with the retarded. In N. R. Ellis (Ed.), International review of research in mental retardation, Vol. 2. New York: Academic Press, 1966.

Tharp, R. G., & Wetzel, R. J. Behavior modification in the natural environment. New York: Academic Press, 1969.

Ullman, L. P., & Krasner, L. (Eds.), Case studies in behavior modification. New York: Holt, Rinehart and Winston, 1965.

Ulrich, R. E., Stachnik, T., & Mabry, J. Control of human behavior, Vol. I. From cure to prevention, Vol. II. New York: Scott-Foresman, 1966.

Zeilberger, J., Sampen, S. E., & Sloane, H. N., Jr. Modification of a child's problem behaviors in the home with the mother as a therapist. Journal of Applied Behavior Analysis, 1968, 1(1):47–53.

Zimmerman, J., Stuckey, T. E., Garlick, B. J., & Miller, M. Effects of token reinforcement on productivity in multiply handicapped clients in a sheltered workshop. Rehabilitation Literature, 1969, 30(2):34–41, 64.

11 A Learning Theory Approach to Counseling Indecisive Clients

Shlomo P. Kravetz
and Kenneth R. Thomas

Rehabilitation counselors are frequently confronted with the task of helping indecisive clients to make appropriate vocational decisions. For example, clients are often indecisive concerning what type of training to pursue, what type of employment to seek, or whether to submit to a rigorous and time-consuming program of vocational evaluation. Such indecisive clients may pose for the counselor what Haley (1963, p. 17), in his communication analysis of psychotherapy, has termed a paradox: On one level, the clients report that they lack the qualifications to evaluate the available vocational possibilities and therefore request the counselor to make a vocational decision for them. On a level of almost equal generality, the clients say that they are sufficiently qualified to judge the appropriateness of the decision the counselor makes for them. The clients both relinquish control over the situation and yet retain ultimate control over it at the same time. Direct counselor suggestions of an appropriate vocational choice may actually reinforce the clients' indecisiveness since they have described the counseling situation in a manner which allows them to pass final judgment over the appropiateness of the counselor's suggestion. If the counselor remains silent or in some other way suggests that the clients make their own decision, the clients can contend that they are not receiving the direct reinforcement that they supposedly demand of the counselor. The counselor seems to be damned whether he or she is directive or nondirective.

This situation can be described in the more explicit terminology of learning theory. The clients' indecisiveness can be viewed as avoidance behavior—indecision in the counselor's office permits them to avoid the possibly aversive effects of acting on a decision in the real world. By interpreting the counselor's silence or direct recommendations as additional confirmations of their inability to decide, the clients transform the counseling context into a situation which further reinforces the indecisiveness.

Handicapped individuals with histories of steady employment until the occurrence of their disability and handicapped individuals with histories of chronic unemployment both before and

Reprinted by permission from the June 1974 *Rehabilitation Counseling Bulletin*, pp. 198–208.

after the occurrence of their disability often place their counselors in this type of paradoxical situation. The former individuals, after once having demonstrated their job acquiring ability and experienced stable employment, suddenly claim they no longer are able to select and find appropriate employment. The latter individuals constantly rationalize their inactivity with regard to seeking employment. Walker (1969, p. 403) actually found that about 90 percent of the clients in the Minneapolis Rehabilitation Center "state one or more untreatable problems as the primary reason they are not working." Haley (1963, p. 15) claimed that clients impose paradoxes on their counselors to gain "control of what is to happen in a relationship with someone else." These clients apparently use the paradoxes to avoid the risk inherent in all human relationships, a risk which is especially salient when the relationship requires that a decision be made.

Although vocational rehabilitation counselors have the resources to place their clients in such manipulatable environments as a sheltered workshop, a vocational trade school or an on-the-job training situation, they continue to use the interview as a principle means for facilitating client change. As Kanfer and Phillips (1970, p. 402) contended, "cases in which the target behaviors are verbal behaviors for efficient assessment of life situations, evaluation of feelings, or decision-making are also well suited for treatment by interviews." The context of the counseling interview can be examined in learning theory terms, and the results of this examination can be used by the counselor to provide a situation that encourages the client to engage in decision making.

VERBAL LEARNING AND THE INTERVIEW

Experimental studies of verbal learning have been considered as partial analogues of what occurs during counseling interviews (Kanfer & Phillips 1970, pp. 371–405). During experimental interviews, researchers have been able to increase the probability of their subjects' emitting a particular category of verbal response by arranging for verbal or nonverbal reinforcement to be contingent upon this response. Counselors can use their own responses contingently to increase the occurrence of those verbal responses of their clients that the counselors judge to facilitate the attainment of the clients' goals. An analysis of a therapy case of Carl Rogers uncovered that his expressions of counselor empathy, warmth, and directiveness seemed to be contingent on those responses of his client that would be consistent with Rogers' theory of client progress. The probability of these latter responses' occurrence increased apparently as a result of the contingent reinforcement (Truax 1966).

Operant principles that only aid counselors to encourage their clients to talk about making decisions without affecting the clients' tendency to avoid decision making outside of the counseling sessions are of limited usefulness. Unfortunately, research has not provided an answer concerning the generalizability of the changes produced by the operant conditioning of verbal behavior. Some experiments demonstrate the generalizability of these changes, and others do not (Kanfer & Phillips 1970, pp. 394–395).

Investigations of the operant conditioning of verbal behavior usually use "such reinforcing stimuli as head nods, smiles, verbal gruntlike signs of affirmation and similar minimal behaviors [Kanfer & Phillips 1970, p. 392]." These reinforcing stimuli are actually kinds of social reinforcement and are subject to all the vagaries of social reinforcements. For one client counselor agreement may be positively reinforcing, whereas for another client this agreement may result in an aversive condition of dissonance which the client may avoid by emitting incompatible behavior (Collins 1969, p. 220). When working with a client who is using self-contradictory behavior to avoid decision making, counselors can use the general operational definition of reinforcement and probe how effectively various kinds of counseling responses increase the occurrence of the desired client behavior.

Since individuals can only analytically be abstracted from their behavior, the general characteristics of the individuals who are attempting to use their own behavior to reinforce another individual's behavior contribute a great deal to the effectiveness of this attempted reinforcement. Counselors who have been associated with the direct or vicarious reinforcement of their clients will probably be liked by the clients and will probably be effective reinforcers of the clients' behavior

(Kanfer & Phillips 1970, p. 471). Lubin (1969, p. 200) deduced from his experimental investigation of the differences in effectiveness of controllers of verbal reinforcement that "(a) experimenters differ from one another in their skill as dispensers of verbal reinforcement; (b) one aspect of this skill, i.e., speed of reinforcement, is related to effectiveness in verbal conditioning; and (c) the need for abasement and endurance (PPS) predict verbal conditioning effectiveness fairly well." Apparently, in addition to carefully considering the effects of the specific behaviors presented to clients at any one point in the counseling interview, counselors must pay equal attention to their style of behavior throughout the whole counseling process.

Transferring operant principles of demonstrated effectiveness in experimental settings to counseling settings requires that counselors actively involve themselves with the issues of the potential generalization of the counselor-client interaction, the effects of specific counselor responses, and the general qualities of the counselor-client relationship. This analysis would seem to be a tedious process, and counselors who are working with an indecisive client might wonder if they could shorten the process by informing the client that as counselors they favor decisiveness and will exhibit approval of decisive behavior every time the client emits it. There are researchers who claim that the slowly arrived at discovery of the experimenter's intention underlies all effective operant verbal conditioning paradigms (Kanfer & Phillips 1970, p. 395). These researchers might consider such a shortcut plausible. However, since part of the indecisive client's problem may be inconsistency, making the reinforcement contingency explicit could result in an increase in the client's indecisiveness. The question of whether awareness is essential to the operant conditioning of verbal behavior is especially pertinent to the potential success of counselors' efforts to create a situation in which an implicit reinforcement contingency can accomplish more than an explicit reinforcement contingency.

The nature of the learning task and the ambiguity of the task requirements are two variables that mediate the relationship between awareness and the effective operant conditioning of verbal behavior (Kanfer & Phillips 1970, p. 396). Learning tasks perceived by the client as problems to be solved are dependent on the client's discovery of the reinforcement contingency for their successful mastery. Task ambiguity interacts with a kind of reinforcement in its effect on verbal conditioning. Social reinforcement is more effective than nonsocial reinforcement when the task requirements are more ambiguous (Kanfer & Phillips 1970, p. 396).

Thus, counseling settings are situations in which implicit reinforcement contingencies should be effective. These settings are not usually perceived by the client as problem solving tasks. Especially in the case of indecisiveness, the requirements of counseling sessions remain ambiguous. The reinforcing stimuli most available to the counselor in counseling sessions are social. A counselor's effort to set up implicit social reinforcing contingencies for re-

sponses that are incompatible with indecisiveness should reduce this indecisiveness and produce increased self-consistency.

Gelatt (1962) describes decision making as a sequence of the following three steps: (a) the organization and consideration of information related to a preselected objective; (b) the weighting of this information according to its relevancy to alternate courses of action and to the outcomes to which these courses of action might lead; and (c) the selection of the most desirable outcome and the course of action that would most likely lead to this outcome. These steps could be summarized as information seeking, deliberation, and decision making. Behavioral expressions of these decision making components occur in counseling sessions usually in the form of client statements. Whether the frequency and variety of these statements can be increased by a counselor reinforcing them and whether this increase in frequency and variety will generalize to noncounseling situations are empirical questions.

Specific studies have been conducted to explore the possibility of increasing the frequency of the behavioral components of decision making by means of the verbal operant conditioning paradigm. Krumboltz and Thoreson (1964) attempted to increase the number of times a student would seek information pertinent to vocational decisions by verbally reinforcing their stated intentions to pursue this information. They then evaluated (a) the extent to which these behaviors were actually carried out in practice, (b) the relative effectiveness of behavioral counseling in group settings compared to behavioral counseling in individual settings, and (c) verbal reinforcement alone compared to verbal reinforcement combined with modeling. The verbal operant conditioning of overt deliberation and decision statements was explored by Ryan and Krumboltz (1964). Although this study provided for a test of the spread of the effects of the operant paradigm from the original learning situation to a story completion situation, it used only an individualized setting and reinforcement alone. Among the conclusions derived from these studies were the following:

1. Reinforcement and model-reinforcement of the stated intention to seek information in counseling sessions raised the level of occupational and educational information seeking behavior to a higher level than did nonspecific attention in similar quasi-counseling sessions.

2. In the case of male students, combined modeling and reinforcement increased this behavior more than reinforcement alone. In the case of females, these factors produced no differential effect on the dependent variable.

3. In the case of male students, the model-reinforcement combination was more effective in the group setting than in the individual setting, whereas the opposite occurred with the reinforcement alone. This interaction did not emerge from the data on female students.

4. Different counselor and/or school settings produced different changes in information seeking behavior for males and females in group and individual counseling.

5. Increasing clients' deliberation and decision responses by counselor reinforcement depends more on counselor characteristics than does increasing client information seeking behavior by the same method.

6. The increase in decision making responses attained by counselor reinforcement appears to be more easily generalized than is a similar increase in deliberation responses.

7. Awareness of the reinforcement contingencies on the part of the client does not appear necessary for either the efficacy of the reinforcement or the generalization of the effects of this reinforcement.

A COUNSELING STRATEGY BASED ON VERBAL OPERANT CONDITIONING

The counseling strategy presented here is aimed specifically at reducing client indecisiveness with regard to vocational planning. It is designed to deal with clients whose indecisiveness provides a means for avoiding the anxiety arising from the risk inherent in all decision making. A basic assumption underlying this strategy is that the client's indecisiveness can be identified as avoidance behavior. A means must be available to rule out other explanations of the client's problem.

Evaluation of the Problem

Three aspects of the client's situation which the counselor can explore to identify those circumstances that are maintaining the client's problem are (a) the client's vocational history, (b) the client's present verbal behavior, and (c) the client's present nonverbal behavior. If clients have been able to gather sufficient vocational information on which to deliberate and arrive at an appropriate vocational decision in the past, their present indecisiveness would appear to result from anxiety rather than from a lack of decision making skills. If clients describe themselves as being incapable of making a decision but stubbornly retain the prerogative of rejecting counselor suggestions as inappropriate, they may be using paradoxical statements to avoid decision making. If the clients make no effort on their own to gather vocational information, they are apparently successfully avoiding decision making. Clients may also report or indicate by facial or bodily expression excessive fear of being rejected for a job or of finding themselves in an inappropriate job situation.

Definition of the Goal

Major behavioral components of decision making are information seeking, deliberation, and decision statements. Once the counselors have decided that the client is avoiding decision making, they can focus on increasing the occurrence of these components in the client's behavioral repertoire by means of counselor-controlled reinforcement contingencies. Information seeking, deliberation statements, and decision statements will constitute the target behaviors for the counseling strategy presented here.

According to Gelatt (1962), decision making is a cyclical process. Information seeking requires some prior deliberation and decision making, and adequate information is necessary for appropriate deliberation and decision making. After devoting sufficient time to initiate a counseling relationship, to explore a client's problem, and tentatively to evaluate the nature of the problem, counselors can decide with which of the three decision components to begin the reinforcement program. They should attempt to have their clients enter the decision making cycle by means of the component most appropriate for each client. Some counselors might begin the program with clients who express total ignorance of the occupational world by reinforcing information seeking behavior. With clients who claim minimal occupational information, they might begin by reinforcing deliberation. To ensure the possibility of evaluating the efficacy of the counselor-selected reinforcement contingency, counselors should reinforce these components successively rather than simultaneously. Counselors should ignore those client self-reports in which clients describe themselves as being unable to seek information, to deliberate, or to make decisions.

Clients whose presenting problem is an inconsistent indecisiveness with regard to vocational choice do not implicitly request that their inconsistency and indecisiveness be reduced. They usually express an interest in finding appropriate employment. Another assumption underlying this counseling strategy is that reducing the clients' inconsistency and indecisiveness will facilitate their finding such employment. The evaluation of this strategy's ultimate effectiveness should be derived from an examination of the degree to which this goal is attained.

Definition of Possible
Reinforcement Contingencies

The verbal and nonverbal social responses used by Krumboltz and Thoreson (1964) and Ryan and Krumboltz (1964) to reinforce information seeking behavior, deliberation statements, and decision statements in experimental settings can be used by counselors during counseling sessions. These social responses probably function as reinforcing stimuli because they reflect the counselors' affirmation of and attention to client behavior. Other interpersonal responses which reflect counselor attention and which can be used as reinforcement by counselors are interpretations, confrontations, and reflections (Kanfer & Phillips 1970, p. 393).

To the extent that the reinforcement value of counselor responses is derived from the desirability of counselor affirmations and attention, the effectiveness of these responses in changing client behavior will be dependent on the nature of the client-counselor relationship. Therefore, for their responses to be of value to the client, counselors will have to demonstrate their genuine interest in the client. They will not be able simply to administer mechanistic responses.

Counselors should use implicit reinforcement contingencies. Explicit reinforcement contingencies might be interpreted by the client as direct suggestions that the client has the capacity to make decisions. Since the client is presumed to be avoiding decision making by denying the capacity to make decisions, direct suggestions might reinforce the client's denial. In addition, task ambiguity has been

shown to increase the reinforcement value of social stimuli (Kanfer & Phillips 1970, p. 396).

Evaluation of the Efficacy
of the Counseling Strategy

Since counselors can differentially reinforce this treatment strategy's target behaviors, they can evaluate whether the relative frequencies of these behaviors changed during the counseling treatment session. Counselors should tape record the counseling treatment sessions. They should divide the responses which the client emitted during that session. If the frequency and seeking responses, deliberation responses, decision responses, and other responses and then compare the variety and frequency of the response category being reinforced during each session to the variety and frequency of the response categories not being reinforced during that session. If the frequency and variety of reinforced responses are not greater than the frequency and variety of nonreinforced responses during any treatment session, the efficacy of the reinforcement contigency employed by the counselors during that treatment session is questionable.

By setting aside a portion of the counseling session to explore with the client the information which the client stated he or she would obtain or the outcome of a decision which the client made, counselors can evaluate the generalization of reinforcement effects to noncounseling settings. Counselors can also confirm the degree to which counselor reinforcement of information seeking and decision making during the counseling session modifies the client's behavior in the desired direction outside the counseling session by directly contacting the resources the client is to use to carry out the information seeking and decision statements. The generalization of deliberation statements emitted in the counseling session can only be evaluated indirectly by examining their effect on information seeking and decision making.

The ultimate sucess of this counseling strategy will be revealed by the client's attainment of appropriate employment. After the client has begun to emit a high frequency of information seeking behavior, deliberation statements, and decision responses both in and out of the counseling situation, appropriate employment should eventually be found. Gonyea (1962), in his investigation of the use of "appropriateness-of-vocational-choice" as a counseling criterion, demonstrated that counselor judgment of this criterion is of doubtful validity. The best that counselors can do is to recall clients for an interview after the clients have been employed for an arbitrary period of time to evaluate whether they are satisfied with the job. With the clients' permission, counselors can also interview the clients' employers, asking them whether they are satisfied with their employee. If the clients do not find appropriate employment after making an intensive effort to find it, counselors should reconsider their original hypothesis concerning the clients' problem.

Alternate Counseling Strategies

The evaluations just outlined could reveal one of the following failures of this counseling strategy:

1. Differential reinforcement of the behavioral components of decision making may not increase the frequency and variety with which these components are emitted by the client during the counseling treatment sessions.

2. Treatment effects produced by differential reinforcement during the counseling sessions may not be followed by increased client decisiveness outside of the counseling session.

3. Increased client decisiveness may not eventuate in the client's finding appropriate employment.

Counselors can attempt to increase the effectiveness of the reinforcement contingencies they are employing by increasing the reinforcement value of the contingent stimuli, by adding modeling to the reinforcement, by punishing competing behaviors, or by increasing client dissonance to the point at which this dissonance becomes aversive for the client. To increase the generalizability of the treatment, desensitization could be combined with the reinforcement of decision making behaviors.

A counselor's evaluation of a client's problem should always remain open to revision. If counselors who originally felt that the client's indecisiveness served as a means of avoiding decision making find the client unable to find appropriate employment even after the client has become an ardent decision maker in the noncounseling world, the counselors should reconsider their own clinical decision. The client's inability to find a job may not be the result of prior avoidance behavior, but it may be the consequence of some other condition. In this case, counselors would need to identify the underlying problem and develop a suitable counseling strategy to alleviate it.

REFERENCES

Collins, B. J. The effect of monetary inducements on the amount of attitude change produced by forced compliance. *In* A. C. Elms (Ed.) Role playing, reward, and attitude change. New York: Van Nostrand Reinhold, 1969, Pp. 209–223.

Gelatt, H. B. Decision-making: A conceptual frame of reference for counseling. Journal of Counseling Psychology, 1962, 9:240–245.

Gonyea, G. G. Appropriateness-of-vocational-choice as a criterion of counseling outcome. Journal of Counseling Psychology, 1962, 9:213–220.

Haley, J. Strategies of psychotherapy. New York: Grune & Stratton, 1963.

Kanfer, F. H., & Phillips, J. S. Learning foundations of behavior therapy. New York: Wiley, 1970.

Krumboltz, J. D. & Thoreson, C. E. The effect of behavioral counseling in group and individual settings on information-seeking behavior. Journal of Counseling Psychology, 1964, 11:324–333.

Lublin, I. Sources of differences in effectiveness among controllers of verbal reinforcement. *In* R. C. Anderson et al. (Eds.), Current research on instruction. Englewood Cliffs, N.J.: Prentice-Hall, 1969. Pp. 202–210.

Ryan, T. A., & Krumboltz, J. D. Effects of planned reinforcement counseling on client decision-making behavior. Journal of Counseling Psychology, 1964, 11:315–323.

Truax, C. B. Reinforcement and non-reinforcement in Rogerian psychotherapy. Journal of Abnormal Psychology, 1966, 71:1–9.

Walker, R. A. "Pounce": Learning responsibility for one's own employment problems. *In* J. D. Krumboltz and C. E. Thoreson (Eds.), Behavioral counseling: Cases and techniques. New York: Holt, Rinehart & Winston, 1969. Pp. 399–414.

12 Interpreting Nonverbal Behavior, a Key to More Effective Counseling
Review of Literature

Duane Brown
and James C. Parks

Rehabilitation counseling as a human enterprise has been conceptualized in many different ways. There is, however, at least one central theme upon which most of these conceptualizations would agree: the need for an optimal level of communication between rehabilitation counselor and client. It is our contention that the vital process of communication can be facilitated if rehabilitation counselors can be sensitized to both the recognition and the interpretation of certain gross nonverbal behaviors.

Within the context of a counseling session, overt and covert behaviors occur which provide input to the counselor. Clients speak and their voice quality affects the reception of the verbal message. They cross and uncross their legs, make gestures, engage in eye contact, increase or decrease their physical proximity, shrug their shoulders, etc. In short, the message that clients verbally transmit is usually amplified, or at least modified by their nonverbal behavior. As Davitz (1964) and Reusch (1955) contend, nonverbal behavior serves a complementary function with verbal behavior; both are intertwined facets of communication. This contention is particularly noteworthy when counseling the clients of the typical rehabilitation counselor, since nonverbal behavior is often the primary mode of communication for some groups such as the mentally retarded, speech handicapped, and certain other clients whose handicaps have caused unsatisfactory experiences with people.

In summary, there exist global techniques through which individuals communicate with one another. For many clients the primary recognized mode of communication is the spoken word, but even within this context messages are often ambiguous. These verbal influences are in a sense confirmed or unconfirmed by nonverbal actions. The focus of this article is on some of these nonverbal aspects of communication, examining primarily eye contact, gestures, and use of personal space. It includes the importance of these variables for the communications process. The objective is to increase the rehabilitation counselor's awareness of both his own and his client's nonverbal behaviors. The inference is that counselors can—by becoming more aware

Reprinted by permission from the March 1972 *Rehabilitation Counseling Bulletin*, pp. 176–184.

of their own and their clients' nonverbal behaviors—enhance the probability of their own effectiveness.

EYE CONTACT

Eye contact is one of the more obvious of the nonverbal dimensions of communication between counselor and client. A review of relevant research has indicated that the meanings that may be attached to eye contact are both numerous and complex. For example, Exline and Winter (1965) found that eye contact was greater when an interviewer was providing positive feedback. Interviewers who engaged in greater amounts of eye contact during positive feedback were judged as preferred by interviewees. Exline, Gray, and Shutte (1965) found that there was less eye contact when personal or embarrassing questions were asked. Argyle and Dean (1965) presented data on the relationship between eye contact and physical proximity. They found that as distance decreased so did eye contact, which they concluded was the result of intimacy that became too intense.

In a study that looked at the popular assumption that lack of eye contact elicits negative reaction, Ellsworth and Carlsmith (1968) found that when the topic of the interview was neutral or positive, subjects liked the interviewer more when he looked at them directly. They rated the interview more favorably than did subjects who were not engaged by the interviewer in eye contact. On the other hand, when the content of the interview was negative, the group not looked at liked the interviewer more and rated the interview more favorably than the looked-at group. Ellsworth and Carlsmith speculated that there is perhaps something rewarding about discussing oneself negatively when the interviewer is not looking. It also seems plausible that the explanation for the phenomenon may lie in the intensity of the embarrassment experienced by a subject when talking to an interviewer about himself in a negative fashion.

Argyle and Dean (1965) have summarized some of the major functions of eye contact in interpersonal relationships:
1. Obtaining social feedback to determine how one is received.
2. Indicating that one is ready to receive feedback.
3. Hiding one's feelings because of past experiences through avoiding eye contact.
4. Seeking to be seen, recognized, and thus confirmed as a "real" person.
5. Accomplishing some or all of the above simultaneously.

Eyeblink rate, although not directly related to eye contact, has been researched by Appel, McCarron, and Manning (1968). Briefly, they found that when subjects were confronted with varying amounts of threat their eye blink rate tended to increase as the amount of threat increased.

What conclusions can rehabilitation counselors draw from these diverse findings? How can eye contact as a variable increase their counseling compotency? Although the data are incomplete, there are a number of inferences that the counselor might draw. First, eye contact with a counselee must generally be considered as a plus factor in a counseling interview. One exception to this assumption is when the counselee discusses himself in a negative fashion. In this instance, lack of eye contact may not be indicative of poor counselor-client communication. Second, eye contact can provide the counselor with insight regarding his moment-to-moment impact upon the counselee. For example, previously cited research indicates that eye contact may be lowered or eye blink rate increased under conditions that could be judged as threatening. Eye contact seems to be an indication of interpersonal intimacy, although there does seem to be a point beyond which this is not true. Third, although eye contact is an important variable, it must be considered within the broader context of client behaviors.

GESTURES

For purposes of this discussion, gestures are limited to definitions given in Rosenfeld's research (1966) regarding the use of nonverbal response in approval-seeking functions in a dyadic relationship. The gestures include smiles, positive and negative head nods, gesticulations, and self-manipulation.

The research does indicate that the counselor can glean information regarding the client's emotional state from gestures. Sainsbury (1955), for example, recorded gestures during high and low stress periods and found that the numbers of gestures increased during high stress periods. Dittman (1962) also studied gestures during various moods. He found that when his subjects were angry, they exhibited many head and leg movements but few hand gestures. When the subjects were in a depressed mood, they exhibited few hand and head movements but many leg movements. Both of these studies are supported by the results of research by Ekman (1965) who found that lower body gestures tended to be manifestations of intense emotion.

Needles (1965) provides what may be a tentative explanation for the findings in the foregoing studies. He suggested that gestures are utilized during periods of great emotion when speech is ineffectual.

Rosenfeld (1966) and Fretz (1966) conducted studies that looked at a broader range of gestural behavior. Rosenfeld found that positive head nods and smiles were associated with approval-seeking and negative head nods with approval avoidance. Further, positive head nods and smiles elicited favorable responses from persons from whom approval was sought. Fretz (1966) studied many of the same factors researched by Rosenfeld but did so within the context of a counseling relationship. His findings, in conjunction with those similar outcomes of the Rosenfeld research, led him to suggest three hypotheses regarding counselor-client interaction:

1. Clients who perceived highly favorable relationships with their counselors as compared with clients who perceived unfavorable relationships, utilize (a)

significantly fewer negative nods/
points and (b) significantly more leaning forward and back.
2. Counselors who perceive highly favorable relationships with their clients,
as compared with counselors who perceive unfavorable relationships, utilize
(a) significantly more hand movements
and (b) significantly more smiles and
laughs.
3. Counselors in approval-seeking
conditions, as compared with counselors in non-approval-seeking conditions, utilize (a) significantly more
positive nods and (b) significantly more
smiles and laughs.

Other hypotheses, in addition to
Fretz's, can be suggested. It seems
likely that clients under stress will be
somewhat restricted in their hand
movement, but trunk and leg movement may be accentuated. This may be
illustrated by the client who grips the
arms of his chair but shuffles his feet
nervously and shifts his position in his
chair. An additional factor to be considered in the interpretation of gestural
behavior, especially for the rehabilitation counselor, is the nature and extent
of the client's handicap and the personal impact of these handicaps upon
his gestures.

PROXEMICS

The term proxemics, introduced into
research literature by Hall (1959), was
coined to represent and delimit certain
categories of nonverbal behavior, i.e.,
distance, touching, and orientation.
Primarily, the proxemic dimensions of
distance and orientation will be examined in this section. Distance is operationally defined as the physical space
that separates the counselor from the
counselee, the addresser from the addressee, etc. Orientation refers both to
the angle through which the median
place of a speaker is turned with regard
to his addressee and other gross torso
movements such as leaning forward
and leaning backward.

Hall (1959) has indicated that the
distance between two speakers is governed by implicit norms within a particular culture, that there is a permissi-
ble range in distance between speakers
which, if violated, will result in the
formation of negative attitudes. He further suggests that the closer a speaker is
to his addressee, the greater the communication of a positive attitude.

Hall's theory has found support.
Argyle and Dean (1965) have cited evidence for an equilibrium level of physical proximity. For example, when talking to a stranger of the same sex,
Americans tend to stand not closer than
18 to 20 inches, they tended to stand
side-to-side or to orient their faces at
right angles to one another. It was also
reported that experimental subjects
who were physically within 2 feet of
one another tried to increase the physical distance, while subjects at 10 feet
tried to reduce the distance, Also, the
subjects who were 2 feet apart reported
that they were uncomfortable or tense.

Steinzor (1950) found that subjects in groups of 10 were least likely to
speak to those nearest to them and were
most likely to address those group
members who were a few paces away.

A study by Sommer (1962) reported that people usually preferred to sit no more than five and one-half feet apart. Sommer's study also indicated that experimental subjects, when physically close, preferred to converse from a corner seat position where they would not be directly facing one another.

Mehrabian, in two articles (1968a, 1968b), reported the results of several experiments that dealt both with the distance between the speaker and the addressee and with the physical posture of the addressee. His finding indicated that greater body relaxation, a forward lean of the torso toward the addressee, and a smaller distance to the addressee tended to communicate a more positive attitude toward the addressee. On the other hand, a backward posture lean, a larger distance between the addresser and addressee, and a tense posture tended to communicate a more negative attitude.

In conclusion, Hall has indicated that there are preferred distances between speakers which tend to be governed by cultural norms and that attitudes tend to be influenced by a violation of these norms. Sommer, Steinzor, and Argyle and Dean have produced evidence for an equilibrium level of physical proximity which lends support to Hall's contention. Mehrabian has indicated that certain variables—degree of relaxation, distance from addressee, lean of torso toward the addressee—communicate a more positive speaker attitude.

Of particular importance to rehabilitation counselors are those variables which, when modified, tend to result in greater probability of a more positive client attitude. Evidence has been cited indicating that the amount of distance that separates the counselor from the client has a bearing upon the communication of attitude. Other data indicate that body relaxation and/or forward lean of the torso toward the addressee (client) conveys a more positive addressor (counselor) attitude. In the interpretation of proxemic behavior for the rehabilitation client, the counselor is cautioned to be cognizant of the specific physical and emotional handicaps of his client. Occasionally the client who comes to the rehabilitation counselor may have feelings about his physical appearance or actual physical handicap which will influence his posture, torso position, or distance from the counselor. The counselor should consider these factors.

SYNTHESIS

The foregoing analysis of nonverbal behavior has been presented in three distinct sections. In reality the counselor rarely encounters nonverbal behavior in this compartmentalized manner. The dilemma for the counselor lies in the interpretation of totality of the client's behavior and the need to respond in a manner that will facilitate client growth. In order to assist the counselor in making judgments about the meaning of nonverbal cues, the following illustration of how a client might react in two counseling climates is provided. Although not all nonverbal behaviors can be expected to occur at a given time in a single counseling session, the presence of several of these behaviors can be indicative of the counseling climate.

Negative Climate

High eye blink rate, little eye contact, lower body movements, reduced hand movements, body lean away from counselor, general orientation away from counselor, negative head nods.

Positive Climate

High eye contact, smiles, positive head nods, hand gestures, forward body lean, direct orientation.

Facilitative action is suggested when a negative climate is detected. Under this condition the counselor may need to focus introspectively upon his own verbal and nonverbal behavior in order to determine the source of threat. The counselor may also deal with his perception of the negative climate by discussing it with his client or in some cases through directly manipulating his proximity, his orientation, etc., in a direct attempt to communicate his desire to improve the relationship. Additionally, the counselor may wish to focus verbally upon both his own and the client's behaviors in order to deal effectively with the emerging interaction.

SUMMARY

The assumptions that provided the framework upon which this article was constructed had two major dimensions: They were related to both an increased *counselor self-awareness* and to an increased *counselor awareness of his client*. These assumptions were that: (a) most rehabilitation counselors have a greater sensitivity to the verbal aspects of their own and of their client's communication processes; (b) certain gross nonverbal client and counselor behaviors are directly related to the counseling relationship; (c) certain nonverbal behaviors can be recognized and their implications assessed; and (d) through an understanding and recognition of these nonverbal behaviors counselors can become aware of their own attitudes toward their clients and of their clients' attitudes toward them.

The meaningfulness of the research reported here will be determined by the degree to which it can be applied to the counseling endeavor. If rehabilitation counselors find that they can better interpret and understand the attitudes that they imply to their clients or the attitudes that their clients imply to them, this article will have relevance.

REFERENCES

Appel, V. H., McCarron, L. T., & Manning, B. A. Eyeblink rate: Behavior index of threat, Journal of Counseling Psychology, 1968, 18:153–157.

Argyle, M., & Dean, J. Eye contact, distance and affiliation. Sociometry. 1965, 28:289–304.

Davitz, J. R. (Ed.) The communication of emotional meaning. New York: McGraw-Hill, 1964.

Dittman, A. T. The relationship between body movements and moods in interviews. Journal of Counseling Psychology, 1962, 26:480.

Ekman, P. Differential communication of affect by head and body cues. Journal of Personality and Social Psychology, 1965, 2:726–735.

Ellsworth, P. C., & Carlsmith, J. M. Effect of eye contact and verbal content on affective response in a dyadic interaction. Journal of Personality and Social Psychology, 1968, 10:15–20.

Exline, R. V., Gray, D., & Schuette, D. Visual behavior in a dyad as affected by interview content and sex of respondent. Journal of Personality and Social Psychology, 1965, 1:201–210.

Exline, R. V., & Winter, L. C. Affective relations and motive glances in dyads. In S. Tompkins and A. C. Izzard (Eds.), Affect, cognition and personality, New York: Springer, 1965.

Fretz, B. R. Postural movements in a counseling dyad. Journal of Counseling Psychology, 1966, 13:344–347.

Hall, E. T. The silent language, New York: Doubleday, 1959.

Mehrabian, A. Inferences of attitudes from the posture, orientation, and distance of a communicator. Journal of Consulting and Clinical Psychology, 1968, 32: 296–308.

Mehrabian, R. Relationship of attitudes to seated posture, orientation, and distance of a communicator. Journal of Personality and Social Psychology, 1968, 10: 26–30.

Needles, W. Gesticulation and speech. International Journal of Psychoanalysis, 1959, 40:291–294.

Rosenfeld, H. M. Approval-seeking and approval-inducing functions of verbal and nonverbal responses in the dyad. Journal of Personality and Social Psychology, 1966, 4:597–605.

Ruesch, J. Nonverbal language and therapy. Psychiatry, 1965, 18:323–330.

Sainsbury, P. Gestural movements during the psychiatric interview. Psychosomatic Medicine, 1955, 17:458–469.

Sommer, R. The distance for comfortable conversations: A further study. Sociometry, 1962, 25:111–116.

Steinzor, B. The spatial factor in face to face discussion groups. Journal of Abnormal and Social Psychology, 1950, 45:582–585.

13 Rational Therapy in Rehabilitation Counseling

Ben N. Ard, Jr.

Rehabilitation counseling probably involves some of the most difficult work in the whole field of counseling, inasmuch as many rehabilitation clients have physical handicaps which radically change the sort of life they can live (as compared to their lives before their handicap). So what follows will be some ideas (radical, too, by the way) that may help the rehabilitation counselor in his work with rehabilitation clients. These ideas stem, in the main, from Albert Ellis, a psychologist in private practice in New York City, where he is the Executive Director of the Institute for Rational Living. A basic source book would be his *Reason and Emotion in Psychotherapy* (1962). Ellis calls his approach rational therapy (often called RT for short); it may be particularly well fitted for counseling with rehabilitation clients.

One of the unique aspects of RT is its emphasis on cognitive aspects in counseling, hence the name rational therapy. Heretofore in the history of counseling and psychotherapy, from Sigmund Freud to Carl Rogers, the major emphasis has been primarily on the client's irrational impulses and feelings, rather than on what the client thinks. That perceptive observer of human beings, Mark Twain, once said that "We all do no end of feeling and mistake it for thinking" (*Life*, May 13, 1966, p. 16).

Ellis suggests that the counselor should get behind the client's feelings and get at his thinking, if counseling is to be of the most effective help. Put in simple *A-B-C* terms, it is rarely the external stimulus situation, *A*, which gives rise directly to an emotional reaction, *C*. Rather, it is almost always *B*—the individual's beliefs regarding, attitudes toward, or interpretation of, *A*—which actually lead to his reaction, *C*. As Epictetus has put it, "Men are disturbed not by things, but by the views which they take of them" (Oates, 1940). Shakespeare, in Hamlet, said, "There's nothing either good or bad but thinking makes it so."

The basic job of counselors, then, is to help clients see for themselves that it is necessary for them to work on the *B* step, their assumptions or internalized sentences, rather than railing at the external situation, *A*, or wallowing in their own miseries at *C*. If clients can be encouraged to work on questioning their assumptions, encouraged to challenge their self-defeating values, they can develop more rational and therefore

This paper was presented at the Bay Area Rehabilitation Counselors' Association meeting in Oakland, California, January 11, 1967.

Reprinted by permission from the December 1968 *Rehabilitation Counseling Bulletin*, pp. 84–88.

more self-satisfying philosophies and lives.

In the rational approach to counseling (as opposed to other approaches), there is an attempt to help the client acquire three levels of insight (Ellis, 1962, pp. 187–188). *Insight 1* is the usual kind of understanding that the Freudians make much of: namely, the individual's seeing that his present actions have a prior or antecedent cause.

An additional and unique contribution of RT, however, is that rational therapy does not stop there but goes on to further insights. That is, *Insight 2:* namely, the understanding that the irrational ideas acquired by the individual in his past life are still existent, and that they largely exist today because he himself keeps reindoctrinating himself with these ideas, consciously or unconsciouly.

And finally, *Insight 3* is the full understanding by the client that he simply has got to change his erroneous and illogical thinking. Unless the client, after acquiring *Insights 1 and 2,* fully sees and accepts the fact that there is no other way for him to get better than by forcefully and consistently attacking his early-acquired and still heartily-held irrational ideas, he will definitely not overcome his emotional disturbance.

The rational approach, then, adds to the rehabilitation counselor's other methods the more direct techniques of confrontation, confutation, deindoctrination, and reeducation, as well as a rather unusual contribution known as "homework assignments." In assigning "homework," the counselor tries to encourage, persuade, and impel clients to do the things they are afraid of (e.g., risk rejection) in order to see more concretely that these things are not actually fearsome. As Epictetus has stated, "Remember that foul words or blows in themselves are no outrage, but (only) your judgment that they are so. So when any one makes you angry, know that it is your own thought that has angered you" (Oates, 1940, pp. 472–472).

Probably many rehabilitation clients implicitly assume that they must be unhappy when they are frustrated. They believe, in other words, the irrational idea that it is terrible, horrible, and catastrophic when things are not going the way one would like them to go.

As long as their actions show that they are implicitly at least presuming this idea, they will not get well (psychologically). The counselor can help a client believing such self-defeating thoughts by getting the client to challenge this basic assumption. Adults can work to end their frustrations, to change their environments, or they can philosophically accept their existing life handicaps when these cannot be changed.

If human beings conducted their lives with consistent intelligence, they would have many different kinds of experiences; they would enjoy some and dislike others; they would keep seeking the experiences they enjoy and calmly avoid those they do not enjoy; and finally, when they could not avoid certain unpleasant experiences—such as losing the use of their arms, eyesight, or legs—they would still calmly accept the fact that life holds certain inevitable unpleasantries and frustrations and that that is too bad—but it is not terrible, atrocious, or catastrophic.

As a rehabilitation counselor employing a rational approach, one might say to his client:

> If you make yourself—yes, make yourself—terribly upset and unhappy about your frustrations, you will almost invariably block yourself from effectively removing them. The more time and energy you expend in lamenting your sorry fate, ranting against your frustrators, and gnashing your teeth in despair, the less effective action you will be able to take in counteracting your handicaps. Whether you like it or not, you simply must accept reality when you cannot change it. Reality is; and if it is unfortunate and frustrating, that is bad; but it is still not necessarily catastrophic (Ellis & Harper, 1961, p. 113).

"When faced with a frustrating set of circumstances, you should first determine whether it is truly handicapping in its own right or whether you are not essentially defining it so" (Ellis & Harper, 1961, p. 117). "If the frustration that you face is truly considerable and there is no way in which you can presently significantly change or control it, then you would better gracefully and realistically accept it. Yes: not with bitterness and despair, but with dignity and grace" (Ellis & Harper, 1961, p. 118). One man put it this way, "If it be my lot to crawl, I will crawl contentedly, if to fly, I will fly with alacrity; but as long as I can avoid it, I will never be unhappy."

A moderate degree of accepting the inevitable frustrations and unpleasantness of life is indispensable for unanxious and unhostile living. If there is nothing more that can be done: tough. That's the way the cards fall. Why make the game of life so much more difficult by fretting and stewing about its existing inequities? If the circumstances one lives under are not changeable, then one can philosophically learn to live under such conditions without making himself panicky about them.

As a rational counselor, one might say something like the following to his client:

> Track your worries and anxieties back to the specific sentences of which they consist. Invariably, you will find that you are telling yourself: "Isn't it terrible that—" or "Wouldn't it be awful if—." Forcefully ask yourself: "Why would it be so terrible that—?" and "Would it really be so awful if—?" Certainly, if this or that happened it might well be inconvenient, annoying, or unfortunate. But would it really be catastrophic? (Ellis & Harper, 1961, p. 140).

"If the situation cannot be minimized, then you have little or no choice and you'd just better accept it. No matter how you slice it, the inevitable is still inevitable; and no amount of worrying will make it less so." Another Stoic philosopher, Marcus Aurelius, has put the matter most succinctly, "If thou are pained by any external thing, it is not this thing that disturbs thee, but thy own judgment about it. And it is in thy power to wipe out this judgment now" (Oates, 1940, p. 550).

Perhaps another relatively common irrational idea might be found among many rehabilitation clients from time to time, namely, the irrational idea that people and things should be different from the way they are and that it is catastrophic if perfect solutions to the grim realities of life are not immediately found. As a rational counselor, one might say to a client that believes this sort of thing:

> When things or events go wrong, that is unfortunate, and may affect you adversely. But the adversity thereby caused you is rarely half so bad as you think it is or as you make it by telling yourself "Things shouldn't be this way. I can't stand it" (Ellis & Harper, 1961, p. 164). When conditions are not the way you would prefer them to be, calmly and determinedly try to change them for the better; and when they cannot be changed, the only sane thing to do is quietly to accept them. If you fail, that is unfortunate; but it rarely is catastrophic. And failure never—no never!—has anything to do with your intrinsic value as a person. Humans only learn by doing and failing—that is probably the main aspect of reality that you must accept (Ellis & Harper, 1961, p. 172).

Since a somewhat Stoic philosophy would seem to be a necessity for many rehabilitation clients, we shall turn to Epictetus for some final, succinct wisdom: "What disturbs men's minds is not events but their judgments on events. . . . And so when we are hindered, or disturbed, or distressed, let us never lay the blame on others, but on ourselves, that is, on our own judgments. To accuse others for one's own misfortune is a sign of want of education; to accuse oneself shows that one's education has begun; to accuse neither oneself nor others shows that one's education is complete" (Oates, 1940, p. 469).

REFERENCES

Ellis, A. Reason and emotion in psychotherapy. New York: Lyle Stuart, 1962.

Ellis, A., and Harper, R. A. A guide to rational living. Englewood Cliffs, N.J.: Prentice-Hall, 1961.

Oates, W. J. (Editor). The stoic and epicurean philosophers. New York: Random House, 1940.

14 The Gestalt Approach to Rehabilitation Counseling

Arnold B. Coven

Rehabilitation counselors and other human services professionals are constantly seeking more powerful means of helping people. The increased impetus to assist the severely disabled has also increased the demand to find more effective counseling procedures. Bozarth and Rubin (1975) in a five-year study obtained results that suggested counselors might raise their level of functioning through increased psychological understanding and increased training in interpersonal skills. Gestalt therapy, which has emerged as a major force in mental health, may partly fulfill the need of rehabilitation counselors to obtain greater psychological insight and increased skill in interventions, which produce changes in disabled clients.

The potential of Gestalt therapy for counselors has been recognized by the American Personnel and Guidance Association's inclusion of two Gestalt programs in its 1976 "Counselor Development workshops" (APGA 1976). In a recent text, Passons (1975) emphasized that Gestalt techniques can be utilized by counselors who have been using aspects of client-centered counseling, rational-emotive therapy, transactional analysis, and other change approaches from the field of psychotherapy. Passons points out that learning Gestalt techniques would not make counselors into Gestalt therapists but would afford trained counselors the opportunity of adding to their helping repertoire. The purpose of this article is to (a) present an overview of the theory of Gestalt therapy, (b) examine the rehabilitation process from this Gestalt perspective, (c) identify Gestalt techniques that can be used effectively by rehabilitation counselors, and (d) show the congruence of rehabilitation counseling philosophy and the Gestalt approach.

GESTALT THEORY

Gestalt theory emphasizes self-awareness, self-integration, and self-fulfillment; the counseling methodology is directed toward achieving these goals. Gestalt therapy is an existential helping approach that assumes human beings have the potential to choose their behavior and thus define their own meaning in life. To facilitate this functioning, Gestalt therapists attempt to help people use their faculties of awareness fully so they can discover

Reprinted by permission from the March 1977 *Rehabilitation Counseling Bulletin*, pp. 167–174.

how to be responsible for choosing their own behavior. Perls believed that without such awareness people are unable to make choices and determine their existence (Yontef 1969).

Gestalt is a German word that, crudely translated, means the forming of an organized, meaningful whole. Perls perceived people as being fragmented and lacking wholeness. He believed that people are aware of only parts of themselves and that they need to become aware of, acknowledge, reclaim, and integrate these fragmented parts in order to become whole. This integration would help in the transition from dependency to self-sufficiency, from authoritarian outer support to authentic inner support (James & Jongeward 1971). The basic concepts supporting this theory are: (a) a person is a total system, (b) a change in one part of the individual affects the "whole" person, and (c) humans seek closure, the completion of unfinished situations. This Gestalt theory, as well as Gestalt principles of figure/ground relationships, have led to the focusing in Gestalt therapy on the aspect of the person that "stands out" or is obvious. The therapist helps the person be aware of "figural" parts and then facilitates their integration into the individual's whole being, thus enabling the individual to achieve a strong personal Gestalt. According to Perls, Hefferline and Goodman (1951, p. 232) "The achievement of a strong Gestalt is the cure."

Gestalt theory is similar to other personality theories that view needs as the organizer of behavior. In Gestalt theory the essential human need is homeostasis; the achievement of an individual balance and integration that occurs when needs have been fulfilled in a way that leaves the person complete. Whatever is missing in a person's system "stands out" as a need in the background of his or her existence. The person then behaves in a way to meet and complete this unfulfilled part of the self. Once this need has been satisfied, another need becomes the figure or dominant dimension of the person's being, and the homeostatic process continues.

In Gestalt therapy theory, heavy dependence on others and the environment for need fulfillment is considered immature. If the person has a self-support system, ways of behaving that use one's own power to meet needs, then the person is considered integrated, complete, and mature. An ideal balance occurs when the organism has equal ways of fulfilling itself and obtaining support from the environment. From the Gestalt viewpoint, a person's struggle toward self- and environmental support, as well as the opposite poles of meeting one's needs and not having them met, reflect the nature of personality and behavior conflicts. These contradictory needs create impasses in an organism's functioning. Gestalt therapists believe that people cannot be understood or helped to change unless this paradoxical nature of human existence is taken into account. Thus, in addition to the previously mentioned emphases, Gestalt counselors also focus on helping individuals become aware of their bipolar nature of being and behaving, using techniques to assist the unblocking of the impasses it creates.

REHABILITATION COUNSELING APPLICATIONS

Initial Interview

The first visit of a client to a rehabilitation agency is undoubtedly vague with no clear figures or boundaries evident. The person does not know what to expect from the agency or the counselor. The client has a poor Gestalt and often experiments with various behaviors for the maintenance of homeostatic balance. The individual may try to meet the need for safety or some other need that is in the foreground. Does the person seek to manipulate the counselor and the environment to meet these needs, or is there an adequate self-support system in the individual? Does the person ask many questions, or wait for the counselor to talk or lead the interview? How does the person sit? What is the client's voice like? The Gestalt rehabilitation counselor is looking for the behavior that stands out and assists the individual to be aware of this obvious behavior and the need it represents. Questions such as, "What are you aware of now?" "How are you presently?" and "What do you need?" facilitate this process.

Gestalt counselors do give a good deal of attention to the client's need to constantly ask questions, as this behavior often represents the passivity of the individual (Levitsky & Perls 1970). The questioner is usually saying, "Give me, tell me, do for me." In this way, the client attempts to influence the counselor to assume the responsibility for the rehabilitation work. The Gestalt rehabilitation counselor strives to help the client be aware of these efforts to give the power to the counselor (Passons 1975). The Gestalt counselor also uses the technique of asking clients to change their questions into statements (e.g., "What should I do with my life now?" into "I want you to tell me what to do"). This highlights the client's dependent behavior and sets the stage for the client choosing whether this is the way he or she wants to be. This is just one step in helping persons begin to take ownership of their problems and start the struggle for self-support. When a client is asked to change questions into statements, the counselor does not necessarily know what will occur. Clients often answer their own questions. In fact, one often used Gestalt technique is to have clients try answering their life questions, which facilitates the development of personal power in problem solving.

Loss and Need

What does the person who has suffered a spinal cord injury and is now paraplegic need in order to maintain his or her unique, individual balance? One Gestalt approach is to determine how the loss has affected the homeostasis. Disabled persons struggle to restore equilibrium to their world. The loss may have changed the ways in which needs are fulfilled. Because every person is different and has had a unique history, nothing can be assumed. In the here-and-now encounter, the counselor has to increase the person's awareness of needs and assist their fulfillment.

The paraplegic, who has suffered a loss in mobility, may need the feeling of movement. What can the client do to fulfill this need in the living counseling situation? The disabled person may be able to fulfill this need with a feeling of moving in life. The counselor can help by moving the person quickly into the beginning rehabilitation stages—the medical examination, psychological testing, and vocational exploration. A heightened awareness of needs and steps that can be followed to satisfy them may also supply the feeling of momentum to the disabled person.

The paraplegic may not have this specific need when first visiting the rehabilitation counselor. He or she may still be in some stage of mourning, such as denial, anger, or depression. The Gestalt counselor can facilitate the expression and completion of the needs of the mourning experience so that a need like "moving on in life" can come to the fore. If we feel the clients should be over the mourning stage when they come to our rehabilitation agency, it is our need that may not be fulfilled by the rehabilitation venture.

Rehabilitation in the Present

The phrase "here and now" is a byword of Gestalt therapy; it helps counselors and clients stay in the present. The counselor who is present centered looks at and listens to the person, observing his or her mannerisms, movement of the body, and use of the voice. The counselor helps the client come in contact with present experiencing; this is done in small steps so that the person may become independent. One technique for following this principle of the now is to ask questions such as "What is your present awareness?" "What is happening now? and "What do you feel at this moment?"

If a person talks in a low, sad voice, he or she may be creating the sadness. The counselor may help the person to stay in the here-and-now as follows:

Client: I feel sad. I feel as if I were standing still in life.
Counselor: Are you aware of your voice right now?
Client: It is quiet, as if I were nonexistent.
Counselor: Could you try saying, "Right now I am making myself sad and deadlike."

The client is being asked to focus on how at the present moment he or she is maintaining the sense of depression and being "nonalive." This also illustrates how the person is asked to own and be responsible for what he or she does to feel this way. The counselor gives attention not only to what the person states but also to the manner of expression. The example also illustrates the Gestalt technique of feeding a person a sentence to see if it fits.

Once awareness and ownership of behavior is heightened, the Gestalt rehabilitation counselor can ask the client to experiment with new behavior (e.g., talking in a louder and firmer voice). The client is then asked, "How is this for you?" This phrase is another key approach in Gestalt counseling. Persons are constantly confronted with being aware of their own experience and judging for themselves how it feels so that they may choose how they want to be. Without this awareness of how they are, they are unable to take responsibility for selecting how they want to be. Asking the person to experiment with new behavior is another major Gestalt counseling method that can enhance the occurrence of rehabilitation in the here and now of the counseling situation itself.

Language and Responsibility

The client's language is another important element that can be attended to by the counselor using a Gestalt approach. Do clients refer to themselves as "you" and to their actions as "it?" Third person language is a common way of referring to ourselves and our behavior in order to keep at a distance from ourselves and avoid taking responsibility. The Gestalt counselor uses the simple technique of asking the person to use "I" instead of "it," and a statement such as "it knocked me off my feet" turns into "I have been knocked off my feet." In this way, the person learns to own and identify with the behavior. Another example that goes one step further moves the person from "it is choked" to "I am choked" and then to "I am choking myself." This dramatically demonstrates the greater degree of responsibility and involvement that can be experienced (Levitsky & Perls 1970). People who use the first person are more likely to be aware of themselves as active agents who can control their lives.

REHABILITATION RESISTANCE AND GESTALT POLARITIES

"She just isn't motivated." "He is resistant to rehabilitation." "She says one thing and then does the opposite." These phrases have been echoed by many rehabilitation counselors and reflect the dilemmas experienced in working with many clients. The Gestalt

view that human nature is bipolar and that people have opposite needs, wants, and ways of being, appears to have significance for the motivational problems encountered in rehabilitation. Guided by this theory, the Gestalt counselor would consider the nonmotivated, resistant part of the client as only one "end" of a person's being. This personality dimension could be a reflection of the person's need to return to the homeostasis experienced in the nondisabled past. This resistance, then, represents an attempt to achieve balance that the counselor should honor and respect.

The client who verbalizes the desire to be rehabilitated and then sabotages efforts in this direction, may be showing opposite needs. The Gestalt counselor should use techniques that would increase the client's awareness of ambivalent, contradictory feelings. One method is to have the person voice silently or to the counselor, "I do not want to be rehabilitated." Another approach is to have the client write down what would be lost or given up if there is a return to work and independence. These procedures often enable the person to contact negative feelings evoked by the rehabilitation process. The client can then take responsibility for the resistance and is then in a position to choose whether to stay the same or change to a behavior congruent with the verbalized goal of "I want to be rehabilitated."

CLOSURE: REHABILITATION AND GESTALT

Closure, the rehabilitation of a person to gainful work and self-sufficiency, is the prime goal of rehabilitation. Closure is also an important concept and goal in Gestalt counseling. According to Perls, Hefferline, and Goodman (1951) most of us are holding on to a lot of "unfinished business." Many of our relationships and life situations are incomplete. Good examples are the difficulty we experience saying good-night or good-bye to a loved one and our constant completion of conversations with people in our imagination. In many ways people feel that they are in limbo and experience many of their needs as unmet. The assumption is that we have learned how not to complete ourselves. This could be connected to the open expression of needs being blocked in the past by our parents or the environment. The anticipation of criticism, pain, or loss can inhibit the completion of needs.

Disabled persons might resist finishing the rehabilitation process, as this would terminate their dependent status and the source of how their needs are met now. There may not be a clear Gestalt of how one would function or have one's needs met when independence is attained. Clients may be accustomed to having other persons finishing things for them. This anticipation of uncertainty, pain, and loss might be the emotional factors operating in our clients who avoid closure. The expectation that the client can move evenly along the rehabilitation trail and end up smoothly is unrealistic.

Rehabilitation counselors are familiar with disabled persons who drop out just before the program is completed or the first day on the job. Therefore, it is critical to help the client

"try out" finishing life situations in the here-and-now of the counseling situation itself. Perls (1969) believes that learning is permission to try out and discover, which is similar to the idea in Gold's (1975) film, "Try Another Way." The counselor who is working on increasing interpersonal skills and power to effect change can facilitate a client's experimenting with finishing life events. Questions such as "Have you completed that statement?" "Have you told me all you wanted to today?" and "If you were to complete your interaction with the person what would you say?" can help the person begin to obtain completion in approximate ways. The disabled person can then confront the task of finishing bigger life situations.

Fantasy is another tool that can help the person finish an important life event (Polster & Polster 1973). The client can try imagining the completion of the rehabilitation process and saying good-bye to the counselor. Earlier in the relationship the client might imagine talking to and saying farewell to lost parts and functions. As "I" write these examples they sound scary, and yet "I" as a counselor remember that the person and "I" usually do not go beyond our own self-support systems. If the client is too threatened, the experiment will be refused. On the other hand, the disabled person may have been afraid from the onset of the disability. This fantasy exercise gives the counselor the opportunity to enter the frightened world of the client. If the rehabilitation counselor enters and survives, the client may begin to know survival is possible. If the rehabilitation counselor does not face the loss with the person and help to reach some closure with the loss, who will? Rehabilitation involves finishing life experiences, even the act of disablement; thus, the act of closure cannot be saved for the end. It is a behavior that can be worked on with the person from the beginning, for even the beginning stage has to be completed.

CONGRUENCE: REHABILITATION AND GESTALT PHILOSOPHY

The Gestalt approach is consistent with rehabilitation philosophy and principles. The Gestalt emphasis on the present concurs with the rehabilitation principle of helping the disabled to not dwell on the past, which facilitates focusing on the present and future. The Gestalt view of an individual as a total system is similar to the practice in rehabilitation of considering the whole person. The Gestalt existential view of humans as beings who define their own meaning, and the subsequently derived techniques that confront individuals with becoming aware of how things are for them, aligns with the rehabilitation philosophy of treating clients as unique individuals. The attention of Gestalt counselors to the development of self-support and individual responsibility is congruent with the mission of rehabilitation to help persons become self-sufficient and independent. Finally, the aim of Gestalt counseling to help per-

sons attain closure by fulfilling needs and attaining personality integration is markedly similar to the closure goal of rehabilitation, which is also the sign of successful completion.

REFERENCES

American Personnel and Guidance Association. APGA workshop programs for continuing professional development, APGA Spring Series, 1976.

Bozarth, J. D., & Rubin, S. E. Empirical observations of rehabilitation counselor performance and outcome: Some implications. Rehabilitation Counseling Bulletin, 1975, 19:294–298.

Gold, M. W. Try another way. Indianapolis, Ind.: Film Productions of Indianapolis, 128 East 36th, 1975. (Film)

James, M., & Jongeward, D. Born to win: Transactional analysis with Gestalt experiments. Reading, Mass.: Addison-Wesley, 1971.

Levitsky, A., & Perls, F. S. The rules and games of gestalt therapy. In J. Fagan and I. L. Shepherd (Eds.), Gestalt therapy now. Palo Alto, Calif.: Science and Behavior, 1970, Pp. 140–149.

Passons, W. R. Gestalt approaches in counseling. New York: Holt, Rinehart & Winston, 1975.

Perls, F. S. Gestalt therapy verbatim. Lafayette, Calif.: Real People Press, 1969.

Perls, F. S., Hefferline, R.; & Goodman, P. Gestalt therapy. New York: Dell, 1951.

Polster, E., & Polster, M. Gestalt therapy integrated. New York: Brunner/Mazel, 1973.

Yontef, F. M. A review of the practice of gestalt therapy. Los Angeles: Trident Shop. California State College, 1969.

Section III

REHABILITATION COUNSELING
System Approaches

15 Editorial Introduction

In addition to working with clients in a counseling relationship, rehabilitation counselors spend a significant proportion of their time arranging for and coordinating various specialized services. The seven articles comprising this section are concerned with the efficient provision of rehabilitation services to disabled clients. Furthermore, the emphasis of these articles is appropriately on severely handicapped clients because they require multiple services of a comprehensive nature over an extended period of time.

Grantham proposes a ten-element service delivery system that encompasses the minimum requirements for a comprehensive rehabilitation program. After describing each of the ten categories of services, he discusses modifications in organizational structure and counselor roles and functions that the adoption of a community-wide service delivery system would necessitate. In the next article twelve critical issues in providing rehabilitation services to severely handicapped clients are discussed. While all but one of the issues are phrased as questions, few answers are given. Rather, each critical issue is explored, and, where possible, implications are tentatively offered. The purpose of the article, then, is to establish a context within which service delivery decisions can be made.

The next two articles each describe specialized rehabilitation treatment strategies that are based on highly contrasting theoretical orientations—technological alterations of behavior in a controlled environment versus personal growth as the result of mutual sharing of common problems, respectively. Walls and Nicholas review the use of token economies, which are behavior modification procedures applied to groups of individuals, with various rehabilitation client populations. The essence of a token economy is the establishment of a system of rules that is "enforced" by rewarding appropriate behaviors and penalizing less desirable behaviors.

Jaques and Patterson describe the emergence of the self-help group as a movement that occurred independently of the development of the professional rehabilitation system. Yet, self-help groups have complemented the professional service system by strengthening their members' motivation and sense of identity and ultimately by contributing to the maintenance of rehabilitation gain and prevention of deterioration of function over time. The authors outline the operational assumptions of self-help groups and provide suggestions for improved relationships between the self-help and professional rehabilitation systems.

The next two articles, which were both published as special research reviews, address very similar topics. Wagner evaluates the expository and research literature concerned with teamwork or interdisciplinary collaboration. He concludes that interdisciplinary teams can deal more effectively with complex problems and respond more efficiently to the multiple needs of clients. Roessler and Mack review the literature pertaining to interagency or interorganizational collaboration. They analyze the critical issue of consensus, distinguish among three levels of coordination, and summarize the current state of knowledge regarding interagency linkage in a list of twelve implications for practice.

The major reason for the emphasis on multidisciplinary approaches in rehabilitation and other health care systems is embodied in the dictum to ''treat the whole person.'' Other reasons are related to the problems of over-specialization, the complex coordination of disparate services, and the shortage of skilled practitioners in some areas. In the final article in this section, Auvenshine argues that much of the work of the rehabilitation counselor can be performed by support personnel, thus allowing professionally trained counselors to devote a greater proportion of their time to less routine functions. The article concludes with a series of implications and recommendations for incorporating support personnel into the rehabilitation service system. The interested reader is referred to an article by Jaques (1972) that addresses several related issues.

REFERENCE

Jaques, M. E. 1972. Rehabilitation counseling and support personnel. Rehab.
Couns. Bull. 15:160–171.

16 A Comprehensive Service Delivery System for Rehabilitation

Robert J. Grantham

If the rehabilitation field is to achieve its national goal of providing all disabled persons in the United States access to needed rehabilitation services, something must be done to alter the present system of service delivery. This task has been complicated by the increased focus on the severely disabled in the Rehabilitation Act of 1973 and its amendments.

Previous observers have criticized the rehabilitation effort from a number of points of view. In 1968, the National Citizens Advisory Committee on Vocational Rehabilitation reported to the Secretary of Health, Education and Welfare that the general level and quality of rehabilitation services suffers from (a) inadequate funding, (b) unavailability of personnel, (c) legislative restrictions, and (d) unimaginative administrative practice (NCACVR 1968).

In June 1969, the National Citizens Conference on Rehabilitation of the Disabled and Disadvantaged (Rusalem & Baxt 1969) cited failures within the present system (a) to develop a program that is additive rather than planful; (b) to carefully delineate a theoretical, conceptual, or philosophical base; (c) to keep service delivery abreast with other advancements; (d) to achieve a healthy dispersion of services in order to achieve our national goal of "giving all disabled persons in the United States access to the rehabilitation services they need . . . by 1975" (pp. 34–35); (e) to provide the total range of counselor duties due to overburdened caseloads and orthodox agency staffing patterns and differentiate counselor role functions adequately; (f) to decentralize service; (g) to equalize financing from region to region; (h) to utilize the interdisciplinary concept; and (i) to develop more appropriate use of staff.

Both committees, assisted by suggestions from the consumers of rehabilitation services, focused on one dimension of the problem—citizen participation—with which the rehabilitation community has long been grappling. In spite of this emphasis, the goal of providing all disabled persons with the services they need has still not been attained.

LEGISLATIVE HELP?

New legislation has since been advanced to make this national goal more possible. The Rehabilitation Act of 1973 (P.L. 93–112) and it amendments (Title I-Amendments to the Rehabilitation Act of 1973; P.L. 93–516) were

Reprinted by permission from the September 1976 *Rehabilitation Counseling Bulletin*, pp. 5–14.

emphatic in their intent to channel services to those with severe physical disabilities. P.L. 93-112 also included new requirements under the state plan regarding program descriptions, annual evaluations of individual programs with the clients or their representative, special technical services, postemployment services, and the individual's eligibility for benefits from other sources.

Recent reviews of the new act (Randolph 1975) have raised considerable doubt concerning the clarity and feasibility of this legislation, and they have defined special problems related to implementation, which range from changing the present state/federal process to redefining the roles of rehabilitation practitioners.

Although numerous problems could be cited as major failures of the presently defined rehabilitation system, there are actually two changes that will move the system in the desired direction: (a) the delineation and implementation of a ten-element comprehensive service delivery cluster and (b) decentralization of the service delivery modality, which is focused on a county level.

"Comprehensive" is operationally defined as a number and category of services available in a community. A system is defined in Churchman's (1968) terms as a series of elements linked together in a coordinated fashion for the overall objective of the whole. Thus, it is not sufficient to have the elements present; they must be coordinated in a synergistic manner to produce their maximum value.

A COMPREHENSIVE SYSTEM: REHABILITATION PROGRAM ELEMENTS

From a review of the history of the field, Rusalem and Baxt (1969) concluded that the field of rehabilitation grew in an additive rather than in a planned fashion. The further development of a national program of habilitation or rehabilitation would require an agreement on some basic programmatic goals and objectives.

Like the mental health field in the 1960s, rehabilitation must ask itself these basic questions: Who are the persons to be served? What services will be provided? What is the organizational structure needed? Where (geographically) will we provide these services? Who will deliver these services? How much will these services cost?

It appears that the field of rehabilitation is on the verge of answering some of these questions in practice and in legislative action. Accepted practice and legislative mandate have provided boundaries within which to function. However, there is still a lack of clarity at the local, state, and national levels. For example, although P.L. 93-112 places explicit emphasis on services to the severely disabled, there is much ambiguity in the language of the act (Institute on Rehabilitation Issues 1975). Further, as pointed out by the Institute, the definition of the severely disabled will probably differ from state to state and region to region. There is no real method for accurately defining, either by number or severity, the disabled clients to be served (Nau & Turem 1975).

Faced with the problem of not being able to accurately identify the disabled and with the various program obstacles (NCACVR 1968; Rusalem & Baxt 1969), the field of rehabilitation must respond with some new approaches to service delivery. The ten-element system proposed here addresses itself to this problem.

The following activities are postulated as representing such a system:

1. Linkage services (intake-information-referral)
2. Medical evaluation, repair, and restoration
3. Psycho-social evaluation and support
4. Residential living facilities
5. Multipurpose vocational evaluation and training programs
6. Educational opportunity programs
7. Placement and follow-through services
8. Transportation services
9. Research and self-evaluation
10. Consultation and education

These elements have not been placed in order of delivery; no one service has preeminence over any other; and there may be other special elements needed. This list is not exhaustive; it is descriptive of a minimum. Once a community has these elements in place it is well on the way to developing a comprehensive service system.

BRIEF DESCRIPTION OF THE TEN-ELEMENTS SYSTEM

In taking some of the services already provided by rehabilitation practitioners and combining them into a compact operational model, I have attempted to respond to the needs of the populations to whom we are responsible. The model was designed after considering the implications of the new legislation and its intent regarding service delivery. The model also offers a variety of options once access to the system has been attained.

Another feature of the proposed system is its applicability to single or multiple groups of disabled persons; each group specified by P.L. 93-112 could use the range of services being proposed. As an organizational scheme, the comprehensive service delivery approach presents a clean, uncomplicated categorization with broad applicability.

None of the elements of the proposed system are new. The rehabilitation profession has already become familiar with and competent in many of these areas. Yet what is unique here is the different configuration of these services.

Linkage Service (Intake-information-referral)

These services are the traditional entry points into the system. Given the widened focus of rehabilitation, these points will be located in a variety of places, but they should be programmatically tied together in order to minimize the overlap, illuminate the gaps in service, and establish a firm treatment-oriented program. Through the application of computer technology we should be able to maintain communication with persons once they come in contact with the system for identification, service, and follow-up purposes.

Medical Evaluation, Repair, and Restoration

This activity involves the traditional medical diagnosis, treatment, and restoration long known to rehabilitation efforts. These services are provided by skilled medical and allied health personnel, and they are vital to the overall rehabilitation program.

Psycho-social Evaluation and Support Services

These activities have an assessment and a therapeutically supportive character. They are designed to discover the level of psychological and social functioning and to provide the necessary supportive milieu to allow an individual to attempt many purposive behaviors. This service includes a range of recreational programs and activities. The underlying theoretical concept of the mastery of developmental, physical, and mental tasks appropriate to age level is especially significant.

Residential Living Facilities

The need for residential living arrangements within the total rehabilitation system has long been felt. Many client groups will be unable to continue living in their present environments if they are to avail themselves of rehabilitation services. Others who have been institutionalized are in need of viable alternatives once they are released from a protective setting. The elimination of environmental barriers must also be assured.

In order to fulfill the housing and living needs of disabled persons, a judicious mixture of halfway houses, group homes, independent apartments, and other living arrangements will be needed. Programmatic emphasis will usually be on skill development as well as on the provision of a living space.

Multipurpose Vocational Evaluation and Training Programs

These programs provide the therapeutic and supportive environments in which rehabilitation practitioners appraise the vocational functioning levels of clients in the system, as well as those activities that provide skill acquisition. Terminal workshops, transitional workshops, on-the-job training, trial work experiences, and a variety of other evaluative training approaches are included.

Educational Opportunity Programs

This category includes programs that provide advanced education and training beyond the high school level for those who qualify. Presently, such programs, available in most states for minority individuals, do not preclude the entry of disabled persons. In the effort to maximize resources for disabled persons, we must explore all avenues that offer productive and effective program possibilities. Thus, rehabilitation practitioners are moving toward mainstreaming.

Placement and Follow-through Services

These services are not new, but they do represent a new conceptual approach.

Placement has traditionally represented a final testing ground for the marketability of the product of the rehabilitation process. Since the goal of rehabilitation is usually to develop the marketable skills of certain candidates, the success or failure of our efforts has often ridden on this phase.

Follow-through

This phase is an extension of placement in that it implies continued service to the individual. Follow-through is distinguished from follow-up, in that follow-up does not connote in actual terms the continued service to clients beyond placement. Follow-up has been linked to the closure notion of the state/federal program, which is more time- than service-oriented. Follow-through, on the other hand, is specifically mandated in P.L. 93-112.

Transportation Services

It is becoming increasingly evident that clients need to transport themselves or be transported, in order to take advantage of opportunities for training, treatment, and other program necessities. P.L. 93-112 has increased the population in need of transportation and has placed new demands on our present transportation systems. Extant transportation systems in most communities are often inadequate to the needs of the total community, offering limited or inappropriate conveyances for the disabled (i.e., they are unable to accommodate wheelchairs, crutches, stretchers, and the like with any degree of ease). An inadequate transportation system is a hindrance to many programs

offered at rehabilitation facilities. The total elimination of all environmental barriers is a focus of this program and the residential living facilities area.

Research and Self-evaluation Services

Basically, this effort is one in which a particular posture is adopted and implemented vis á vis efforts at rehabilitation. The following seven subareas are required for adequate coverage: (a) analysis of need, (b) assessment of program design, (c) program-client congruence evaluation, (d) program improvement, (e) cost benefit analyses, (f) program standardization, and (g) research utilization. Contrary to the position of research and self-evaluation in this scheme, this element should be one of the first considered in the formulation of comprehensive rehabilitation programs.

Consultation and Education

Consulation may be thought of as those problem-centered activities that, when shared with others, extend our influence and effectiveness. This may result in direct contact with assisting agencies or with other significant individuals in the rehabilitation process, such as medical doctors, nurses, occupational therapists, other allied health workers, and employers. Rehabilitation practitioners may serve as either consultants or consultees. Education is both the formal, curriculum-centered process geared toward the professionals in the rehabilitation field as well as the public education process aimed at influencing attitudes and behavior toward the disabled. Preventive programming, which stems from an educational base, is also included.

ORGANIZATIONAL STRUCTURE

In order to implement the program outlined in the essential elements concept, a new organizational structure is proposed that features (a) a decentralized planning function on the county level and (b) the delegation of authority for the dispersal of program funds at the local level, which is an added characteristic separate from the usual purchase-of-service method for funding client services. The structure may eventually include program-sized funding for agencies and programs of whole communities based on the ten-element model.

State plan requirements call for a variety of persons to be included in the plan development process. If done logically, rather that through a noncontinuous approach that does not tie into ongoing groups, the inclusion of diverse groups in the state plan could lead to specific area programming. The recent work of Nau and Turem (1975) points convincingly to the need to localize data collection and, by implication, programming.

The annual report to the president on activities related to the administration of the Rehabilitation Act of 1973 for FY '75 (U.S. Department of Health, Education and Welfare, Office of the Secretary 1974) points out that state plans have been implemented in a variety of ways. Incentive programs have been developed by several states to serve severely disabled persons. In other states, training was provided for staff members and special counselors assigned to the problem. In addition, it is fair to say that some states indicated problem areas with the legislation that did not specifically indicate a need for a change in the state/federal structure.

However, changes in the structure and focus of the state-federal relationship would not be entirely new (Grantham 1970; Rusalem & Baxt 1969). The potential for implementation of the minimum service elements concept is already available. The creation of a configuration of minimal service elements and localized planning and program implementation would significantly upgrade the minimum rehabilitation services available to disabled persons on a county level.

The advantages of the present proposal are threefold: (a) more local participation in the planning, implementation, and evaluation of services by the disabled and disadvantaged can be secured on a continuing basis; (b) more services will be provided to smaller areas; and (c) the opportunity to monitor services on a county and state level can be developed so as to improve the system's ability to identify more accurately and to service appropriate client groups. P.L. 93-112 and its amendments, P.L. 93-516, are keyed to severe disabilities; there is an obvious need for additional service elements to be applied to the problems.

At present, the rehabilitation system is not entirely equipped to reorganize its service elements to fit the needs of the severely disabled. Considerable attention will need to be paid to readapting service centers to the needs of the severely disabled. Agencies may find it necessary to change their philosophy, training, placement programs, and public relations approaches to accommodate the severely disabled (Randolph 1975). All these issues will have an impact on the service delivery system.

DIFFERENT ROLES AND FUNCTIONS

The coordinated system suggested here requires a rethinking of the roles and functions of workers in the field. More specifically, it necessitates additional manpower. There are three new roles to be filled by the disabled and the disadvantaged: *articulator* of the problem: *advocate* within the system, and *referral and resource person*. Jaques (1972) has suggested taking on these new persons through the use of the career ladder for support personnel. Reiff and Reissman (1965) and Kelly (1969) have also pointed out the value of indigenous workers and have urged their use in the rehabilitation system.

Professional workers, those with a master's degree and above, have had their duties and functions scrutinized over a long period of time (Johnson & Koch 1969; Muthard & Salomone 1969; Sussman, Haug & Joynes 1969). Many roles were delineated and legitimized from such efforts, such as that of counselor, administrator, workshop evaluator, teacher, and so on. Each is valid both in the present system and the one proposed here. The new roles to come out of the comprehensive system will be additions rather than replacements. Another significant feature of these new roles will be an expansion of their definition with a resultant functional specificity that takes into account new goals and objectives.

CONCLUSION

Rehabilitation is still a developing profession. The creation of the expanded comprehensive services concept will move rehabilitation further toward its goal of providing service to all those in need. It is imperative that the notions of comprehensive services be expanded as the target population widens. The increased workload necessitated by a focus on the severely disabled forecasts the need for a change in roles, duties, and responsibilities within the profession. Perhaps each level within the manpower tract will have to reassess its role in the selection, training, and employment of rehabilitation practitioners. Self-selection can no longer be relied on to achieve the desired client-practitioner congruence necessary in a multiservice system. Some method of selection that differentiates among counselors, placement-personnel, planners, and other necessary roles will have to be developed.

The ten-element service system proposed in this article is posited as a necessary complement of services for a county-sized program. Although service to each disability group can be measured against these standards, there is no inherent need to devise a separate system for each disability group. The carry-over of skills, personnel, and other ingredients is highly probable. In addition, disabled and disadvantaged clients will have greater access to and interaction with rehabilitation programs and personnel, thus bringing us closer to the goal of providing service to all.

Finally, the ability to establish reasonable cost accounting procedures that approach uniformity cannot be overlooked. It may become possible to achieve a more accurate estimate of the cost of the system as a result of the ten-element proposal (Conley 1975). In the future, cost-sharing approaches with local governments can be determined, based on services to a given geographic area.

Thus, all rehabilitation needs within a given location will achieve greater specificity in terms of the identification of clients in need of service and the sharing of costs on a local basis. In such a scheme it will be less likely that disabled persons will be overlooked because a level of accountability, heretofore unknown to rehabilitation services, will be built into the system.

REFERENCES

Churchman, O. W. The systems approach. New York: Dell, 1968.

Conley, R. W. Issues in benefit cost analyses of the vocational rehabilitation program. American Rehabilitation, 1975, 1:19–23.

Grantham, R. J. Toward an effective community service system. Paper presented at NRA Convention, September 1970, San Diego, California.

Institute on Rehabilitation Issues. Critical issues in rehabilitating the severely handicapped. Rehabilitation Counseling Bulletin, 1975, 18(4):205–213.

Jaques, M. E. Rehabilitation counseling and support personnel. Rehabilitation Counseling Bulletin, 1972, 15(3):160–171.

Johnson, B. G., & Koch, R. A. Study of the effectiveness of rehabilitation counselors as related to their level and type of education, In J. E. Muthard, N. Dumas, & P. Salomone (Eds.), The profession, functions, roles and practices of the rehabilitation counselor. Gainesville, Fla.: University of Florida Regional Rehabilitation Institute, 1969. Pp. 89–100.

Kelly, J. G. The mental health agent in the urban community. In A. Budman & A. Spiegel (Eds.), Perspectives in community mental health. Chicago, Ill.: Aldine, 1969. Pp. 620–634.

Muthard, J. E., & Salomone, P. R. Rehabilitation counselor roles and functions: Implications for preparation and practice. In J. E. Muthard, N. S. Dumas, & P. R. Salomone (Eds.), The profession, functions, roles and practices of the rehabilitation counselor. Gainesville, Fla.: University of Florida Regional Rehabilitation Research Institute, 1969. Pp. 3–20.

National Citizens Advisory Committee on Vocational Rehabilitation Report, Washington, D.C., June 26, 1968.

Nau, L., & Turem, J. The comprehensive needs study. American Rehabilitation, 1975, 1(2):9–12.

Randolph, A. H. The Rehabilitation Act of 1973: Implementation and implications. Rehabilitation Counseling Bulletin, 1975, 18(4):200–204.

Rehabilitation Act of 1973, P.L. 93-112.

Rehabilitation Act of 1973. Amendment P.L. 93-516, Title I, Amendments to the Rehabilitation Act of 1973.

Reiff, R., & Reissman, F. The indigenous non-professional: A strategy for change in community action and community mental health programs. Community Mental Health Journal Monograph Series, No. 1. New York: Behavioral Publications, 1965.

Rusalem, H., & Baxt, R. Delivering rehabilitation services. Paper presented at the National Citizens Conference on Rehabilitation of the Disabled and Disadvantaged, Washington, D.C., U.S. Dept. of Health, Education and Welfare, Social Rehabilitation Services, June 1969.

Sussman, M. B.; Haug, M. R.; & Joynes, V. A. Rehabilitation counseling as a second career. *In* J. E. Muthard, N. S. Dumas, & P. R. Salomone (Eds.), The profession, functions, roles and practices of the rehabilitation counselor. Gaines-ville, Fla.: University of Florida Regional Rehabilitation Research Institute, 1969. Pp. 73–81.

U.S. Department of Health, Education and Welfare. Office of the Secretary. The annual report of the president on activities related to the administration of the Rehabilitation Act of 1973, Washington, D.C., March 21, 1975.

17 Critical Issues in Rehabilitating the Severely Handicapped

Institute on Rehabilitation Issues[1]

The 1973 Rehabilitation Act's mandate to give service priority to the severely handicapped creates many issues for rehabilitation agencies. Some of the issues revolve around the problems expected when any change of emphasis occurs in a system, but other issues center around the more controversial definitions of "severely handicapped" and "services" as they are presented in the Act.

The Institute on Rehabilitation Issues is a cooperative effort by state vocational rehabilitation agencies, selected research and training centers, and the Rehabilitation Services Administration (DHEW) to develop resource materials on topics of common concern (Massie 1974). Overall objectives of the Institute on Rehabilitation Issues (IRI) include identification and study of issues and problems that are barriers to optimal vocational rehabilitation services and the development of methods for resolving problems and incorporating solutions into state programs.

Since a previous Institute on Rehabilitation Services on the Severely Disabled (1973) dealt with many of the same problems, it would have been presumptuous for this prime study group to propose solutions to these complex issues. The purpose of this Institute on Rehabilitation Issues was to help bring the issues, their origins, and their implications before rehabilitation administrators, rehabilitation supervisors, and the general rehabilitation populace for examination and perhaps constructive clarification.

Central to the discussions is the overriding problem of ambiguity created by the language contained in the 1973 Act. Because the severely handicapped are clients who require multiple services of a comprehensive nature over extended time periods, the entire rehabilitation process is affected from the top administrators down through the ranks of counselors and general service personnel. These complexities are increased when the system is not sure of who the severely handicapped are by legal definition and when some judgment must be made in relation to those clients now receiving rehabilitation services.

STATEMENT OF THE PROBLEM

The Rehabilitation Act provides both general and specific categories of the

---

[1]John A. Fenoglio, Chairman; B. Douglas Rice, University Coordinator; Henry W. Aston, Larry Biscamp, Jon Kissinger, Pat Lavery, Young M. Orsburn, Richard Santos, Thomas J. Skelley, C. Leon Thornton, William F. Twomey, Royce L. Vernon, and Henry C. Warner, Prime Study Group members.

Reprinted by permission from the June 1975 *Rehabilitation Counseling Bulletin,* pp. 205–213.

severely handicapped, but it offers no guidelines for determining the degree of severity within the individual categories; thus, the issue of whom, within these categories, shall be served remains rather nebulous. For example, the following statements illustrate the problem:

General definition (Program Instruction RSA-PI-74-16) (HEW 1973)

That physical or mental impairment which seriously limits the functional capacities (mobility, communication, self-care, self-direction, work tolerance, work skills) of a handicapped individual to the extent that the person is unable, to a substantial degree, to cope with the physical or mental demands of gainful employment and whose rehabilitation normally requires multiple services (restorative, compensatory training, selective placement) over an extended period of time.

Specific definition (PL93-112)

The disability which requires multiple services over an extended period of time and results from amputations, blindness, cancer, cerebral palsy, cystic fibrosis, deafness, heart disease, hemiplegia, mental illness, multiple sclerosis, neurological disorders (including stroke and epilepsy), paraplegia and spinal pulmonary dysfunction, and any other disability specified by the Secretary in regulations he shall prescribe.

The Act's lack of clarity leads to a whole series of issues that influence the rehabilitation process. When clients and services cannot be clearly identified, there can be only limited implementation of systematic changes in the rehabilitation agencies. Interim guidelines for identifying these clients have been developed in attempts to interpret the intent of the Act by various federal, regional, and state administrators and officials. However, this is only temporary since no national standards for procedures, selection, and evaluation have as yet been devised for implementation.

IMPLICATIONS

The implications that these issues have for the rehabilitation agencies and personnel are that two kinds of actions must occur simultaneously. First, the rehabilitation system must make some type of immediate response by interpreting the Act to the best of its ability and begin selecting clients, coordinating and creating necessary services, gathering personnel, and so on. Second, the rehabilitation field must begin identifying, clarifying, and solving the problems that impede the most meaningful fulfillment of the Act as it was intended.

OVERVIEW OF THE ISSUES

As part of the IRI charge, the following prominent issues and problem areas have been discussed in light of the implications most seriously affecting the rehabilitation of all other clients.

Issue 1: Legislation Designed to Assist Disabled People May Create Barriers to the Expansion of Rehabilitation Services for the Severely Handicapped

Numerous laws enacted to assist the severely handicapped have created duplication of services by various agencies with overlapping and often conflicting responsibilities. Many of these programs do not have adequate funds to carry out their intent. The result is that severely handicapped individuals lose motivation and become confused and frustrated.

The Act directs rehabilitation agencies to continue serving the traditional clients. As a result of limited funding, rehabilitation agencies are placed in an almost untenable position since they have substantial sums of money invested in facilities, personnel, and special programs for the "nonseverely handicapped," including alcoholics, drug abusers, and public offenders. The change of emphasis undoubtedly will adversely affect these programs.

Legislative conflicts for the severely handicapped also exist in health services, public assistance, vocational rehabilitation, and workmen's compensation programs. Clients can frequently lose benefits if they receive services from more than one agency which often mitigates the gains that could be attained through rehabilitation services. Proliferating programs in health services such as Medicaid and Medicare present problems to the rehabilitation counselor. From this context, medical problems may assume priority over vocational problems, or the counselor may have difficulty obtaining reports from other agencies. Thus, the counselor, in serving the client, may have to duplicate previous services which in reality are a loss of time and money resulting in inefficiency and a waste of health care resources.

Because of the various legislation, rehabilitation counselors may experience a mixed blessing. All rehabilitation personnel should be aware of additional provisions in the Acts and must be able to utilitize all available resources. These provisions will make it possible to serve more handicapped clients, particularly the severely handicapped, by appropriate referrals from sources such as workmen's compensation, Supplemental Security Income (SSI), national health programs, etc.

Issue 2: Are Adequate Funds Available to Serve First the Severely Handicapped as Mandated in the Rehabilitation Act of 1973 While Maintaining the Present Level of Services to Other Clients?

Advanced funding provides for planning and program development at least for two successful years. Joint funding, however, will need more study, but its potential benefits should not be overlooked. Beneficiaries of Trust Fund, Social Security Disability Insurance, and Social Security Supplemental Income can be served, and, in turn, rehabilitation can be reinbursed for these services. There will be a number of handicapped persons who could be screened out of the rehabilitation process as a direct result of inadequate funding, especially those with limited vocational potential and no personal resources with which to purchase needed services. Counselors, therefore, must utilize all available resources in order to serve clients.

Unquestionably, service costs will continue to increase in training, medical, vocational, and other areas. This will be especially true with the severely handicapped, since rehabilitation will involve multiple services and extend over longer periods of time. Accountability will be a vital facet of rehabilitation services; thus, every possible benefit must be gleaned from every dollar dispensed for services. Programs will be monitored to ensure that handicapped people are receiving needed services in accordance with the Rehabilitation Act.

It is evident that rehabilitation's already inadequate funding will be taxed; therefore, the use of all available resources for the client's maximum benefit will be essential.

Issue 3: Should the Severely Handicapped Be Given Special Consideration for Rehabilitation Services in Reference to an Economic-Needs Test?

The decision to use an economic-needs test is to be made by each individual state. If used, it must be incorporated into the state plan to ensure that resources are used for the rehabilitation of the client. Sufficient resources, however, should remain available for the handicapped person to maintain a reasonable standard of living. An economic-needs test should not be used to deny services to severely handicapped individuals but should be a process to ensure equal treatment for all concerned.

Issue 4: Will It Be Advantageous for Rehabilitation Not to Close Cases of Severely Handicapped Clients But to Retain Them in Open-ended Status in Order That Follow-up and Follow-along Services Can Be Provided Without Reopening Closed Cases?

The severely handicapped will require services beyond traditional closure, which in itself will have far-reaching implications for rehabilitation agencies. Open-ended rather than closed cases may be a system that will permit rehabilitation to provide follow-up and follow-along services to the severely handicapped. Because of the severe limitations of these individuals, supportive counseling, medical attention, and other services may be needed in order for them to maintain employment. Since closing and reopening a case is both time-consuming and costly, open-ended status could possibly conserve time and money. A further implication of this procedure would be the need for some process for measuring counselor performance without special emphasis on the number of closures. The benefit from open-ended cases, however, seems to be client-centered; that is, rehabilitation will not neglect the client after the traditional rehabilitation services have been rendered.

Issue 5: Is the Emphasis on Numbers of Production a Primary Barrier to Serving the Severely Handicapped?

Since serving the severely handicapped is to receive priority, the traditional quantity of closures becomes a prominent issue to rehabilitation agencies. Because of the emphasis on this clientele and increased costs for multiple services over longer periods of time, the number of closures will be reduced, resulting in a need for a different method of assessing counselor performance. One possible approach is some type of qualitative measurement rather than a quantitative system. This indicates a possible need for specialists rather than generalists in reference to rehabilitation personnel, since specialization tends to de-emphasize production of numbers and to emphasize services. Specialists in mental retardation, deafness, trust fund, and the mentally ill are examples.

Issue 6: Is the Vocational Rehabilitation Process Obsolete, or Can It Function to Serve the Needs of the Severely Handicapped?

Several attempts have been made to revise, alter, and/or change the rehabilitation process and the provision of services to handicapped clients. The process is not the issue. Proper use of the process by rehabilitation personnel is the real issue, since it is designed to move clients through growth and development, from dependence to independence.

Several vital components, including outreach and referral, evaluation, assessment, adjustment, vocational objectives, the counselor's role, job development, and placement, are vital functions in the rehabilitation of the severely handicapped.

Issue 7: It Is Becoming More Difficult for Rehabilitation Agencies to Recruit, Train, and Retain Competent Front-line Counselors, Other Professional Staff, and Secretarial Personnel, and the Effects of Turnover and Inexperience Represent a Major Barrier to Serving the More Severely Handicapped.

A major issue that has always confronted rehabilitation agencies is that of recruiting and retaining competent personnel. The problem seems to develop in one of two ways: promotions or resignations. In either case, competent

people are removed from direct contact with clients. The result is that handicapped clients are all too often dealing with inexperienced staff who are frequently transitional in their employment.

The lack of staff stability has several implications for rehabilitation, including development of cooperative relationships, inappropriate use of case-service funds, personnel costs, and duplication of efforts. Frequent staff turnover also demands that the supervisor devote a large percentage of time to the training of new personnel. Staff changes in turn affect the development of good working relationships among consumer groups, professional organizations, referral sources, and other helping or cooperating agencies.

Several suggestions that merit careful consideration on the part of rehabilitation administrators are: initiation of competitive salary scales, careful selection of rehabilitation staff, early identification of personnel with supervisory potential, more and better use of volunteers and support personnel, and training of supervisory staff.

Issue 8: Will the Use of Extended Evaluation Enable Rehabilitation Agencies to Provide Services to the Severely Handicapped before Determining Rehabilitation Potential?

The use of extended evaluation should enable rehabilitation personnel to meet the intent of Congress to serve the severely handicapped, especially the provisions for a complete and comprehensive evaluation of a severely handicapped client prior to determination of rehabilitation potential. With the advent of services to the severely handicapped on a priority basis, extended evaluation should serve as the technique to validly determine the feasibility of eligibility. Nevertheless, its use will require better knowledge of evaluation methods, assistive devices, training demands, adjustment services, job placement, jobs, and opportunities. Better use must be made of physical therapy, occupational therapy, research analysis, rehabilitation engineers, vocational evaluation, and others in order to determine potential. Most important, however, is the emphasis on individualized programs rather than stereotyping individuals into disability groups.

Issue 9: Will Facilities Be Able to Meet the Needs of the Severely Handicapped?

A major problem that has always existed with rehabilitation, especially between referral sources and facilities, is the area of communication. It is possible that the rapid growth of both field and facility programs has accelerated the problem's growth. Nevertheless, with the advent of the severely handicapped into the rehabilitation process, two-way communication becomes essential. The framework for communication must involve more than administrative directives; it must provide for the inclusion of line staff in decision making, program planning, program evaluation, and establishing goals and objectives.

Since, unquestionably, facilities will play a very prominent role in providing services to the severely handicapped, proper utilization will be essential. Comprehensive services will be the rule rather than the exception. With the added responsibility of accountability, facilities will have to demonstrate how clients benefit from their services.

Because of their severe limitations, the severely handicapped will require multiple services over extended periods of time, which implies that facilities must re-evaluate such programs as vocational evaluation, adjustment services, vocational training, and medical services.

Issue 10: Can Vocational Rehabilitation Agencies Meet the Challenge of Job Development and Placement of the Severely Handicapped?

It is estimated that 3 million severely handicapped Americans are now in the labor force, with a large percentage of this group involved in consumer services such as clerks and sales personnel, light assembly work, or in piece work jobs. Nevertheless, the unemployment and underemployment rates among the severely handicapped are significantly higher than the national employment rate.

Rehabilitation personnel must devote careful attention to the development and placement of the severely handicapped. Suitable and satisfactory placement of the handicapped individual depends on much more than proper training. Special consideration must be given to transportation (public or private), architectural barriers, job locations, and sheltered employment. Extensive efforts must be made to inform employers of the outstanding performances, loyalty, and dependability of handicapped individuals. Further, employers could be encouraged to employ the handicapped through subsidized training or other types of tax-break programs.

Job development possibilities for the severely handicapped exist but need to be identified. Specific jobs that can be performed by persons with severe restrictions or limitations in industry, state and federal government, business, and service occupations can be classified and made known to employers and employment agencies.

Issue 11: Can Consumer Participation in the Rehabilitation Process Improve the Function, Development, and Delivery of Services to the More Severely Handicapped?

Increased consumer involvement in the rehabilitation process is stressed in the Rehabilitation Act of 1973. Before active consumer participation becomes reality several major factors must be resolved, including the following:
1. Coordination among all resources, such as community programs, vocational rehabilitation, health services, social services, etc.
2. Compilation of directories of community resources.
3. Cooperation of vocational rehabilitation and consumer in obtaining needed services—FHA loans, wheelchair ramps, readers, interpreters, etc.
4. Use of task forces composed of vocational rehabilitation personnel and rehabilitation consumers to achieve maximum benefit from available community resources.

There are other issues involved, such as the following:
1. Limitations of various rehabilitation facilities, family counseling, and psychological counseling.
2. Lack of specialists (psychiatric, physicians, etc.), acceptable child care facilities, family counseling, and psychological counseling.
3. Architectural barriers.
4. Lack of adequate housing and training facilities and employment discrimination practices of businesses, industries, and others.
5. Lack of evaluations of benefits derived by the severely handicapped from services available in the community.

Issue 12: Can Research, Program Planning, and Evaluation Improve the Quality and Quantity of Rehabilitation Services for the Severely Handicapped?

Research, program planning, and evaluation are essential components of improving services to the severely handicapped. Issues involved include: (a) employment of capable personnel to conduct rehabilitation research, program planning, and program evaluation; (b) translation of useful results into action without an undue time lag; and (c) consideration for research relevant to client satisfaction, case-cost benefits, client benefits, and client outcome.

The Rehabilitation Act of 1973 emphasizes that research, program planning, and evaluation units are to be vital factors in rehabilitation services for the severely handicapped. These sections can assist rehabilitation agencies to become more accountable and more efficient in the delivery of appropriate services.

SUMMARY

It was not the charge of the prime study group to take positions or to offer solutions to the many issues confronting rehabilitation's effort to provide services to the severely handicapped. Its purpose is to bring the issues to the attention of rehabilitation workers, with the understanding that time, research, and experience will lead to appropriate solutions.

Providing comprehensive services, not only to the more severely handicapped, but to other less disabled individuals, presents a definite challenge to vocational rehabilitation agencies. Significant efforts have been and are being made to identify and to alter, redirect, or modify ongoing programs in order to absorb more of the most severely handicapped individuals into the rehabilitation process. Only time, experience, research, and the evaluation of results will tell how successful vocational rehabilitation was in meeting this challenge.

REFERENCE

Massie, W. A. Partners in improving rehabilitation practices. Social and Rehabilitation Record, 1974, 1(7):6–8.

18 Token Economies in Rehabilitation

Richard T. Walls
and Heather Nicholas

The term behavior modification or behavior change has become widely known in rehabilitation circles during the past decade. In general, it implies the improvement of a given behavior as a result of the pleasant or unpleasant consequences of the behavior. That is, positive or negative reinforcement following a response tends to increase the probability of the response, while punishment following a response tends to decrease the probability that it will be repeated.

A good deal of research has described the schedules of reinforcement and the conditions under which such changes take place most efficiently (e.g., Bandura 1969; Skinner 1969). To cite a few examples from our work, successful applications of behavior modification have been demonstrated at the West Virginia Rehabilitation Center—using tokens with reluctant or retarded clients in speech therapy, using workcard checkmarks as tokens on prevocational training, hole lacing in occupational therapy, parallel bar walking in physical therapy, self-recording and public charting in hysterical acting-out behavior, and with retarded clients' reading and math. We

have also achieved favorable outcomes at the Kennedy Federal Youth Center, a federal correctional institution for juveniles (maximum age 23 years). These projects with individual student inmates have reduced or eliminated such behaviors as class absences, tardiness to group meetings, knuckle biting, excessive cursing, disruption of commissary or classroom activities, cigarette butts on the floor, and late sleeping. Points, praise, an extra hour on town trips, and many other reinforcers have been used.

It is thus apparent that the use of behavior modification techniques ranges across the entire spectrum of rehabilitation, i.e., where individual behavioral difficulties exist. Application of behavior change techniques to rehabilitation of individuals has been reviewed elsewhere (Bandura 1969; Walls 1969) and need not be considered here.

Much less work has been done with group application. Although rehabilitation of individual clients is of course the ultimate objective, individual treatments *within groups* have been attempted in a number of cases. That is, a system of rules is established;

The investigation was supported in part by the Social and Rehabilitation Service, U.S. Department of Health, Education and Welfare through the Regional Rehabilitation Research and Training Center. Special appreciation is expressed to Frank Falbo, Workshop Director and to Mary Cain, Donna Lough Saffron, and Charlotte Dadisman, Prevocational Instructors.

Reprinted by permission from the June 1973 *Rehabilitation Counseling Bulletin,* pp. 244–257.

the extent to which each group member meets the requirements is recorded; and appropriate consequences follow. For example, with a group of patients in a psychiatric ward, hitting another patient might be a "costly behavior," whereas putting magazines in the rack after using them could be a "rewarded behavior." The patients may be given the option of paying not to do something they dislike. The system of rewards (and punishment) applies to each group member and is delivered as soon after the behavior has occurred as possible.

A convenient medium of exchange is typically used to facilitate transactions. Tokens such as IBM cards, British half-pennies, or points on a workcard may be delivered immediately and later traded in sufficient amounts for such backup reinforcers as cigarettes, entrance into the dining hall, a good bed, etc. Thus, a token economy is created in which, to a greater or lesser extent, the group member earns and pays for what he gets. When goals are well-defined and the individual understands the contingency relationships between responses and reinforcements, responsibility is placed squarely upon the shoulders of the patient.

Although a number of studies have dealt with the use of token reinforcement in relatively normal classroom environments, the present review primarily focuses upon groups of individuals usually considered target rehabilitation populations. The research can largely be categorized into studies attempting to help (a) psychiatric patients, (b) the mentally and socially retarded, and (c) juvenile and adult offenders.

PSYCHIATRIC POPULATIONS

Perhaps the most widely known research in this area has been compiled by Ayllon and Azrin (1968). In a series of experiments, they attempted to strengthen desired behavior of psychotics through the use of operant reinforcement principles on a mental hospital ward. Popular activities—entrance into the dining hall, tobacco, a better bed, rugs, night stands—served as reinforcers. Tokens were given to mediate the time between the occurrence of a behavior which was necessary or useful for the patient's functioning and his purchase of backup reinforcements with tokens earned. This procedure was effective in maintaining the desired behaviors as long as it was in effect; however, these behaviors decreased when the reinforcement was discontinued or disrupted. The program appeared to be successful in maintaining higher performance for the majority of patients (ages ranging from 24 to 74), not merely for isolated individuals. Further, the program was helpful in supporting both simple performance, such as washing dishes or self-grooming, and full-time job performance.

A similar contingency program for 86 subjects labeled chronic schizophrenics or brain damaged consisted of "every important phase of ward life" (Atthowe & Krasner 1968). The earned tokens could be exchanged for movies, cigarettes, watching television, and so forth. Results at the end of a year indicated gains in social interaction, responsibility, and initiative. Patients with severe behavior disorders and unfavorable prognosis evidenced genuine progress toward more adaptive behaviors. An ultimate goal of Atthowe's program is to help the patient tolerate and deal with the delay of reinforcement, a circumstance more in keeping with the real world (Walls & Smith 1970; Walls, Miller & Cox 1970).

Winkler (1970) described a closed, refractory psychiatric ward of female patients and a token system similar to that used by Ayllon and Azrin (1968). He reports success in promoting rewarded performances such as getting up in the morning, dressing, exercising, making the bed, being at meals on time, and cleaning. And such behaviors as violence, tantrums, screaming, and banging were dramatically reduced.

A point system was set up by Boren and Colman (1970) for delinquent soldiers in a psychiatric ward. They could earn points by attending classes, dressing neatly, working, and talking. These points could be exchanged for privileges such as semiprivate rooms, free coffee, access to a television set, poolroom privileges, and weekend passes. To the surprise of some supervising personnel, the point system was much more effective than conventional procedures or providing a model (ward officer) to illustrate appropriate behaviors.

A unique token economy experiment was reported by Ellsworth (1969). At a VA hospital, the previously locked doors of a mental ward were opened; the men were informed that they could now go to meals and activities on their own. They would be treated as responsible individuals and rewarded for positive behavior. Along with the general ways of earning tokens such as shaving,

making beds, and keeping themselves neat and clean, each individual was rewarded for specific activities geared to his own unique problems or needs. For instance, if a particular individual rarely spoke, he received extra tokens when he did talk. Anyone who tried to escape from the newly unlocked ward had to pay another patient to babysit for him. Subsequent improvement and discharge from the hospital of many long-term patients is indeed encouraging.

Several other unique variations on the token economy theme have been used. Guyett (1968) used four different colors of tokens (white=self-care, blue=work, red=socialization, orange =creative spontaneity) to increase the informational value of the reward system. Token reinforcement was also used to control bedtime behavior of severely regressed and aggressive female patients (Steffy, Hart, Craw, Torney & Marlett 1969). A red token was hung on a nail inside a girl's door if she properly undressed and collected her laundry before going to bed. If she caused no disturbance in the night and dressed appropriately the next morning, the token was left on the nail. She could then choose a treat from the tray that was passed around.

Sanders and Walters (1970) have demonstrated the effectiveness of a mechanical counter for recording points worth a penny each in promoting increased verbal responding of chronic schizophrenics on a workshop assembly line. In the token economy established by Garlington and Lloyd (1966), a plan was developed whereby patients could work themselves through various incentive levels of the program and eventually earn positions as member-employees of the hospital. They could earn a monthly salary and, while still living in the ward, could function quite independently.

SPECIAL EDUCATION

Token reinforcement systems have also been introduced into a number of classrooms and wards for retarded pupils and clients who do not cooperate or study under normal conditions. A number of such programs have been established for adults and adolescents. For example, in a closed ward of assaultive, retarded females (IQ 5 to 25), food stealing and other maladaptive mealtime behaviors were attacked (Edwards & Lilly 1966). Contingency management involving satiation was effective in decreasing unacceptable patterns of dining room behavior. The hospital was able to reduce the staff required to manage this group at mealtime.

In another report of special education for mentally retarded adults, Hunt, Fitzhugh, and Fitzhugh (1968) describe an interesting technique for teaching exit ward clients appropriate on-the-job appearance. A checklist was used to record appropriate appearance behaviors, and each patient was awarded 10 points for each day that he met the criteria. Using a progressively leaner or more intermittent schedule, they were able to raise appropriate work appearance from 25 percent to 90 percent.

Work production has also been an element of rehabilitation concern. Zimmerman, Stuckey, Garlick, and Miller (1969) describe a successful attempt to increase productivity in a sheltered workshop for retarded exit ward patients.

Tokens of different types have proven effective in a cottage for mentally retarded girls (Lent 1967). The girls were given extensive instruction in physical appearance, hygiene, walking, sitting, and social interaction; they earned points on a workcard or coin tokens toward desired objects or privileges through successive approximation to desired performance. Thus, the emphasis is on social and living adaptation skills. Similarly, Girardeau and Spradlin (1964) reported favorable progress with an extensive behavioral checklist for moderately and severely retarded teenage girls.

Pupils in a junior high school special education class with multiple cognitive, behavioral, and emotional problems were subjects in an experiment comparing social and token reinforcement (Broden, Hall, Dunlap & Clark 1970). The opportunity to spend points for activities and privileges that they proposed themselves proved much more reinforcing that the teacher's compliments for good study and work behaviors. The investigators stated that such contingency procedures could be easily used even by beginning special education teachers.

Kazdin (1971) presented case material from a sheltered workshop setting to suggest that involving clients in the dispensing of tokens may have some advantages over contingencies administered by staff. Involving clients in recording and graphing their own behaviors or helping with programs for other clients has been demonstrated to be beneficial to both dispenser and receiver, as well as reducing staff administration time (Walls 1970).

Crosson (1969) works with what he terms the "ecology of retardate adjustment." Crosson has broken down even such simple vocational responses as drilling a hole or wiping a table into their component movements. The separate movements are taught through reinforcement procedures and then chained together to make the complete response or act. The Murdoch Center workshop at Butner, North Carolina similarly uses a programmed step-by-step, complex motor-skill teaching approach (Tate & Baroff 1967). As in any efficient teaching-learning situation, the objectives and required skills are defined. This is done by breaking down the jobs required for the construction of electronic equipment into a graded series of assembly line operations. Output is recorded and appropriate rewards follow. Some screwdrivers and pliers are even wired to a mechanical counter board so that an accurate rate of tool use can be obtained.

Schroeder (Schroeder & Yarbrough 1971) uses tokens exchangable for small items. These items are purchased at a cost of less than $35 per month for the entire workshop. Because of the varied nature of the different jobs, clients are initially on a variable, 10-minute-interval schedule, in which they are given a token on the average of every 10 minutes if they are judged by the staff to be doing their job when the time elapses.

Reinforcement systems can be particularly effective with children, as a research program by Birnbrauer

has demonstrated. For example, Birnbrauer, Wolf, Kidder, and Tague (1965) found sizable gains by 15 retarded pupils when their teacher gave tokens for (a) correct response to items, (b) production of an error-free assignment, and (c) being cooperative or doing extra work. Thus, academic skills were emphasized. Substantial improvement occurred in reading, writing, addition, time-telling, etc. Small candies or trinkets worth an average of two cents a day per pupil were sufficient to keep the children working hard.

Similarly, Hewett (1967) reports a successful, engineered classroom using checkmarks on a workcard with a class of emotionally disturbed children. A pupil was given two checkmarks for starting the assignment, three for following through, and five for functioning to the best of his ability as a student. O'Leary's studies (e.g., O'Leary & Becker 1967) similarly show abrupt reduction in deviant behavior; further, there was transference to other school situations. Effective use of of token reinforcement has even been demonstrated with preschool children having deficient language abilities (aphasia) (Fygetakis & Gray 1970).

Instruction-following behavior in such areas as verbalization, motor performance, and imitation was the focus of a program for retarded children discussed by Zimmerman, Zimmerman, and Russell (1969). Each student was assigned a differently colored transparent tumbler into which tokens could be dropped at appropriate times. A 16-compartment box called "the store" contained all the goodies for sale. Over the course of the experiment the children who were most hyperactive and disruptive showed great improvement in following instructions. The emergence of helping behavior was also evident in the form of cooperation with, and assisting, one another in earning reinforcement.

An even more dramatic example of reinforcement of cooperative behaviors was described by Carlin and Armstrong (1968). Several boys who were termed uncontrollable due to brain damage or childhood schizophrenia were brought together for the purpose of encouraging cooperative play. After the authors had observed several days of hitting, kicking, spitting, and the destruction of projects, they instructed the boys as follows: "We notice that you guys have a terrible time playing together, and you don't seem to be having as much fun as you might because you are always fighting. We have decided that we are going to pay you to play together" [p. 171]. When at least three of the children were playing together agreeably, they were paid a substantial amount in tokens, placed into a common pool. Any fighting or hitting resulted in a fine being taken from the pool. At the end of the play period, the tokens in the pool were divided evenly. With proper motivation these children were quite capable of controlling their aggressiveness and working together in harmony for mutual benefit.

Orlando, Schoelkopf, and Tobias (1967) made several observations about their program relevant to the common concerns of administrators, teachers, and other staff. The students did not work only for tokens. There was a general cooperativeness and social-academic effectiveness that extended beyond those situations in which they received tokens. These was no jealousy or bickering when some students received more tokens than others. The students often showed that they were happy for the recipient. The system was effective in reaching some students who had been labeled unreachable in motivation for learning and constructive social interaction.

CORRECTIONS

A third general area in which token economies has been implemented is corrections. For example, Tyler and Brown (1968) attempted to improve the academic functioning of a group of court-committed delinquent youth. Boys who received tokens contingent on test performance had higher test scores than those who received tokens on a noncontingent (straight salary) basis.

Similarly, a point system was effective in a rehabilitation program with predelinquent boys living at Achievement Place under the department of social welfare (Phillips, Phillips, Fixsen & Wolf 1971). Subjects were boys from low-income families who had committed minor offenses. Points were given and taken away for specified appropriate or inappropriate behaviors. Aggressive statements and poor grammar decreased; amount of good academic performance, homework, money saving, punctuality, and tidiness increased. A similar program for the reintegration of extreme adolescent behavior deviates is described by Martin, Burkholder, Rosenthal, Tharp, and Thorne (1968).

Graebner (1967) describes a rein-forcement system used in two girls' rehabilitation cottages at Austin State School in Texas. The program was designed to reduce fighting, hitting and kicking, cursing, name-calling, and vulgarity. Checkmarks for acceptable behavior and points off for unacceptable behavior were placed on a large chart so that the girls could observe their progress as often as they liked, and could thus obtain immediate feedback. Tokens could be used for such desirable activities as shopping off-campus, all day trips off-campus, going to a show, or going to church with a boy. The short-term program dramatically reduced aggressive behavior and apparently was well accepted by the girls.

Even older prison inmates at the Draper Correctional Center in Elmore, Alabama have improved academic and adaptation behaviors. Clements and McKee (1968) constructed performance contracts providing a given period of time in the reinforcing event area with the "Reinforcing Event Menu," following the satisfactory completion of a specified number of programmed instruction frames. Other projects in "ecological control" at Draper have dealt with inappropriate requests, cursing, getting to work on time, etc.

These projects have attempted to identify a broad range of reinforcers available within the typical prison environment and have listed over 100 items and activities of potential reward value (Milan 1971). The rehabilitation research at Draper attempts to make earned tokens or good behaviors buy genuinely reinforcing items or privileges, all of which are legitimate, hard-to-get, and very much in demand by inmates: fishing for two hours, renting a television set, writing four or more letters per week (instead of the institutional limit of three), making a telephone call to someone outside the institution, visiting a women's prison with the Draper band, interviewing with a parole board member, receiving a copy of *Playboy,* and taking a programmed instruction course of his own choice.

Probably the most notable example of a token economy in corrections is the Robert F. Kennedy Federal Youth Center, Morgantown, West Virginia. The entire 300-student coeducational center operates on a system of "hard" and "soft" points. Each of the cottages devises its own soft (privilege) point system to fit the needs of the students in the particular behavior category assigned to that cottage. Hard points worth one cent each are earned in academic-vocational work and may be banked or used to buy commissary items. As a student meets his goals, he advances from trainee to apprentice and finally to honor student status. Built into these student levels is a privilege system by which students enjoy additional privileges as they advance, including a private room, civilian clothing, town trips, furloughs, and work-study release.

STATE VOCATIONAL REHABILITATION CENTER

The foregoing review has presented an encouraging argument for the use of group behavior modification systems with psychiatric, mentally retarded, and correctional populations. A more pessimistic view has been presented by Kuypers, Becker, and O'Leary (1968) in "How to Make a Token System Fail." With proper planning and operation, however, the probability of success is high. The following examples from the West Virginia Vocational Rehabilitation Center will illustrate.

A short-term demonstration project in the Center workshop addressed the competitive-employment grooming problems of a group of men working there. These 27 clients (mean age of 22 years and IQ of 73) were selected from the total workshop population on the basis of their relatively poor appearance and grooming habits in five behavior categories: daily shaving, hair neat and clean, lack of body odor, clothing neat and clean, hands and face clean. The study involved four phases, each lasting for one week (Monday to Friday). Supervisors rated each client as he arrived for work in the morning. The rating for each of the five categories was made on a 5-point scale from very poor (5) to very good (1).

The results are depicted in Figure 1 (lower means indicate improvement). Following the baseline week of private recording, in which clients were told nothing of the project, an awareness week was recorded. As may be noted, when clients were told about the five categories being recorded, average grooming behavior improved, even though no instruction to try to improve was given. When clients were told they could earn five cents for each very good (or a maximum of 25 cents per day), grooming was near perfect (5). During the extinction week, the good performance did not diminish markedly. A follow-up one week later indicated grooming ratings considerably higher than those during phase 1. The maximum amount of money paid to any client in this study was $1.25. If long-term gains can be made in terms of suitability for competitive employment, this is a real bargain for rehabilitation.

When ratings are involved, the reliability of such judgments is often weak. Clearly defined yes and no criteria are much better. Such a point system involving grooming, punctuality, interpersonal behavior, quantity of work, and quality of work is currently in formative stages for the Center workshop. For example, a client is either on time or he is not; he is either out of line with staff or another client during the day or he is not; he either meets his morning production goal or he does not.

Another example of a relatively minor investment with possible large dividends is the token system currently in use with prevocational classes at the Center. The questions often raised but seldom answered are "What is prevocation training and how does one know when it has been successfully completed?" To address these questions, educational, emotional, personal, social, and vocational goals were formulated. These areas were subdivided into the 28 criterion behavior classifications indicated in Figure 2.

Relatively easy (Form 1) and medium (Form 2) difficulty tests were made for the criterion behavior classifications. A client passes as many of these tests as she is able when she enters prevocational training. Passing a combination of Form 1 and Form 2 tests

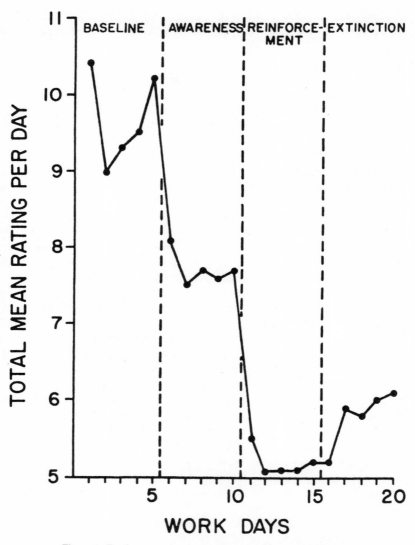

Figure 1. Total mean rating per workday for five target behaviors.

not passed then becomes her goal. She works at her own rate toward meeting these goals; she may study independently, get tutoring from the instructor or a more advanced client, work in groups, etc. She may take a test on any of the 28 classifications when she believes she is ready.

A system of progress stars, completion stars, and points earned indicates each client's progress on her criterion behaviors chart. Tokens in the

	Points	Progress Stars	Completion Star	Date

Educational Goals
1. Arithmetic
2. Money management
3. Reading
4. Spelling—vocabulary
5. Telling time
6. Science
7. Government
8. Current events
9. Following Instructions
10. English grammar

Emotional Goals
1. Working in groups
2. Strengthening self-image
3. Making decisions

Social Goals
1. Manners
2. Recreation
3. Appreciation

Personal Goals
1. Grooming
2. Exercise
3. Safety rules
4. Use of telephone
5. Use of post office
6. Mobility training and self-reliance

Vocational Goals
1. Work habits
2. Housekeeping
3. Laundry
4. Meals
5. Writing business letters
6. Sewing

Figure 2. Prevocational training criterion behaviors chart.

form of different colored IBM cards for different denominations are given to the client as she earns points. The client signs her name to each card as she receives it to prevent its loss. These tokens may be traded in appropriate amounts for backup reinforcers from the class country store.

The recently initiated system operates for approximately 10 cents per client per day. The system allows immediate and constant feedback to both client and instructor concerning accomplishments in the course. Clients are interested, and even excited, not only by the extrinsic reinforcers, but also by their own rehabilitation progress. The Woodrow Wilson Vocational Rehabilitation Center in Virginia puts each new client on a point system for his first month.

The examples of token reinforcement systems cited in this article illustrate the benefits to be derived from appropriate contingency management. Rehabilitation personnel should examine their portion of the service spectrum for opportunities to make creative application of improved service delivery (Walls 1971). Dedication to facilitating client progress from intake to successful rehabilitation requires the seeking out and use of tools bearing undeniable credentials. Behavior improvement techniques constitute one such tool.

REFERENCES

Atthowe, J. M., Jr., & Krasner, L. Preliminary report on the application of contingent reinforcement procedures (token economy) on a "chronic" psychiatric ward. Journal of Abnormal Psychology, 1968, 73:37–43.

Ayllon, T., & Azrin, N. H. The token economy: A motivational system for therapy and rehabilitation. New York: Appleton-Century-Crofts, 1968.

Bandura, A. Principles of behavior modification. New York: Holt, Rinehart & Winston, 1969.

Birnbrauer, J. S.; Wolf, M. M.; Kidder, J. D.; & Tague, C. E. Classroom behavior of retarded pupils with token reinforcement. Journal of Experimental Child Psychology, 1965, 2:219–235.

Broden, M.; Hall, R. V.; Dunlap, A.; & Clark, R. Effects of teacher attention and a token reinforcement system in a junior high school special education class. Exceptional Children, 1970, 36:341–349.

Boren, J. J., & Colman, A. D. Some experiments on reinforcement principles within a psychiatric ward for delinquent soldiers. Journal of Applied Behavior Analysis, 1970, 3:29–37.

Carlin, A. S., & Armstrong, H. E. Rewarding social responsibility in disturbed children: A group play technique. Psychotherapy: Theory, Research and Practice, 1968, 5:169–174.

Clements, C. B., & McKee, J. M. Programmed instruction for institutionalized offenders: Contingency management and performance contracts. Psychological Reports, 1968, 22:957–964.

Crosson, J. E. A technique for programming sheltered workshop environments for training severely retarded workers. American Journal of Mental Deficiency, 1969, 73:814–818.

Edwards, M., & Lilly, R. T. Operant conditioning: An application to behavioral problems in groups. Mental Retardation, 1966, 4:18–20.

Ellsworth, J. R. Reinforcement therapy with chronic patients. Hospital and Community Psychiatry, 1969, 20:238–240.

Fygetakis, L., & Gray, B. B. Programmed conditioning of linguistic competence. Behavioral Research and Therapy, 1970, 8:153–163.

Garlington, W. K., & Lloyd, K. E. The establishment of a token economy ward at the State Hospital North in Orofino, Idaho. Unpublished mimeo, Washington State University, 1966.

Girardeau, F. L., & Spradlin, J. E. Token rewards in a cottage program. Mental Retardation Journal, 1964, 2:345–351.

Graebner, O. E. Token reinforcement at Azalea and Begonia, girl's rehabilitation cottages. Unpublished mimeo, Austin State School, Austin, Texas, 1967.

Guyett, I. Behavior modification using resocialization and token economy for the rehabilitation of chronic schizophrenic patients. Unpublished manuscript, Dixmont State Hospital, Pennsylvania, 1968.

Hewett, F. M. Educational engineering with emotionally disturbed children. Exceptional Children, 1967, 33:459–467.

Hunt, J. G.; Fitzhugh, L. C.; & Fitzhugh, K. B. Teaching "exit-ward" patients appropriate personal appearance behaviors by using reinforcement techniques. American Journal of Mental Deficiency, 1968, 73:41–45.

Kazdin, A. E. Toward a client administered token reinforcement program. Education and Training of the Mentally Retarded, 1971, 6:52–55.

Kuypers, D. S.; Becker, W. C.; & O'Leary, K. D. How to make a token system fail. Exceptional Children, 1968, 35:101–109.

Lent, J. R. Mimosa Cottage: Experiment in hope. Unpublished mimeo. Parsons, Kansas: Parsons Research Center, 1966–67.

Martin, M.; Burkholder, R.; Rosenthal, T. L.; Tharp, R. G.; & Thorne, G. L. Programming behavior change and reintegration into school milieux of extreme adolescent deviates. Behavior Research and Therapy, 1968, 6:371–383.

Milan, M. A. An ecological experiment in corrections: A programmed environment for behavior modification. Unpublished mimeo, Experimental Manpower Laboratory for Corrections, Draper Correctional Center, Elmore, Alabama, 1971.

O'Leary, K. D., & Becker, W. C. Behavior modification of an adjustment class: A token reinforcement program, Exceptional Children, 1967, 33:637–642.

Orlando, R.; Schoelkopf, A.; & Tobias, L. Tokens as reinforcers: Classroom applications by teachers of the retarded. Institute on Mental Retardation and Intellectual Development, 1967, 4:1–26.

Phillips, E. L.; Phillips, E. A.; Fixsen, D. L.; & Wolf, M. M. Achievement place: Modification of the behaviors of predelinquent boys within a token economy. Journal of Applied Behavior Analysis, 1971, 4:45–49.

Sanders, R. M., & Walters, G. M. Behavior modification on the assembly line: Collateral behaviors. Unpublished mimeo, Southern Illinois University, 1970.

Schroeder, S. R., & Yarbrough, C. C. A system for applying the principles of programmed learning to the rehabilitation of skills among the retarded. Unpublished mimeo. University of North Carolina, 1971.

Skinner, B. F. Contingencies of reinforcement: A theoretical analysis. New York: Appleton-Century-Crofts, 1969.

Steffy, R. A.; Hart, J.; Craw, M.; Torney, D.; & Marlett, N. Operant behavior modification techniques applied to a ward of severely regressed and aggressive patients. Canadian Psychiatric Association Journal, 1969, 14:59–67.

Tate, B., & Baroff, G. Training the mentally retarded in the production of a complex product: A demonstration of work potential. Exceptional Children, 1967, 33:405–408.

Tyler, V. O., Jr., & Brown, G. D. Token reinforcement of academic performance with institutionalized delinquent boys. Journal of Educational Psychology, 1968, 59:164–168.

Walls, R. T. Behavior modification and rehabilitation. Rehabilitation Counseling Bulletin, 1969, 13:173–183.

Walls, R. T. The teacher as a behavior therapist. In O. G. Mink (Ed.), Behavior change process. New York: Harper & Row, 1970. Pp. 169–183.

Walls, R. T. A reinforcement contingency analysis of rehabilitation. Rehabilitation Research and Practice Review, 1971, 2:29–35.

Walls, R. T.; Miller, J. J.; & Cox J. Delay of reinforcement and training choice behavior of rehabilitation clients. Rehabilitation Counseling Bulletin, 1970, 14:69–77.

Walls, R. T., & Smith, T. S. Development of preference for delayed reinforcement in disadvantaged children. Journal of Education Psychology, 1970, 61:118–123.

Winkler, R. C. Management of chronic psychiatric patients by a token reinforcement system. Journal of Applied Behavior Analysis, 1970, 3:44–55.

Zimmerman, J.; Stuckey, T. E.; Garlick, B. J.; & Miller, M. Effects of token reinforcement on productivity in multiply handicapped clients in a sheltered workshop. Rehabilitation Literature, 1969, 30:34–41.

Zimmerman, E. H.; Zimmerman, J.; & Russell, C. D. Differential effects of token reinforcement on instruction-following behavior in retarded students instructed as a group. Journal of Applied Behavioral Analysis, 1969, 2:101–112.

19 The Self-Help Group Model

A Review

Marceline E. Jaques
and Kathleen M. Patterson

The decade of the thirties saw the beginning of parallel movements in rehabilitative care. One was counseling and psychotherapy, developed on a traditional base of professional care; the other was a "people's movement" of self-help. For more than thirty-five years, these two helping systems have existed side by side. They have expanded, matured, and grown beyond the expectations of their adherents; yet they have ignored or denied each other, rarely communicated, and have gone about their business as if the other did not exist. Occasionally rumblings were heard, and more often than not they were critical of the other's practices. A few individuals from each system showed interest in the practices of the other, but interactions were rare and superficial. Primarily, each seemed convinced of its "rightness of approach" and chose not to examine its relationship or be examined.

The questions remain: What do the two approaches have in common? Is it possible to share or move between the professional and the self-help model? Or is the self-help process a unique modality of care not now widely known, acknowledged, or accepted by

the professions, but a functional part of a total rehabilitative system?

Recently, the professional world has shown more interest in the self-help world as it has become progressively more difficult to ignore its growth in numbers, size, and benefits. The reports of satisfaction by self-help group members and the pragmatic results they have achieved for themselves have been impressive, if not disturbing, to some professionals. These reports seem to be in contrast to the general aura of self-doubt and dissatisfaction permeating the professionals' helping fields. Hard evidence that the professional service system works effectively for those seeking help is sparse. Too many persons with problems are either not cared for or cared for in an unsatisfactory manner.

GROUP TYPES AND PURPOSES

There are two basic types of self-help groups: (a) individuals with a certain condition or problem who have suffered a personal-social deprivation, such as Alcoholics Anonymous (AA) and Recovery, Inc., and (b) groups of families or friends of persons who have

Reprinted by permission from the September 1974 *Rehabilitation Counseling Bulletin*, pp. 48–58.

a condition or problem, such as Alanon, Alateen, and Parents of Retarded Children. Groups are also referred to as mutual aid groups. The labels, self-help and mutual aid, state concretely the purpose and method of these groups. Help for each member around specific problem areas is the group goal. Although groups of the first type are usually occupied with their personal problem solving and programs, the group members often fulfill an information-giving function to the interested public. Groups of the second type more often engage in advocacy, social action, and program development.

There seems to be a fine line of demarcation between a families/friends self-help group and a voluntary agency, with no clear cut criteria of distinction. As the group grows in size it tends to develop structure and add services, usually given by professionals. This, of course, changes the original self-help and mutual aid function. The volunteers who join the group help the programs and support a common cause, though they may not share the problem. Examples are hundreds of college students and persons from all walks of life who volunteer their services as companions, foster grandparents, big brothers and sisters, and in other aspects of planning, program development, public information, and fund raising in large and small private agencies. The self-help and mutual aid may not be as clear cut, at least not explicitly, although Riessman's helper principle (1965) of receiving therapeutic help in the process of helping others may apply.

Katz (1970) described five phases of development by which some self-help groups evolve a more complex organization: origin by disadvantaged persons and relatives, informal organization spread through friends and acquaintances, emergence of leaders, formal organization through rules and by-laws, and use of professional methods and staff. Zola (1972) described the development occurring in another order from voluntary lay associations of American pioneer days to mutual aid societies with membership based on social characteristics of race, religion, and country of origin. The original mutual aid was of a tangible, material type, like money lending, Zola reported. The tangible aid members gave to each other was followed by "aid of a more social psychological nature" (p. 180).

GROWTH AND DEVELOPMENT OF SELF-HELP MODEL

Self-help groups have undergone an impressive growth, although there is no up-to-date total directory or census. Mowrer (1964) reported that Maurice Jackson developed a directory in 1961–62 entitled *Their Brother's Keepers* and listed 265 different types of self-help groups. A recent survey of self-help organizations for the physically handicapped reported over 1,200 groups nationwide (Massachusetts Council of Organizations of the Handicapped, Inc. 1973). In their most recent directory, Alcoholics Anonymous (1973) reported 600,000 members throughout the world, with 405,858 United States members in 14,037 groups. This is a phenomenal story of growth and development, which began with two members in 1935. The Oxford group movement of that day is credited with providing some background for the AA method, though its tenets were considered too rigid by the AA founders (*Alcoholics Anonymous* 1955; *Alcoholics Anonymous Comes of Age* 1957). AA has been used as a model for the development of other self-help groups, such as Synanon, Gamblers Anonymous, Neurotics Anonymous, Weight Watchers, and Overeaters Anonymous. Recovery, Inc., reported in their 1973 directory that they have 950 groups in 46 states and 5 Canadian provinces and 1 group each in Puerto Rico and Israel.

Self-help groups have spread not only across the nation but throughout the world. It is safe to say that more groups exist in the United States and Canada than in other parts of the world. They have spread, at least in contemporary times, from the United States to other countries in the manner of AA and Recovery, Inc. Katz (1964, 1965) reported two quite different self-help programs in England and Poland. The Psychiatric Rehabilitation Association in England has a program of social clubs or groups where numerous self-help functions are carried out for both former and present patients. Although these are done with official support and in offical health centers, professionals are in the background with the patients or clients actually planning, organizing, and directing the programs from counseling to planning job interviews and training. The programs are not limited to professional activities, but may include cultural and social functions.

The Polish Union of Invalid Cooperatives exists so that disabled persons and their families may prepare themselves for work through both treatment and training. The cooperatives, not state-owned or managed, are set up on a self-help model. The disabled persons belong to the cooperatives, share in planning, and participate in the rehabilitation programs. Apartments, workshops, and business enterprises, along with counseling, training, and placement, are integral parts of the cooperative program. Participation in the planning and policymaking seems to provide high incentive and motivation toward self-help.

There is no end to the possible number and type of self-help groups. Their potential may be as variable as unsolved human problems or the special needs not met by existing social arrangements. Some behavioral scientists believe that the small group is in fact a new dimension in social organizations, counteracting the isolation of our time and the rigidity of an institution. Rogers (1973) described the emergence of a new kind of person, who uses the small informal group as an alternative to the structured bureaucratic institution. The traditions and structure of AA, for example, permit few organizational structures within or influences from outside. For example, chairpersons rotate monthly, and the work of the group is assumed by members' small contributions; no contributions from outside are permitted, therefore eliminating a potential source of control.

The Integrity Group movement described by Mowrer (1972) and the

Self-Directed Therapeutic Group reported by Berzon and Solomon (1966) are related developments by professionals in counseling and psychotherapy who have used several aspects of the self-help mutual aid model. Frankel and Sloat (1971) described the total process of development of a self-help group for persons with physical, emotional, and social disabilities who wanted group involvement, but existing groups were not available to them. Colbert (1969) reported a program of planned mutual help at the Veterans Administration Hospital at Brentwood, Los Angeles, where the opportunity of giving as well as receiving help was incorporated into the rehabilitation program. This is an example of the use by professionals of a concept long known and practiced by self-help organizations.

EFFECTIVENESS OF THE SELF-HELP PROCESS

The nature of the self-help process has been commented on by a number of authors (Grosz 1972, 1973; Hurvitz 1970; Jaques 1972, 1974; Katz 1965, 1967, 1970; Mowrer 1972; Riessman 1965; Wechsler 1960; Wright 1971; Yalom 1970). In most cases authors, usually professionals, have read the sparse literature, attended meetings of self-help groups, collected self-reports of members, and, from an outsider's viewpoint, attempted to be objective, empirical observers. Two survey research projects were reported by Grosz and Wechsler. From the perspective of self-help group participant members

some reports have appeared in their own publications, such as the Recovery Reporter, the AA Grapevine, and Paraplegic News. In addition, an AA survey of its own membership was reported (Bailey & Leach 1965).

Positive aspects to members of self-help groups include the following knowledge, therapeutic, and skill dimensions: (a) gaining facts and knowledge of the condition; (b) social learning of coping mechanisms from those who are successfully living with the condition; (c) motivation and support by communicating with others who have shared a similar life experience; (d) the modeling effect of successful problem-solving behaviors which provides reinforcement for new members and for long-term members; (e) self-evaluation of process resulting from feedback and sharing with members at various stages of problem, knowledge, and levels of coping behavior; (f) identification with the group providing a tangible sense of belonging, of an individual and social nature, and minimizing isolation and alienation; and (g) in the mutuality of the altruistic concern for others, finding self-help.

The self-help mutual aid group cannot be ignored as a system for maintaining rehabilitation gain and preventing deterioration of function over time. Modeling effect is provided by members who are coping with stigma problems and functioning adequately in life roles. Positive impact on social attitudes may be an additional gain from the coping behaviors demonstrated. Too frequently negative succumbing aspects of disadvantaged disability are emphasized in the media, particularly for fund-raising purposes (Wright 1969). Observing persons with handicapping problems functioning in the community and living "like other people" cannot help but enhance the quality of life for the able and disabled alike. AA group members report that persons are coming to their groups at earlier ages, which seems to demonstrate a more hopeful and accepting view of the problems presented. And, of course, the value of seeking help early cannot be over-emphasized in rehabilitation.

A case study of Recovery, Inc., reported by Wechsler (1960) included the results of two surveys, one of the characteristics and opinions of members and the other of selected psychiatrists, members of the American Psychiatric Association in Detroit and Chicago. The results reported certain potential problem areas which concerned the psychiatrists sampled. These areas included the lack of medical or professional supervision, no system for the screening of members or of training leaders, and certain professional reservations about the Recovery method. The respondents did agree that the group aspect satisfied "the needs of some ex-patients for various forms of group support" (p. 309). The basic criticism resulted from a professional view of services giving little recognition to the validity of the self-help mutual aid group model as part of the total service system.

Recovery was founded in 1937 by Abraham A. Low, a psychiatrist (Recovery, Inc. 1973b). Until his death in 1954, Low underwent years of attack and rejection by his colleagues. His biography (Rau 1971) documented his struggles to establish the self-help method. A recent survey by Grosz (1972, 1973) reflected a change in attitude on the part of the psychiatric profession to the Recovery approach. Grosz related this in part to the general climate of acceptance of the important role of paraprofessionals in mental health. For the last three years Recovery panels have been a regular event at the annual meeting of the American Psychiatric Association.

OPERATIONAL ASSUMPTIONS

The basic operational assumptions of the self-help group approach are as follows:

1. Individuals come together because they have a specific personal problem or condition which they share (e.g., alcoholism, weight-loss, paraplegia).

2. The status of peer relationships is maintained for all members within the group.

3. Peers, sharing the condition or problem, come together with the expectation of helping themselves and each other; that is, both the self-help and mutual aid aspects are central to the group process.

4. Behavior change is expected by and for each member. Learning a new way of life, presumably more satisfying, is undertaken at the individual's own pace.

5. Peers identify with the specific program developed by the group, become committed to its basic beliefs,

tenets, and procedures, and actively support the program through practicing its principles in daily life.

6. Although the basic form of interaction is a regularly scheduled group meeting, peers are readily accessible and available to each other as needed outside of group meetings. This interaction is of a one-to-one type relationship, so both group and individual modes of contact are used.

7. The group process consists of actively relating, "owning," and revealing problems, receiving and giving feedback to each other, sharing hope, experiences, encouragement, and criticism in relation to the day-to-day goals of individual behavior change.

8. Members are held responsible for themselves and their behavior. This involves being honest about themselves, both within and outside the context of the group interaction.

9. Group leadership develops and changes from within the group on the basis of giving and receiving help in keeping with the program's purposes and principles.

10. Status comes from helping and being helped effectively, which in turn provides the validity for the program. Status achieved outside the group is of little, if any, value after joining the group; in fact, if it is used manipulatively, it can work against a member's status within the group.

These assumptions have been experientially derived and remain untested, but they are supported pragmatically by the demonstrated help group members receive. Why and how the self-help methods work for so many

individuals are common and challenging questions to the professional. Basic themes of many self-help stories shared in the groups are of past experiences and relationships with professionals which were not satisfactory or helpful with their problems. Part of the cathartic value of self-help groups is in sharing past frustrations with other members who have experienced them, knowing there is hope and help within "their program." The self-help experience was described in the words of one member as "a weight of despair being lifted from my life" and "at last I can experience some joy in living" (personal communication, April 1972). It is a common observation and sometimes a surprise to new members and visitors that self-help group meetings are happy occasions with much humor and laughter shared.

THE PROFESSIONAL MODEL: A LOOK WITHIN

The feeling held by many self-help group members is that their professional experience or contact has not been helpful and, in some instances, even harmful. That these perceptions are not unrealistic has been verified by the experience of many persons, both professional and nonprofessional, who have attested to the ineffectiveness and fragmentation of much service delivery. By and large professionals still ignore, if not downgrade, the self-help model, although there is evidence that a change in attitude is occurring (Wright 1973). Self-help and professional groups alike seem to be increasingly more open, trustful, and appreciative of each others' unique experience and knowledge.

Tyler (1973) referred to a shift on the part of persons needing help away from the professional therapist to others who understand because they have had the same problems. "Alcoholics Anonymous was perhaps the first herald of this change in the manner in which psychological difficulties were to be dealt with" (p. 1022).

The Lasker Award was given to AA in 1951 by the American Public Health Association. The citation stated: "Historians may one day recognize Alcoholics Anonymous to have been a great venture in social pioneering which forged a new instrument for social action; a new therapy based on the kinship of common suffering; one having a vast potential for the myriad other ills of mankind" (*Alcoholics Anonymous* 1955, p. 573). The role of the helping professional changed from that of a therapist in the medical model to a consultant who suggests rather than prescribes. An equally dramatic change is emerging in the role of the person needing help, from a passive recipient of a service to a consumer who can not only make choices among alternatives, but who also assumes responsibility as the manager of a personal rehabilitative plan. Some problems of professional service delivery may be inherent in the rigid impersonal nature of the bureaucracy and organization within which agencies exist. Some organizational shifts are apparent in rehabilitation service delivery systems generally, and others are underway (Morris 1973).

Programs of client advocacy have developed over the last decade. The provisions within the Rehabilitation Act of 1973 for consumer participation in program planning and evaluation, a specific client-counselor program planning review process, and program review by a third party make these concerns explicit. They attempt to assure that the clients are truly co-managers of the rehabilitation process. Whether or not the reforms contemplated will be more than paper plans, honestly reflecting humanness and personal concern for individuals with problems in concrete ways, is yet to be tested in practice.

A number of groups have developed statements of need or codes outlining their basic human rights as individuals. Geist and others (1973) called for agencies to develop codes of ethical practices, pointing out the necessity for agency ethic accountability to consumers if individual professional codes of ethical standards are to have real meaning in practice. Clearly, consumer input has already had considerable effect on the service providers, both institutions' and professionals' practices, but this is only a small beginning. The professional enterprise itself is in need of careful re-examination. Change in organizations, institutions, and service delivery systems will not modify negative or unhelpful professional attitudes and practices, and it is here that the self-help group experience can be most useful. Its essence of helpfulness seems to pinpoint the areas where professional blind spots and insensitivity exist.

History shows that a self-help group appeared where professionals did not or could not help. The self-help movement is a reflection of professional pressure points due, in part, to a lack of knowledge but also due to rigidity in professional behavior and beliefs. Yet at each junction of new self-help group development, a few professionals out of step with their colleagues and the times, in thinking and practice, turned the tide to a new approach. For example, the founders of AA, a stockbroker and a physician, both hopeless alcoholics, credit the work of three professionals for the ideas and inspiration that brought AA into existence (*Alcoholics Anonymous Comes of Age* 1957, p. 262): W. D. Silkworth, "benign little doctor who loved drunks," William James' great wisdom in his *Varieties of Religious Experience,* and Carl Jung's statement that "science had no answer for the alcoholic." Abraham Low's persistence against professional attacks, referred to earlier, showed the way to a major self-help movement. Charles Dederich, founder of Synanon, is another example of a person whose beliefs, practices, and courageous struggles were in tune with the needs of persons fighting addiction.

THE RELATIONSHIP
OF THE PROFESSIONAL
TO THE SELF-HELP MODEL

During the last three years both authors have had occasion to relate to the two systems of self-care and professional care in new and highly personal ways. The first author moved from a primary professional stance to the study and experience of the self-help approach, and the second author from self-help group experience of long standing to graduate training in rehabilitation counseling. A unique opportunity to share and learn from each helping modality resulted. Although the experiences of self-help and the professional process are unique, it is possible to share and move between these systems, but only under certain conditions. For example, a professional cannot be a self-help group member or leader unless the conditions of common problem, peer relationship, and mutual aid exist. Any other arrangement would be a violation of the self-help model. Professionals who do not or choose not to meet these conditions can relate only in the capacity of visitor-observer. On invitation a professional can act as a consultant or speaker. The professional therapeutic skills as such cannot be used inside the self-help group. That, of course, would also be a violation of self-help precepts.

It may be that both parties to the helping contract can learn what to expect and what to ask of each other and how they relate to the total rehabilitation task. For example, self-help groups might be able to ask professionals to help study aspects of the process self-help groups do so well. The variables of effectiveness within the helping system could be more precisely defined and isolated to study the patterns of this process. Some members drop out of groups while others stay. How many are in each category, and what characteristics differentiate them? What are the characteristics of those who return again and again?

Professionals could learn to ask self-help group members for specific and regular feedback on their help-getting experiences. Members' reactions and suggestions, as consumers of these services, could be effective in improving and humanizing the total service delivery functions. A plan for evaluation of each individual service interaction might be initiated just as courses and professors' performance are evaluated by students. Better Business Bureaus exist to protect consumers and monitor practices. Certainly as much vigilance should be given to human-helping services. Plans might be developed for confronting the social and community barriers that plague both groups, such as public understanding of problems of disability, deprivation, and job and other types of discrimination.

Raising these issues and other questions could lead to an openness in communication which does not now exist between helpers and those on the receiving end of service delivery. The feedback from this interaction might significantly modify therapeutic practices, rehabilitation outcomes, and professional attitudes, resulting in help being given and received more effectively to the contractual standards set by both parties. A more humanized service delivery system could result. Clearly, both models, the self-help and the professional, are necessary parts of a total rehabilitation service system.

REFERENCES

Alcoholics Anonymous. Alcoholics Anonymous: The story of how many thousands of men and women have recovered from alcoholism. New York: Alcoholics Anonymous World Services, 1955.

Alcoholics Anonymous. Alcoholics Anonymous comes of age. New York: Alcoholics Anonymous Publishing, 1957.

Alcoholics Anonymous. Alcoholics Anonymous world directory, New York: Alcoholics Anonymous World Services, spring 1973.

Bailey, M. B., & Leach, B. Alcoholics Anonymous: Pathway to recovery. New York: National Council on Alcoholism, July 1965.

Berzon, B., & Solomon, L. N. The self-directed therapeutic group: Three studies, Journal of Counseling Psychology, 1966, 13(4).

Colbert, J. N. Philosophia habilitatus: Toward a policy of human rehabilitation in the post-institutional phase of disability. Journal of Rehabilitation, 1969, 35(5): 18–20.

Frankel, A., & Sloat, W. E. The odyssey of a self-help group. Psychological Aspects of Disability, 1971, 18(1):41–42.

Geist, G. O.; Curin, S.,; Prestridge, R.; & Schelb, G. Ethics and the counselor-agency relationship. Rehabilitation Counseling Bulletin, 1973, 17(1):15–21.

Grosz, H. J. Recovery, Inc., Survey: A preliminary report. Chicago: Recovery, Inc., May 1972.

Grosz, H. J. Recovery, Inc., Survey: Second report. Chicago: Recovery, Inc., May 1973.

Hurvitz, N. Peer self-help psychotherapy groups and their implications for psychotherapy. Psychotherapy: Theory, Research and Practice, 1970, 7(1):41–49.

Jaques, M. E. Rehabilitation counseling and support personnel. Rehabilitation Counseling Bulletin, 1972, 15(3):160–171.

Jaques, M. E., & Perry, J. W. Education in the health and helping professions: Philosophic context, multidisciplinary team models and cultural components. In J. Hamburg (Ed.), Review of Allied Health Education, Vol. 1. Lexington, Ky.: University Press of Kentucky, 1974.

Katz, A. Poland's self-help rehabilitation program. Rehabilitation Record, 1964, 5(3):30–32.

Katz, A. Application of self-help concepts in current social welfare. Social Work, 1965, 10(3):68–74.

Katz, A. Self-help in rehabilitation: Some theoretical aspects. Rehabilitation Literature, 1967, 28(1):10–11, 30.

Katz, A. Self-help organizations and volunteer participation in social welfare. Social Work, 1970, 15(1):51–60.

Massachusetts Council of Organizations of the Handicapped, Inc. A directory of organizations of the handicapped in the United States. Hyde Park, Mass.: Author, 1973.

Morris, R. Welfare reform 1973: The social service dimension. Science, August 10, 1973, 181(4099):515–522.

Mowrer, O. H. The new group therapy. Princeton, N.J.: Van Nostrand, 1964.

Mowrer, O. H. Integrity groups: Basic principles and objectives. Counseling Psychologist, 1972, 3(2):7–33.

Rau, N., & Rau, R. R. My dear ones. Englewood Cliffs, N.J.: Prentice-Hall, 1971.

Recovery, Inc. Recovery, Inc., National directory. Chicago, Ill.: Author (60603), January 1973. (a)

Recovery, Inc. Recovery, Inc., What it is and how it developed. Chicago, Ill.: Author, 1973. (b)

Riessman, F. The "helper" therapy principle. Social Work, 1965, 10(2):27–32.

Rogers, C. R. The emerging person: A new revolution. La Jolla, Calif.: Center for Studies of the Person, 1973.

Tyler, L. E. Design for a hopeful psychology. American Psychologist, 1973, 28(12):1021–1029.

Wechsler, H. The self-help organization in the mental health field: Recovery, Inc., A case study. Journal of Nervous and Mental Disorders, 1960, 130(4):297–314.

Wright, B. A. Activism versus passivism in coping with disability. In Ireland National Rehabilitation Board (Ed.), Proceedings of the Eleventh World Congress of Rehabilitation International, Community Responsibility for Rehabilitation. Dublin, Ireland: National Rehabilitation Board, 1969.

Wright, B. A. Changes in attitudes toward people with handicaps. Rehabilitation Literature, 1973, 34(12):354–357, 368.

Wright, M. E. Self-help groups in the rehabilitation enterprise. Psychological Aspects of Disability, 1971, 18(1):43–45.

Yalom, I. The theory and practice of group psychotherapy. New York: Basic Books, 1970.

Zola, I. K. The problems and prospects of mutual aid groups. Rehabilitation Psychology, 1972, 19(4):180–183.

20 Rehabilitation Team Practice

Robert J. Wagner

Team work has been conceptualized as a necessary ingredient to successful rehabilitation of disabled persons. Team practice has further been revealed as a process that permits practitioners to respond to the total person with multiple needs. The team is the full realization that no one profession or person can meet all the needs of the person with multiple problems.

Although conceptual justification, description, and suggestions for team practice are extensive, empirical observation is in short supply. Some research clearly supports the teamwork model, though many dimensions of effective team practice have not been studied.

TEAMWORK: A COHERENT MODEL

Team practice has been viewed as a reaction to fragmentation of service (Haselkorn 1958, p. 396), a phenomenon attributed to specialization and high-level training programs that ordinarily do not include multidiscipline team training for health-related fields (Flack 1971). Whitehouse (1951, p. 45), arguing against fragmentation, claims that "no treatment is medical, social, psychological, or vocational; all treatment is total."

Horwitz (1967, p. 10) ventured to say that technology has influenced the development of teams, resulting in a "trend toward delimiting areas of individual responsibility and increasing the proportion of professional work performed in collaborative processes articulating the segmental skill of different persons." In the helping professions, Horwitz explains, this trend has led to a proliferation of technical and subprofessional occupations and toward "institutionalization of interdisciplinary practice."

Institutionalization has extended the meaning of team practice beyond interprofessional collaboration; team practice has become the methodology of rehabilitation, that is, the essential response to the challenge of rehabilitation and "irreplaceable requirement of success" (Krusen 1964, p. 12). The multidisciplinary effort is idealized in a review by Jaques (1970), who characterizes rehabilitation as a "social movement used to label a process of providing coordinated and multiprofessional assistance to persons faced with the problems of disability and deviance in their lives" (p. 11). According to Jones (1968), no amount of individual skill in one's own particular profession can circumvent the need for group skills with a view to understanding the dynamics of individuals and the problems of decision making. "Multiple

Reprinted by permission from the March 1977 *Rehabilitation Counseling Bulletin,* pp. 206–217.

leadership is an essential goal which coordinated services must set for themselves'' (p. 37).

Although philosophy combined with various prescriptions for team practice suggest strong model coherency, actual team practice has not always been viewed as successful or consistent with the rationale and underlying principles of rehabilitation. For example, "treating the person as a whole," a value basic to rehabilitation and multidisciplinary treatment planning, is often confounded or prevented by communication barriers, status problems, and vested interests, which are three obstacles to "interprofessional collaboration" (Haselkorn 1958, p. 397). Barriers to collaborative effort among professionals also include differences in training, methodology of action and goals of the various groups of workers in the health field, and those noncooperative principles that place great value on individual achievement rather than on accomplishment of tasks through collaboration (Szasz 1970, p. 386).

New (1968) has suggested that underlying assumptions of effective teamwork, such as equality in professional competence, status, authority, task delineation, and operational domain, are essentially incongruent with the reality that sometimes emerges in group interaction. The lack of congruence and lip service to equality, New contends, causes team practice to fail.

Success of the team can be achieved if the following processes are implemented: (a) freedom of communication, (b) sharing of responsibility for decision making and leadership, (c) respect for individual status and competence, (d) encouragement of both independent functioning, (e) development of congenial interpersonal feelings and role consensus among staff members, and (f) continuous evaluation of clinical functioning in the light of shared reality (Stone 1970, p. 837).

Allen (1958) has suggested that professionals on a team might be unable to overcome organizational barriers, interprofessional jealousies, and professional inflexibility, problems that Allen contends can be resolved by close interpersonal relationships, joint staff evaluations, and administrative pressure for communication. Szasz (1970) also sets forth a strategy for overcoming the barriers to effective team practice. The approach includes the following considerations: first, the selection of goals based on the needs and interest of both the client and the professional; second, the fusing among the so-called preventive, diagnostic, therapeutic, and rehabilitative functions of professional personnel; and third, deliberate combination or extension of traditional roles and the invention of services.

Horwitz's (1967) comprehensive look at "interdisciplinary team practice" reveals that team process does not relate unobstructively to client needs and problems but that it is extensively affected by individual differences among practitioners, the structure and processes through which services are provided in a specific facility, professionalization, and the bureaucracy of the complex organization within which the team operates. Szasz (1970, p. 386) pointed out that economic and organization factors inherent in the present health care system "discourage sharing and delegation or surrender of functions even in the face of obvious needs." Team process is obstructed, for example, when in the middle of a conference team members are beset with agency policy decisions regarding their role, which directly or indirectly affects the client being staffed. The severely disabled client with multiple needs, the very reason for the idealized position of teamwork, is often not even considered when the team meets. Nagi (1975, p. 84) recommends consumer participation on teams and has summarized the conviction most service providers have that the client should contribute to the health care planning of the team.

Although teamwork has often been described as unsuccessful, the literature never ceases to claim the value of its practice. Improvement of multidisciplinary team practice is an issue that has evoked concern from those authors who have idealized teamwork. Generally, these writers visualize successful team practice as that which focuses on case material and the total needs of a client and unsuccessful team practice as that which responds to multiple tasks related to agency decisions, role differentiation, status problems, professionalization, and protection of one's discipline.

Whitehouse (1951, p. 45) has defined teamwork as "an interacting partnership of professions which specialize in client needs." Obstacles to "interprofessional collaboration" can be minimized if "we draw upon case material more fully in interprofessional exchange" (Haselkorn, 1958, p. 397).

Patterson (1959, p. 28) suggests that the group should coordinate and direct the activities and services needed by clients. Teamwork "is the best model yet constructed for working with clients as total persons with multiple needs" (Jaques 1970, p. 7). The focus on case material is so well accepted as the fundamental problem-solving activity of teams that Szasz's (1970, p. 390) primary recommendation for interdisciplinary training is a course for students of allied health professions that offers group exercises in management of patient problems. In 1971, the Departments of Counselor Education and Allied Health Professions at the State University of New York at Buffalo coordinated efforts to establish a common laboratory in which students of physical therapy, nursing, medicine, occupational therapy, and rehabilitation counseling worked together on case material extracted from their respective practicum and internship experiences in community rehabilitation settings (Jaques & Perry 1974).

Wright and Hardy (1970, p. 30) also suggest that examining case material and monitoring treatment planning behavior constitute the basics of team practice. The evaluation of clients prior to delivery of services must take into account the interrelatedness of the medical, social, psychological, educational, economic, and vocational problem areas. A major conclusion of Nagi's (1975, p. 82) sociological perspective on teamwork is that commitment to services, and not to the organization or facility, orients health practitioners to the uniqueness of clients.

Lacks, Landsbaum, and Stern's (1970) study, which was designed to improve the communication process of teams in a children's psychiatric unit through training laboratories, utilized treatment planning exercises as group problems because they were considered by the psychiatric unit staff to be the only tasks valid for the training program evaluation. Tasks relevant to the unit staff were developed from data obtained from individual interviews given prior to the workshop. Case material, treatment suggestions, and discharge planning were the problems believed to be important by those interviewed. The implication of the Lacks, Landsbaum, and Stern study is that service planning is the job to be done by teams and the only relevant task on which teams should be measured.

The research of Wagner (1973) examines teamwork performance only in terms of the output on a client case conference. The service plans made by teams are compared with service plans made by practitioners working independent of the team. Output of a number of professions and a number of persons from each profession were incorporated into the experimental design of this research to control for and to determine differences in professional orientations.

TEAMWORK, PERFORMANCE CHARACTERISTICS

The literature on teams is for the most part descriptive or prescriptive, with little effort put forth to evaluate the work of the team. Lowe and Alexander (1974), reporting on the health care of poor children, credited the comprehensive team approach for a dramatic reduction of 50 percent of hospital admissions for children registered in maternal and infant care and child and youth centers. These programs were not experimentally studied, and the success attributed to teamwork, therefore, is not validated.

The *Wisconsin Studies in Vocational Rehabilitation* (Wright & Butler 1968) identify approximately 20 references that relate to teamwork or "interdisciplinary collaboration." The literature is primarily concerned with supporting team service as the ultimate in treatment of people with disabilities. Selected studies deal with developing a rehabilitation program that serves the whole person and the totality of needs rather than isolated services delimited by the various professional specialties. These include the work of Stotsky, Mason, and Samaras (1958), Chenven (1956), Allen (1960), Rappaport and Dorst (1960), Wilson (1972), Schlesinger (1963), Olshansky and Margolin (1963), and Krusen (1964). A special study committee on the professional role of the National Rehabilitation Association (NRA) in 1965 focused on the recommended changes in the structure of NRA and became tangentially involved in a strong support of the multidisciplinary effort (Wright & Butler 1968).

Several articles referred to by Wright and Butler (1968) deal more specifically with communication problems among professionals of different disciplines. Pohlmann (1959), Spangler and Thomas (1964), Mill (1960), and Richardson (1960) have discussed the importance of positive interpersonal relationships among multidisciplinary team members and the issues of professionalism, fragmentation of service, and reduction of the interdisciplinary conflict.

There has been extensive material written about the kinds of variables found interacting in multidisciplinary team situations. Rushing (1964) has suggested that leadership, influence, authority, power, and status are clearly germane to understanding a multidisciplinary setting. Rubin and Bechhard (1972) called for "leadership skills" on the part of some members and "membership skills" on the part of everyone.

Pruyser (1963) has pointed out that, regardless of one's professional discipline, team members have to find their unique roles, places, and functions on the team. Nagi (1975) asks that professionals express their individual points of view; this articulation will help them understand alternate approaches expressed by others. "This articulation constitutes the difference between integrated teamwork and a collection of independent professionals who are disparate in their education and modes of service" (Nagi 1975, p. 80).

Improvement of team communication was the objective of Lacks, Landsbaum, and Stern (1970) who utilized a training laboratory experience for members of a psychiatric team. Improvement in communication skill (i.e., people talking to each other more), they indicate, means improvement in team performance.

Trela and Falkenstein (1972) observed client responsiveness to three-person teams over a two-year period and concluded that some individuals do not respond to the team but instead "seek a more personal relationship with a single worker and employ that person as a link to other services and resources" (p. 1). Weiner and Raths (1959) approached carefully controlled evaluation of the team with their study of diagnoses and prognoses made by individual members of interdisciplinary mental hygiene clinic teams, independently, before and after team meetings. These ratings were compared with each other and with those made by other therapists at the termination of treatment.

Although Weiner and Raths (1959) have evaluated certain aspects of the diagnostic and prognostic accuracy of team members, they did not actually compare team performance with individual practitioner performance; the treatment plans of individual practitioners were compared with treatment plans of the same individuals after they had participated in a team discussion. The study of Wagner (1973) controls the comparison of team performance with individual practitioner performance by first taking a stratified sample of individuals of several professions and then assigning them to either a team situation, in which the individual is a part of a real group, or to an individual work situation, in which the individual is a part of a nominal group. A review of the literature contrasting individual and group performance will demonstrate that a methodology utilizing nominal groups is necessary if the effects of interaction in the team situation are to be measured.

RESEARCH CONTRASTING INDIVIDUAL AND GROUP PERFORMANCE

Much research has been done on the comparative effectiveness of individuals as opposed to groups and nominal as opposed to interacting group processes in decision situations that require participants to generate information concerning a problem. The "effectiveness" measured in most studies is defined as either solving for the correct solution or just productivity in terms of the number of ideas produced.

Kelley and Thibaut (1968) offer an interesting dichotomy that helps to explain how differences in the requirements of tasks can affect the experimental results of research comparing individual with group performance. Requirements of the task are either disjunctive, as when any group member's report of the correct answer constitutes group success, or conjunctive, as when success depends on several persons making proper response to the task. Multidisciplinary teams asked to develop a service plan for a severely disabled client with multiple needs are faced with conjunctive requirements, that is, meeting the total needs of the client requiring the integration of the different skills of several professions.

Marquart (1955) compared groups not only with individuals but with collections of noninteracting individuals, so that a three-person collection was given credit for solving a problem if any one of the three solved it. Taylor and Faust (1952) first referred to this basis for evaluating groups as the method of nominal groups, the collections of independently working individuals constituting a group only for analytical purposes and not in an interactional sense. Utilizing the collective response of nominal groups to represent the individual's performance is necessary in order to assess the addition of interpersonal interaction that occurs in "real" groups. Without this control, the superiority of group performance could be attributed to the abilities of the most competent individual in the group and not to group interaction.

Although early studies supported group superiority (Faust 1959; Lorge & Solomon 1955; Marquart 1955; Shaw 1932), the point of view advocated by more recent research is that generation of solutions is accomplished better by nominal group processes. Such a conclusion is not credible or appropriate to the research on team practice for two reasons. First, most of the studies, which deal with groups that attempt to solve problems, are not complex or conjunctive in that the solutions of problems did not require the input of all team members and the variety of skills that are unlikely to be found in a single individual. Second, the evidence is not all in one direction but in direct conflict with the Hall, Moutin, and Blake (1963) study and an earlier study by Barnlund (1959), which clearly point out that group discussion contributes something beyond the pooling of individual judgments.

Most of the later studies (Anderson 1961; Campbell 1968; Rotter & Portugal 1969), especially those on brainstorming, do not show group superiority. Dunnette, Campbell, and Jaastad (1963) have interpreted such results by suggesting that interacting groups should be used exclusively for sharing and evaluating information and that the generation of ideas or solutions is better accomplished by nominal group patterns. Whether or not group problem solving is superior to individual problem solving, it is clear that group approaches requiring integration of resources of several disciplines are becoming more necessary as the accumulation and fractionation of knowledge in health-related professions increases.

A more recent investigation by Winter (1976) compared individual decisions of practitioners with group decisions regarding service contracts with severely disabled rehabilitation clients. Although the effects of different professional orientations were not accounted for, this study found that "group interaction led to more liberal decisions about providing services, particularly to those clients who are initially considered to be poor rehabilitation prospects" (p. 586). Winter contends that group decisions, risky in terms of increased tendencies to develop minimally feasible service plans, might facilitate the idea that "responsibility for carrying out the rehabilitation plan rests more firmly with every single member of that team" (p. 586).

A major conclusion of the research by Wagner (1973) is that team service plans are more holistic and that team practitioners, when compared with nominal groups of independent practitioners, expressed more of a need to become involved in the totality of the client's life. Teams considered the contributions of several professions more

of the time and attended to needs of the client's significant others. Practitioners working independently, however, produced a greater number of specific recommendations regarding specialized modalities and also offered a greater number of unique service plans.

PERFORMANCE RELATED TO GROUP STRUCTURE

Generally, the research on communication networks has investigated group structure by imposing certain networks on small groups. Structure is thus treated as an independent variable, and the consequences of a particular structure may be observed with regard to group performance, interpersonal response, and the personal reactions of members.

Social structure is invariant at a particular point in time (Kelley & Thibaut 1968). The implication of this theoretical notion for research on team performance is that practitioners on teams and those functioning independently of the team are each doing treatment planning within a specific social structure at a particular point in time. The type of communication structure within which the health practitioner will do service planning, therefore, might be considered an independent variable in this area of research.

Bavelas (1948) advanced the structural model referred to as the theory of communication networks. Although most research compared groups on simple tasks, the communication networks notion allows for the study of any kind of task, not just those with identifiable correct or incorrect solutions. Even if rehabilitation plans were stated as correct or incorrect, it is quite unlikely that one team member could solve the problem individually. The nature of the team task, meeting multiple needs of a client, is one that requires a variety of skills that are not likely to be found in a single person.

Glanzer and Glazer (1961) have defined communication structure as a set of positions with specific communication channels. The channel is the probability that a message can pass in either direction between two positions.

Applied to research on team practice, the "wheel" would be used to represent the independent practitioner. The formal structure of the team, however, is best represented by the "all-channel" network, a structure introduced by Guetzkow and Simon (1955). The all-channel network provides each person in the group with a communication link to every other person in the group.

The idea of restricting the number of persons in a small group so that each member can potentially communicate with some members but not others has led to several empirical studies that have imposed a variety of communication networks on groups and subsequently asked whether the imposed structure made any difference at all in the performance of a group on some task.

Leavitt (1951) and Guetzkow and Simon (1955) have demonstrated that structure alone, the distances between positions, can affect performance in an orderly way; performance varies with each slight change in position distance.

The research of Shaw (1964) supports the idea that the networks with more channels perform best on complex tasks, while networks with few channels do best with simple communication of information tasks. This conclusion is supported in the work of Davis and Hornseth (1967). All-channel network groups, comparable to a team situation, are much more effective with complex human relations problems than the wheel network would be, compared with practitioners working independently of teams.

SUMMARY AND CONCLUSIONS

The literature describing teamwork suggests that the team process is the one rehabilitation tool that can respond to the multiple needs of the disabled client. In addition, team practice is believed to be successful only when service planning and case review are considered its primary function. Although early research contrasting individual and group performance is inconclusive, recent studies suggest that teams provide more holistic response to clients and that teams are inclined to make riskier decisions than practitioners not on teams.

The use of multidisciplinary teams to make service plans for the severely disabled person suggests a consistency of rehabilitation ideology with the democratic and collaborative principles of teamwork. Responding to individuals' multiple problems and their interdependent quality is thoroughly harmonious with the elements of team practice as they are idealized in the literature. This strong model coherency illuminates the centrality of team practice to the rehabilitation program.

Generally, these results are consistent with data reported in the literature that compares groups with individuals and all-channel networks with wheel networks research. Individual group research is highlighted by studies that indicate group interaction, as on the teams that produced holistic behaviors, offers something beyond pooled responses.

REFERENCES

Allen, W. S. Rehabilitation: A community challenge. New York: Wiley, 1958.

Allen, R. M. The cerebral palsied, the rehabilitation team, and adjustment: An overview. Journal of Rehabilitation, 1960, 26(3):22–25; 42–44.

Anderson, N. H. Group performance in an anagram task. Journal of Social Psychology, 1961, 55:67–75.

Barnlund, D. C. A comparative study of individual, majority and group judgment. Journal of Abnormal and Social Psychology, 1959, 58:5–60.

Bavelas, A. A mathematical model for group structure. Applied Anthropology, 1948, 7(3):16–30.

Campbell, J. P. Individual vs. group problem-solving in an industrial sample. Journal of Applied Psychology, 1968, 52:205–210.

Chenven, H. The mental hygiene team in a rehabilitation center. In National Rehabilitation Association (Ed.), Mental illness and health. Journal of Rehabilitation, 1956, 22(4). (Special Issue)

Davis, J. C., & Hornseth, J. Discussion patterns and word problems. Sociometry, 1967, 30(1):91–103.

Dunnette, M. D.; Campbell, J.; & Jaastad, E. The effect of group brainstorming effectiveness for two industrial samples. Journal of Applied Psychology, 1963, 47:30–37.

Faust, W. L. Group versus individual problem-solving. Journal of Abnormal and Social Psychology, 1959, 59:68–72.

Flack, H. On becoming gate openers for minority health manpower. Paper presented at the American Hospital Association Workshop on Minority Group Recruitment and Retention, Chicago, 1971.

Glanzer, M., & Glazer, R. Techniques for the study of group structure and behavior: Empirical studies of the effects of structure in small groups. Psychological Bulletin, 1961, 58:1–27.

Guetzkow, H., & Simon, H. A. The impact of certain communication nets upon organization and performance in task-oriented groups. Management Science, 1955, 1:233–250.

Hall, E. J.; Mouton, J. S.; & Blake, R. R. Group problem-solving effectiveness under conditions of pooling vs. interaction. Journal of Social Psychology, 1963, 59:147–157.

Haselkorn, F. Some dynamic aspects of interprofessional practice in rehabilitation. Social Casework, 1958, 37:396–400.

Horwitz, J. J. Interdisciplinary practice teams in the helping professions: A critical review with perspectives for future research. Unpublished doctoral dissertation. State University of New York at Buffalo, 1967.

Jaques, M. Rehabilitation counseling: Scope and services. In the Guidance Monograph Series by S. I. Stone & B. Shertzers. Boston: Houghton Mifflin, 1970.

Jaques, M. E., and Perry, J. W., Education in the health and helping professions. In J. Hamburg (Ed.), Review of Allied Health Education: 1. Lexington, Ky.: University Press of Kentucky, 1974.

Jones, M. Beyond the therapeutic community: Social learning and social psychiatry. New Haven, Conn.: Yale University Press, 1968.

Kelley, H. H., & Thibaut, J. W. Group problem solving. *In* G. Lindzey & E. Aronson, (Eds.), The handbook of social psychology. Reading, Mass.: Addison-Wesley, 1968.

Krusen F. H. Concepts in rehabilitation of the handicapped. Philadelphia: W. B. Saunders, 1964.

Lacks, P.; Landsbaum, J.; & Stern, M. Workshop in communication for members of a psychiatric team. Psychological Reports, 1970, 26:423–430.

Leavitt, H. J. Some effects of certain communication patterns on group performance. Journal of Abnormal and Social Psychology, 1951, 46:38–50.

Lorge, I., & Solomon, H. Two models of group behavior in the solution of eureka-type problems. Psychometrika, 1955, 20:139–148.

Lowe, C., & Alexander, D. Health care of poor children. *In* A. Schorr (Ed.), Children of decent people. New York: Basic Books, 1974.

Marquart, D. J. Group problem solving. Journal of Social Psychology, 1955, 41:103–113.

Mill, C. R. Interprofessional awareness of roles. Journal of Clinical Psychology, 1960, 16:411–413.

Nagi, S. Z. Teamwork in health care in the United States: A sociological perspective. The Milbank Memorial Fundamental Quarterly, Health and Society, 1975, 53(1):75–91.

New, P. An analysis of the concept of teamwork. Community Mental Health Journal, 1968, 4(4):326–33.

Olshansky, S., & Margolin, R. J. Rehabilitation as a dynamic interaction of systems. Journal of Rehabilitation, 1963, 29(3):17–18; 38–39.

Patterson, C. H. Is the team concept obsolete? Journal of Rehabilitation, 1959, 25:9–10; 27–28.

Pohlman, K. E. Social research in physical disability. Journal of Rehabilitation, 1959, 25(6):7–9; 40–41.

Pruyser, P. W. Existential notes on professional education. Social Work, 1963, VIII.

Rappaport, L., & Dorst, K. S. Teamwork in a rehabilitation setting: A case illustration. Social Casework, 1960, 41:291–297.

Richardson, S. A. Psychological problems in rehabilitation. Journal of Rehabilitation, 1960, 26(5):20–22.

Rotter, G. S., & Portugal, S. M. Group and individual effects in problem-solving, Journal of Applied Psychology, 1969, 53:338–341.

Rubin, R., & Bechhard, R. Factors influencing effectiveness of health teams. Milbank Memorial Fundamental Quarterly, Health and Society, 1972, 3:317–335.

Rushing, W. A. The psychiatric professions: power, conflict and adaptation in a psychiatric hospital staff. Chapel Hill: University of North Carolina, 1964.

Schlesinger, L. E. Patient motivation for rehabilitation: Integrating staff forces. American Journal of Occupational Therapy, 1963, 17:5–8.

Shaw, M. Comparison of individuals and small groups in a rational solution of complex problems. American Journal of Psychology, 1932, 44:491–504.

Shaw, M. Communication networks. *In* L. Berkowitz (Ed.), Advances in experimental social psychology (Vol. 1). New York: Academic Press, 1964.

Spangler, D. P., & Thomas, C. W. Vocational rehabilitation services in a long-term medical setting. Journal of Rehabilitation, 1964, 30(2):20–22.

Stone, N. D. Effecting interdisciplinary co-ordination in clinical services to the mentally retarded. American Journal of Orthopsychiatry, 1970, 40(5):835–840.

Stotsky, B. A.; Mason, A. S.; & Samaras, M. Significant figures in the rehabilitation of chronic mental patients. Journal of Chronic Diseases, 1958, 7:131–139.

Szasz, G. Education for the health team. Canadian Journal of Public Health, 1970, 61 (September-October):386–390.

Taylor, D. W., & Faust, W. L. Twenty questions: Efficiency in problem solving as a function of size of group. Journal of

Experimental Psychology, 1952, 44: 360–368.

Trela, J. E., & Falkenstein, H. R. A note on rehabilitation teams and socially disadvantaged clients. Rehabilitation Research and Practice Review, 1972, 3(3):1–6.

Wagner, R. J. A comparison of the performance of multidisciplinary teams in rehabilitation settings with independent practitioners. Unpublished doctoral dissertation, State University of New York at Buffalo, 1973.

Weiner, D., & Raths, O. Contributions of the mental hygiene clinic team to clinic decisions. American Journal of Orthopsychiatry, 1959, 29, 350–356.

Whitehouse, F. A. Teamwork—a democracy of professions. Exceptional Children, 1951, 18:5–52.

Wilson, A. J. Teamwork conference yields high dividends. Journal of Rehabilitation, 1962, 28(2):23–25.

Winter, M. The rehabilitation team: A catalyst to risky rehabilitation decisions? Rehabilitation Counseling Bulletin, 1976, 19(4):581–586.

Wright, G. N., & Butler, A. J. Rehabilitation counselor functions: Annotated references. Wisconsin studies in vocation rehabilitation (Monograph I). Madison, Wisc.: The University of Wisconsin Regional Rehabilitation Research Institute, 1968.

Wright, K. C., & Hardy, R. E. An alternative to duplication. Journal of Rehabilitation, 1970, November-December, 30–32.

21 Strategies for Expanded Interagency Linkages
Rehabilitation Implications

Richard Roessler
and Greta Mack

For both philosophical and practical reasons, the Rehabilitation Services Adminstration has long stressed the importance of interagency linkages. Philosophically, rehabilitation's approach has always been multidisciplinary; practically, rehabilitation recognizes that no one agency can meet all the needs of the disabled individual.

Current trends in delivery of rehabilitation services make interagency coordination more important than ever. Increased emphasis on serving severely disabled persons requires multiple agency involvement. The concept of total household need, part of the holistic approach to rehabilitation, demands involvement of many agencies to serve handicapped persons and their household members.

Interest in interagency linkages is not confined to rehabilitation. The Department of Health, Education and Welfare has funded 44 Services Integration Targets of Opportunity (SITO) projects to test components of integrated human-service systems (U.S. Department of Health, Education & Welfare 1974). Preliminary feedback from SITO projects and other coordination efforts provides useful information about the issues that must be clarified for rehabilitation to improve linkages with other agencies.

Interagency-linkage issues are discussed in this article in terms of domain, ideological, and interorganizational consensus. Lack of consensus impedes progress toward improving interagency coordination at each of the organizational levels presented: ad hoc case coordination, systematic case coordination, or program coordination.

CONSENSUS: THE BASIS OF INTERAGENCY LINKAGES

Initiation of interagency linkages is often impaired by attitude. As one observer commented, "Linkages are cast in the mold of a threat to the status quo rather than as a means to improve services to clients" (Pecarchik 1974, p. 2).

To lessen the threat and improve attitudes toward coordination, several types of consensus among involved individuals are required (Benson and Kunce 1974): (a) domain consensus,

This research was supported by Arkansas Regional Service Intergration Project NHR-000009-01 from the Department of Social and Rehabilitation Services (Little Rock) and 16-P-56812, RT 13, from Social and Rehabilitation Services, U.S. DHEW (Washington, D.C.).

Reprinted by permission from the September 1975 *Rehabilitation Counseling Bulletin*, pp. 344–352.

agreement among organizations regarding the appropriate role and scope of an agency: (b) ideological consensus, agreement regarding the nature of tasks confronted by the organizations and the appropriate approaches to those tasks; and (c) interorganizational evaluation consensus, judgment by workers in one organization of the value of work in another organization. As Benson and Kunce (1974, p. 29) note, "An interagency relationship is equilibrated when levels of these components are high."

Domain Consensus

Domain consensus is threatened when agencies fear loss of autonomy and power to some coordinating organization or superagency. Since 38 states have combined at least two major program areas under a human resource agency, this type of organizational trend raises concerns about loss of identity (Carlucci 1974). In Arkansas, the comprehensive human resource agency is a loose confederation of divisions retaining their individual identities (Roessler & Mack 1974). Arizona, by contrast, has vested its line authority over service delivery in the regional directors of the Department of Economic Security.

Issues of domain consensus are heightened by many projects' failures to define coordination operationally (Roessler & Mack 1975; Services Integration Targets of Opportunity Project 1974). A recent study of five integrated approaches to mental retardation services (Aiken et al. 1972) noted such disparate coordination concepts as a fixed point of referrals and continuum of care, a lack of duplication of services, a mechanism for communication

and client interchange, an absence of rancorous conflict, a joint planning or coordination committee, or a single superagency.

However, the Cleveland Rehabilitation Complex demonstrated that expectations regarding participation can be defined. Taking as its goal "people renewal," the Cleveland project initiated coordination by (a) specifying values to be gained by each agency's participation, (b) stipulating membership contingencies so that agencies could work together without fear of loss of autonomy, (c) providing communication links between agencies, (d) providing positive influence for interagency involvements, (e) providing for maintenance of the system and mechanisms to work through agency misunderstandings, (f) providing consultation toward helping agencies with one another, and (g) illustrating areas of common interest among agencies (O'Toole et al. 1972, pp. 7–8).

Ideological Consensus

Although logical and supported by some research (Margolin 1955; Stotsky, Mason & Samaras 1958; Wright, Reagles & Butler 1969), the ideology of coordination is not shared by all service providers. If not threatened by the loss of autonomy, some are at least skeptical of the claim made for coordination that services provided in concert are more effective than services sequentially scheduled. Taking another tack, Bruml and Miller (1972) argue that coordination of services is merely a structural reorganization effort that reinforces the dominance of the traditional rehabilitative/social-service approach and fails to make a significant impact on societal problems.

To counter ideological skepticism, evidence of co-ordination's effectiveness, efficiency, and responsiveness is needed. Indeed, preliminary data from a Florida project indicate substantial savings to agencies in workers' time use and in transportation, medical, and system areas. The number of clients receiving services for which they were referred was greater in the coordination project than in a comparable uncoordinated region. In the comprehensive center, clients tended to complete multiservice programs at a higher rate and were somewhat more satisfied with services received (Comprehensive Services Delivery System 1974).

Interorganizational Evaluation Consensus

Coordination projects often place one group in the position of suggesting or mandating changes in service tasks for other groups. Such changes are viewed as negative evaluations of current activities, thus decreasing interorganizational evaluation consensus. Though it takes time, this consensus can be attained by positive actions. For example, in Mon Valley's voluntary service integration system (Pecarchik 1974), the effectiveness of core intake was sufficiently demonstrated so that it completely supplanted the intake procedures of two affiliated agencies.

CONSENSUS ISSUES: RESOLUTION

Reaching consensus can be accomplished if agency representatives participate in the planning stages of a coordinated system. In retrospect, commitment to the Duluth system would have been greater had local groups been involved in early planning stages (Dobmeyer, Russell & Todd 1972).

But consensus also requires time to develop. According to O'Toole et al. (1972):

> One reason behind the lack of coordination among agencies may be that coordination is often viewed as a short-term event that should be accomplished quickly and with relative ease or it is seen as a failure. It is relatively simple from a planning standpoint to draw up a coordination program involving two or more agencies; ... then, from this oversimplified view, programs are integrated and full blown coordination should take place. However, past failures show that this does not take place. It is felt that one of the reasons behind the success of CRS (Cleveland Rehabilitation Complex) has been the slow developmental process whereby inter-agency coordination has evolved gradually. (p. 20)

Experiences at the Cleveland Rehabilitation Complex seem to support the concept of social change labeled "incrementalism" by Henton (1974). Incrementalism allows consensus to build and coordination to develop out of a slow recognition of mutual needs and benefits rather than from an overarching rational scheme to bring agencies immediately into some type of coordinated relationship.

LEVELS OF COORDINATION

Coordinated relationships can occur on three levels (Reid 1969): (a) ad hoc case coordination, informal coordination in which individual practitioners cooperate to meet the needs of particular clients, and to which colocation or physical proximity is central; (b) systematic case coordination, which meshes services from different agencies on an individual case level, which has specific rules and procedures developed for it (case conference committees, referral routines, etc.), and which involves planned exchange of services to meet client needs; (c) program coordination, a method that is centered not on individual cases but on agency programs and that emphasizes joining or expanding agency programs, often into some sort of overall service program for different client types.

Ad Hoc Case Coordination

Colocation is an important approach to improving interagency linkages. Indeed, the first step toward coordination in Arizona was the development of one-stop multiservice centers (Human Ecology Institute 1973). Experiences in Florida reinforce the notion that one-stop service centers make it more probable that joint planning will occur (Comprehensive Services Delivery System 1974). However, colocation itself or ad hoc case planning does not insure case coordination (University of Arkansas Graduate School of Social Work 1973). Real improvement of interagency linkages must come through activities at the case and program levels.

Systematic Case Coordination

Lead-agency and core-staff are two approaches to systematic case coordina-tion. A lead agency may informally take the initiative to provide leadership, support, and technique for case coordination (e.g., the Cleveland Rehabilitation Complex). A core-staff approach base on an overarching coordination structure is found in most projects funded under the service integration banner. Next to single-point funding, the most important linkage in either approach is a management information system (MIS) for clients that tracks the clients and reports outcome data (Spencer 1973).

The initial step in a client MIS is the development of an intake procedure. Several coordination projects use a central site employing trained intake personnel who complete a common intake form for each client. In the Florida Project, a social worker assistant and a general-services intake person complete intake functions (Comprehensive Services Delivery System 1974). In Mon Valley, the intake procedures are completed by information specialists with bachelor's degrees trained in relating client problems to the spectrum of available services (Pecarchik 1974, p. 3). Arkansas, however, depends on regular agency field personnel to gather the common intake information (Roessler & Mack 1972).

In passing, it should be noted that orientation to the coordination program itself is necessary, not only for individuals in the common intake role, but for those who provide support to a central intake site, such as secretaries, receptionists, and persons in service-provider roles. For training purposes, Arizona (Human Ecology Institute 1973) has developed aids such as a film clip and tape presenting the services of one-stop centers and a standardized screening manual describing eligibility requirements of different programs.

Development of a method for sharing intake data among agencies is another key step in systematic case coordination. In South Dakota, SPAARS (Single Purpose Application with Automatic Referral System) includes "a common client intake point from which accurate referral, complete client information, and systemwide coordination of services emanates" (Flaten 1974, p. 4). Arkansas's nonautomated data-sharing system requires a copy of the common intake form completed by agency field representatives to be sent to a central point for circulation to agencies who have some potential for helping the client or his family (Roessler & Mack 1974).

Assessment of clients' needs and referral determination can be aided by computers, as in the Des Moines SITO project. Each agency has a case manager to develop a service plan with the client. Using on-line teleprocessing displays of available agency services (specified in terms of priorities, distance from the client, and delay in available openings), client and case manager can arrange an appropriate schedule for services (Polk/Des Moines Integrated Services Project, 1974). At the Crossroads Community Center, the referral function is performed by central intake workers (Breedlove 1974). In Arkansas, where regular agency field personnel are charged with intake, core staff members screen common intake forms for referral determination (Roessler & Mack 1974).

Systematic data coordination goes beyond information and referral systems. The experiences of SITO projects suggest that the likelihood of comprehensive and effective service delivery increases as the client is moved along a specified pathway based on assessed needs (U.S. DHEW 1974). In some service integration projects, a case manager, independent of any specific agency, is in charge of coordinating multidivision or multiagency cases (Comprehensive Services Delivery System 1974; Roessler & Mack 1974). In the Des Moines project, case managers designated by agencies are responsible for monitoring, evaluation, and follow-up (Polk/Des Moines Integrated Services Project 1974).

Program Coordination

Coordination is also evident on the program level as agencies cooperate to meet certain clearly shared needs. A case in point is the Cleveland Rehabilitation Complex, where program coordination resulted in new projects such as a neighborhood recreational facility and a housing improvement program (O'Toole et al. 1972).

Program coordination is often evident in the sharing of support services such as in-house medical examinations, inservice training, transportation services, a behavorial vocational assessment unit, a policy advisory council, case management, a case review committee, an automated client information system, a common application form, a referral form, a client services record file, equipment, food services, meeting rooms, parking and security, maintenance, adult basic education, child-care service, and emergency financial assistance (Comprehensive Services Delivery System 1974; O'Toole et al. 1972).

Other approaches to improving interagency linkages, which are being used in Brookings, South Dakota (Faris 1974), are joint funding, staff outstationing, joint planning, consolidated grants management, referral for services, case cooperation through agreements on joint use of staff, and purchase of service agreements.

The foregoing discussion of program cooperation completes our analysis of levels of coordination, making it possible to consider an interagency linkage model for rehabilitation.

A COORDINATION
MODEL FOR REHABILITATION

By employing a lead-agency model, drawing mostly from the systematic case coordination level, rehabilitation could formalize a process of interagency coordination. The lead-agency approach requires inservice training of personnel on the use of a common intake form, on activities and services of other agencies, and on some monitoring or follow-along techniques (Human Ecology Institute 1973). Each agency included in the linkage completes common intake forms and circulates information to all agencies having some potential for helping the applicants and their families (Polk/Des Moines Integrated Services Project 1974). If a common computer system exists, information can be consolidated and distributed on a regular basis to agencies (Pecarchik 1974). Although all counselors can assume intake and referral

functions, another approach involves assigning to one person intake and/or management responsibilities for all multiagency clients while other counselors provide rehabilitation services (Polk/Des Moines Integrated Services Project 1974).

Because the common intake and referral procedures themselves are oriented to the needs of the total household (Roessler & Mack 1972), case coordination is required. In case management, the rehabilitation counselor identifies household needs, assists the client and household in initiating services, and ascertains that household members are receiving services necessary to complete the coordinated plan. Additional support, such as an interagency review committee (Comprehensive Services Delivery System 1974), may be required for difficult cases. Finally, rehabilitation could initiate collaborative efforts among agencies to share support services and to meet acknowledged client and community needs.

Coordination, whether by lead-agency or other administrative approach, requires time, planning, and, most of all, commitment. In addition to providing moral support for interagency linkages, rehabilitation planners and supervisors must develop a streamlined system that eliminates redundant activities and is not merely an addition to everything else expected of the rehabilitation counselor.

THE HUMAN ELEMENT

It appears that the human element is still and probably always will be the crucial variable in developing interagency linkages. Where there are understanding, a commitment to the philosophy of coordination, and adequate guarantees for agency identity, coordination seems to work. As is noted by observers of the Cleveland Rehabilitation Project:

> Finally, throughout this report we have stressed the role of the informal coordinating agency. While formal meetings of agency leaders were held, the real work, building the complex, took place informally. It is not enough to have cooperative support for a plan, a philosophy, or an idea. Someone must assume the responsibility of initiating and sustaining the necessary day-to-day leadership tasks in order to attain coordinated goals. (O'Toole et al. 1972, p. 28)

IMPLICATIONS FOR PRACTICE

1. Emphasis on interagency linkages stems from needs to (a) minimize service duplication, (b) serve comprehensively the severely disabled, and (c) meet the needs of a total household.

2. Service coordination efforts are often perceived as a threat, or as the first step toward a superagency that threatens interagency consensus and equilibrium.

3. Domain consensus can be increased by establishing a common goal for and specifying contingencies of interagency linkage.

4. Ideological consensus can be increased by providing evidence of the benefits possible through coordinative activities and by identifying agency actions necessary to implement the coordinated relationship.

5. Interorganization evaluation concerns occur naturally whenever change is suggested or mandated, but do lessen with time as the changes are shown to be effective.

6. Experience suggests that interagency linkages should result from activities to meet acknowledged mutual needs faced by agencies (incrementalism) rather than from short-term, comprehensive master plans.

7. Interagency coordination can occur at three levels: (a) ad hoc case coordination, (b) systematic case coordination, and (c) program coordination.

8. Colocation is an approach to ad hoc case coordination, but in and of itself it is insufficient to bring agencies into cooperative relationships.

9. Though a variety of systematic case coordination approaches exist, all emphasize functions of common intake, case management, and information sharing.

10. Administering systematic case coordination requires either a lead-agency or a core-staff approach. Aspects of systematic case coordination are central to a formalized coordination model for rehabilitation.

11. Program coordination occurs on two levels: (a) agencies cooperating to implement joint projects such as a housing improvement program or a neighborhood recreational center, and (b) agencies pooling resources to meet common needs such as client transportation, medical examinations, case management, security, or maintenance.

12. Human factors such as mutual commitment and understanding are probably the most crucial variables in improving interagency linkages.

REFERENCES

Aiken, M.; Dewar, R.; DiTomaso, N.; Hage, J.; & Zeitz, G. The coordination of services for the mentally retarded: A comparison of five community efforts (Final Report, SRS Grant No. 15-P-55213/5-03. Madison, Wisc.: University of Wisconsin, 1972.

Benson, J., & Kunce, J. Coordinating human services: A case study of an inter-agency network. Social and Rehabilitation Record, 1974, 7: 28–33.

Breedlove, F. The crossroads community services center concept and relationships: Human services integration (HEW Grant No. 12-P-55954/3-01). Washington, D.C.: American Society for Public Administration, 1974. Pp. 68–71.

Bruml, E., & Miller, M. The integration of social services (SRS Grant No. 10-P-56020/5-02). Chicago, Ill.: University of Chicago, September 1972.

Carlucci, F. Statement of Frank Carlucci, Under Secretary of the Department of Health, Education and Welfare, before the Committee on Education and Labor of the United States House of Representatives on the Allied Services Act. Washington, D.C.: Department of Health, Education and Welfare, July 1974.

Comprehensive Services Delivery System. Evaluation. Tallahassee, Fla.: Bureau of Research and Evaluation, Department of Health and Rehabilitative Services, 1974.

Dobmeyer, T. W.; Russell, J. E.; & Todd, S. P. Improved coordination of human services. The concept and its application: A summary report (Final Report, Vol. I) (HUD and HEW Contract H-1343). Minneapolis: Human Services Coordination Program, Institute for Interdisciplinary Studies, August 1972.

Faris, J. Human services integration project. Paper presented at the Services Integration/Capacity-Building Conference, San Francisco, November 1974.

Flaten, G. Services integration efforts in the context of state/local relations. Paper presented at the Services Integration/Capacity-Building Conference, San Francisco, November 1974.

Henton, D. Goals and objectives in services integration planning: A non-traditional approach. Paper presented at the Services Integration/Capacity-Building Conference, San Francisco, November 1974.

Human Ecology Institute. Site reports. Wellesley, Mass.: Human Ecology Institute, 1973.

Margolin, R. Member-employee program: New hope for the mentally ill. American Archives of Rehabilitation Therapy, 1955, 3: 69–81.

O'Toole, R; O'Toole, A.; McMillan, R.; & Lefton, M. The Cleveland Rehabilitation Complex (Final Report, SRS Grant RD-2594-G). Cleveland, Ohio: Vocational Guidance and Rehabilitation Services, 1972.

Pecarchik, R. Mon Valley services integration program. Paper presented at the Services Integration/Capacity-Building Conference, San Francisco, November 1974.

Polk/Des Moines Integrated Services Project. Client pathway. Paper presented at the Services Integration/Capacity-Building Conference, San Francisco, November 1974.

Reid, W. Inter-organizational coordination in social welfare: A theoretical approach to an analysis and intervention. In R. Kramer & H. Specht (Eds.), Readings in community organization practice. Englewood Cliffs, N.J.: Prentice-Hall, 1969.

Roessler, R., & Mack, G. Progress report—Services integration (December 1972) (Arkansas Regional Integration Service Project NHR 000009-01). Fayetteville, Ark.: Arkansas Rehabilitation Research and Training Center, 1972.

Roessler, R., & Mack, G. Second annual report—Services Integration (September 1974) (Arkansas Regional Integration Service Project NHR000009-01). Fayetteville, Ark.: Arkansas Rehabilitation Research and Training Center, 1974.

Roessler, R., & Mack, G. Quarterly progress report—Services integration (January-March 1975) (Arkansas Regional Integration Service Project NHR00000-01). Fayetteville, Ark.: Arkansas Rehabilitation Research and Training Center, 1975.

Services Integration Targets of Opportunity Project. An evaluation of the Waianae-Nanakuli Human Services Center. Summary and recommendations (Vol. I) (SRS Grant No. 12-P—55890/9-01). Hawaii: Office of the Governor, July 1974.

Spencer, L. M., Jr. Planning and organizing human services delivery systems. Proceedings of a seminar on human services integration (SRS Grant No. 09-56027/8-03). Denver, Colo.: University of Denver, April 1973.

Stotsky, B.; Mason, A.; & Samaras, M. Significant figures in the rehabilitation of chronic mental patients. Journal of Chronic Diseases, 1958, 7: 131–139.

University of Arkansas Graduate School of Social Work. An evaluation to determine the effectiveness of coordination, administration, and delivery of services by a multiservice center in rural Arkansas. Little Rock: University of Arkansas, 1973.

U.S. Department of Health, Education, and Welfare, Office of Intergovernmental Systems. Services integration targets of opportunity (SITO) project descriptions. Washington, D.C.: DHEW, September 1974.

Wright, G.; Reagles, K.; & Butler, A. The Wood County project (Final Report, RD Grant 1629), Wisc.: University of Wisconsin Rehabilitation Research Institute, 1969.

22 Support Personnel and Counseling in Vocational Rehabilitation

C. D. Auvenshine

In recent years there has been considerable concern about the use of support personnel in providing rehabilitation services. This concern is widespread and has been reflected in national conferences of state directors of rehabilitation services, university training program coordinators, and representatives of the Rehabilitation Services Administration. Two publications (McAlees and Warren, 1966; Lucas, 1968) have been used widely as working papers on the subject. This article represents an attempt to bring into sharper focus some of the issues related to the use of support personnel in rehabilitation.

NEED FOR SUPPORT PERSONNEL

The job of the counselor/agent in rehabilitation services is becoming increasingly complex. The kinds of activities he must engage in are essential to the dispensing of services to rehabilitation clients. Usually these activities are administrative, technical, or clerical in nature. The fact that the agency representative is a professionally trained counselor affects the rehabilitation process in its entirety. It affects the kind and quality of services provided to the client and the way the client utilizes the services. Yet, because of the time-consuming demands he often must neglect the very activity for which he has been professionally trained, i.e., counseling. For those clients who need counseling (for personal adjustment, self-knowledge, selection of appropriate job objectives or training programs, etc.) the service is too often not available. Such clients often must obtain counseling outside the ongoing rehabilitation process by referral to another agency. Thus, it is evident that the services of the rehabilitation counselor as *counselor* are needed.

Initially, the state-federal program of vocational rehabilitation offered services, primarily, to persons with physical impairments. In recent years services have been extended to include persons handicapped by virtue of mental retardation or mental illness. Now, of even more recent origin, services have been extended and intensified to alcohol and drug addicts, public offenders, and the culturally disadvantaged. These recent additions to the range of clients served by rehabilitation place a still greater burden on the relatively small cadre of professionally-trained rehabilitation counselors across the

Reprinted by permission from the December 1971 *Rehabilitation Counseling Bulletin*, pp. 116–127.

country. Both the greater number of clients and their special problems create this added burden.

The basic program of vocational rehabilitation continues to be modified and expanded to meet the service needs of its clientele. Often expansion of services takes the program to the clients. Rehabilitation services offices now exist in a wide variety of settings including public schools, welfare offices, narcotic hospitals, mental hospitals, institutions for mentally retarded, prisons, and vocational training centers. With the increases, the programs become more visible, better known and better understood, resulting in a continued increase in vocational rehabilitation referrals.

The supply of professionally-trained rehabilitation counselors is also being tapped in the filling of administrative and supervisory positions. Due to rapid program expansion and development, many new supervisory positions have been created. A logical source of personnel qualified to fill these positions is the group of professionally-trained and experienced counselors. The salary structure of most agencies tempts senior counselors to move into administrative or supervisory positions rather than staying in the counselor career line. This is unfortunate both from the standpoint of the shortage of effective counselors and because of the well-known fact that effectiveness as a counselor does not bear a direct relationship to effectiveness as a supervisor or administrator. This problem is a crucial one needing further study. For the purpose of this paper, however, it is sufficient to say

that a sizeable number of the most productive counselors are taken out of their jobs each year and moved into administrative positions. Although these people continue to contribute to service programs, they no longer contribute in their primary specialty of counseling.

Other factors contribute to the shortage of trained counselors. The nature of the counselor's training, work experience, and agency duties renders him fair game for employers in other social service, business and industrial settings. The counselor is typically a specialist who qualified for training by virtue of his intelligence, social service interests, and motivation to improve himself. He is a trained specialist in human relations and in helping services. As a result of his training and work experience he often has acquired considerable poise and effectiveness in interpersonal relations. Furthermore, his job involves considerable local community mobility and visibility, providing him with a great deal of exposure to other job opportunities. Consequently, he is frequently sought by other employers and offered a salary that is considerably greater than he is currently earning and, thus, difficult to refuse. There is, consequently, some loss of counselors to jobs outside of rehabilitation.

The number of rehabilitation counselors graduated each year from the university graduate training programs is small in relation to the number of job vacancies. In fact, the number of graduates from these programs would scarcely be enough to fill turnover vacancies in the state-federal program even if all graduates from these were to seek employment there. Smits (1964), reported that only 30 percent of the graduates enter specifically into state rehabilitation programs (another 40 percent, however, enter other private and public rehabilitation agencies). So with the drop-out of counselors and the number of new jobs being opened each year, it is apparent that the supply of professionally-trained counselors falls far short of the demand.

To summarize to this point: The shortages of counselors and of time for counseling arise from several sources. The duties expected of counselors are growing, new clientele in new settings have new needs, and yet the supply of counselors is limited by promotions, drop-outs, and low numbers of university-trained professionals.

Since there are so few counselors in service agencies, it is essential that the existing ones be utilized as fully as possible. One way in which the counselor can contribute maximally is to have assistance doing those non-counseling functions of the rehabilitation process. The shortage of professional personnel would not be so acute if certain duties now performed by the respective professionals were assigned to assistants, aides, and other helping hands. Mase (1964) maintained that manpower in the health professions is not being effectively utilized. He indicated that most professionals spend considerable time on tasks which could be done by not-so-highly trained personnel. No business or industry could operate with the poor management procedures and use of manpower which characterize health, education, and welfare programs supported by tax

and voluntary dollars without cost-plus government contracts. The profit motive makes effective management essential in industry. Time and motion studies with respect to the effective use of professionals and support personnel in rehabilitation and related disciplines should lead to a reduction of manpower loss.

Whitten (1966), pointing to the varying demands on the counselor, recommended breaking down the total job into components, establishing new job classifications. This would better make it possible ". . . to apply the skills most difficult to acquire to functions of the rehabilitation process that require such skills." He urged also that the possibility of using volunteer workers to a greater extent be carefully explored. Patterson (1966) suggested that if existing professional counselors were used as *counselors* and if all non-counseling functions were assigned to other personnel, fewer professional counselors would be needed.

Lucas and Wolfe (1968), referring to severely-disabled and multiple-handicapped clients, stated that these clients ". . . must have the benefit of those counselors who possess not only the skill but also sufficient time to practice that skill. These two facets are responsible for the greatest number of clients remaining in the unserved disability category."

Truax (1968) reported significantly better outcomes for certain types of clients when counseled by counselor-aides than by either professional counselor or aide-counselor combinations. The aides were reported to have spent considerably more time per client on the average than did the counselor and to have shown greater "non-possessive" warmth and greater empathy. Truax attributed the time differential to "the enthusiasm of the aides and their motivation to spend time with the clients." He also reported that aides with high case loads spent considerably more time with clients than did aides with low case loads. The opposite was true for counselors wherein the larger the case load, the less time spent with clients. Truax concluded that, given the high level of training required for the professional practice of rehabilitation counseling, the complexities involved in the counseling process, and the extensive reservoir of expert knowledge required, a support personnel model should be considered by rehabilitation agencies. Such a model can demonstrably increase not only the available manpower pool, but it would do so with increased client benefit. Truax recommended a vertical administrative structure that provided a one-to-one relationship between the professional counselor and supportive personnel for his own case load.

Varying notions exist among rehabilitation professionals as to precisely who support personnel should be. The conceived role and function of these workers varies widely. It is not unlike the proverbial tale of the blind man and the elephant, i.e., each agency perceives support personnel as they relate to the needs of their particular agency. And, too, this perception is nebulous and ill-defined because of the many kinds of tasks support personnel can perform.

There are several dimensions on which support personnel may be considered. Some have to do with *worker* characteristics, others with characteristics of the *job*. These include general education, amount of independence, extent of client contact, and nature of work assignment (i.e., administrative, technical, or clerical). With regard to education, such workers may vary from indigenous workers with up to a high school education through those with graduate degrees. Some may work with minimal supervision while others must be supervised closely and directly, and some will rarely see clients while others will make many client contacts. Some can be administrators or case managers, others technicians, and still others primarily clerical workers. There are numerous combinations of personal and work characteristics among persons now employed as support personnel.

It seems apparent that the roles that support personnel will assume must be determined by the purpose for which they are used. Schlossberg (1967), in reference to "subprofessionals" in guidance, pointed out that three goals would be served by using them: (1) to provide jobs for the poor, (2) to provide manpower for the agency, and (3) to improve effectiveness of services. Savino and Schlamp (1968) suggested that these goal activities can also be therapeutic and educational for the support persons. The goals most frequently mentioned in the literature are related to provision of manpower and improvement of services. To a lesser extent, provision of jobs for those employed as support personnel may be another purpose in rehabilitation. It would appear that any decision as to who is to be employed and what he is to do would have to be made in relation to these purposes.

Some authors (Mase, 1964; Whitten, 1966; Patterson, 1966) have advocated a job analysis of rehabilitation counseling, splitting off certain of the tasks. This approach is based primarily on the goals related to manpower needs. On the other hand, the use of indigenous non-professionals to break down educational, cultural, linguistic, and color barriers seems related more to goals of improving services than to manpower goals. In addition to concerns of purpose and role, another consideration is the nature of the tasks, i.e., skills and activities required in the performance of the tasks. This has the most immediate implications for recruitment and training of support personnel.

In addition to matters related to purpose, role, tasks, recruitment, and training, an additional aspect adds even more confusion to the issue. Most administrators are in the postiton of having to classify the personnel they employ. Usually this means that some kind of job description has to be on file in the department that does the hiring before a position can be filled. Although the administrator may have a reasonably good idea of the kinds of tasks a support person might provide, he is often faced with the immediacy of establishing a personnel category or series of categories, fait accompli, prior to actual use of support personnel. In this regard Galloway and Kelso (1966) state:

These concerns are leading to demands to define the aide role before there has been time to find out what that role should be. The tendency to impose immediate structure seems to assume that aides are a necessary evil to be closely contained through the magic of job description. It is better to assume that there may be intrinsic advantages in the employment of aides. This view allows the period of experimentation and risk taking which is essential before job description and training guidelines are firmly established [p. 2].

They recommend considerable flexibility, recognizing initially that the role of the support person will necessarily vary with the setting.

The American Personnel and Guidance Association has an official position on the use and training of support personnel. This policy statement was prepared by the Professional Preparation and Standards Committee consisting of individuals from a broad spectrum of counseling interests (Strowig & Kennedy, 1967). This association acknowledged, by this action, the crucial need for support personnel and made an attempt to differentiate, in job tasks, the work of the counselor from the work of the support person:

1. The counselor performs the counseling function described in the professional policy statements while support personnel may perform important and necessary activities that contribute to the over-all service.

2. The work of the counselor involves synthesis and integration of interrelated parts of the total range of services with and on behalf of, the counselee. The work of support personnel tends toward

the particular and becomes an integral part of the larger whole only as this is developed under the leadership of the counselor.

3. The counselor bases his performance on the use of relevant theory, authoritative knowledge of effective procedures, and evaluation of the total endeavor. Functions of support personnel are characterized by more limited theoretical background and specialization in one or more support functions.

At a conference on support personnel held at the University of Maryland (Waldrop, 1966) agreement was reached that support personnel should be "technical" rather than "professional." It was also generally agreed that support personnel should be trained at the baccalaureate level. The report contains a list of specific functions believed appropriate to this technical definition of support personnel.

Bregman (1966) has suggested that support personnel fall into two categories. He classified them according to "First Order Personnel" and "Second Order Personnel." His first category included persons qualified by virtue of training to provide technical services for the rehabilitation process. His second-order-personnel category included persons not providing a technical service and those for whom it is incidental or not requiring special training. According to this system, selection and training of personnel would be according to the tasks performed in each category.

It is apparent from the foregoing considerations that support personnel may vary in qualifications and in tasks perf med. The way a particular agency perceives and utilizes these workers may be an expression of its unique needs as well as an expression of its creative planning and organization.

SOME IMPLICATIONS

Several major considerations emerge from the premise that support personnel can be used as adjuncts to the counselor.

1. The rehabilitation process consists of several levels and types of rehabilitation services covering a broad spectrum. The delivery of this spectrum of services requires a wide range of skills.

2. Explicit criteria must be applied in recruitment and selection of support personnel. These criteria must be based on the intended goals for the use of support personnel. And such criteria must also reflect the nature of the tasks, amount of supervision, implications for training and promotion, and relationships to existing personnel.

3. At all levels of education and skill some orientation and training are essential in order for the support person to become an effective contributor to the rehabilitation process. Such training needs to be short-term in nature and close to practice. Thus, it appears that state vocational rehabilitation agencies or regional training institutes are the appropriate settings in which the training should occur. If colleges and universities are to be used, either separately or in conjunction with the above, it would seem appropriate to select community colleges or state universities with viable continuing education programs.

4. The support persons must be supervised by someone; and the logical persons to supervise them are professional rehabilitation counselors. Amount and kinds of supervision will have to be determined by the nature of the tasks he is to perform.

5. The support person is, by definition, a technician. He is not a "shake and bake" counselor. This means, among other things, that he is probably not cognizant of the counselor's professional code of ethics. Yet, he will be required to implement the counselor's professional decisions and, in doing so, make judgments which have ethical ramifications for the entire rehabilitation process. The training of support personnel, therefore, must include instruction on ethical standards adhered to by counselors in the provision of rehabilitation services.

6. Since the need for support personnel is so great and their potential duties so diverse, we will probably see an increasing use of these workers in rehabilitation. In order to gain maximum effectiveness in recruitment, productivity, and longevity among them, an effective incentive and reward system must be established. For some of them, the job may represent a stepping-stone to becoming a rehabilitation counselor, while for others the job may represent their maximum level of aspiration. So the agency's personnel structure should provide flexibility in providing rewards consistent with the contributions made.

7. It may be that some degree of standardization in the employment, training and functioning of support personnel on a national or regional scale is desirable.

If so, this could be implemented by a series of research and demonstration projects under controlled conditions. Some variables which could be studied systematically are outcome, effectiveness, role, education, sex, age, race, cultural background and personal characteristics; organizational structure of the agency; rural-urban location of workers; and attitudes of other agency personnel toward these workers. Out of such projects should emerge a clearer understanding of how best to use support personnel. In addition to the apparent uses perhaps some imaginative and innovative uses would emerge which will further enhance the rehabilitation process.

It is inevitable that support personnel will be used in the rehabilitation process. Adequate thought, planning and research can help insure that such workers are used with maximum effectiveness.

REFERENCES

American Personnel and Guidance Association. Support personnel for the counselor: Their technical and non-technical roles and preparation. Personnel and Guidance Journal, 1967, 45: 858–861.

Arkansas Rehabilitation Research and Training Center & Association of Rehabilitation Center, Inc. (Conference co-sponsors). Selection, training, and utilization of supportive personnel in rehabilitation facilities. Hot Springs, Arkansas: Arkansas Rehabilitation Research and Training Center, 1966.

Arkansas Rehabilitation Service. This is one way. Little Rock, Arkansas: Arkansas Rehabilitation Service, 1961.

Bregman, M. H. The utilization of rehabilitation counseling and support personnel.

NRCA Professional Bulletin, 1966, 7, No. 6.

Cantoni, L. J. & Canton, L. Lay and professional counseling. Rehabilitation Literature, 1965, 26: 169–171.

Di Michael, S. G. New directions and expectations in rehabilitation counseling. Journal of Rehabilitation, 1967, 33: 38–39.

DiMichael, S. G. Preparation of rehabilitation technicians in community colleges. Rehabilitation Counseling Bulletin, 1968, 12: 76–83.

Fahy, E. W. The utilization of rehabilitation counseling support personnel. *In* Leslie, G. R. (Ed.) Supportive Personnel in Rehabilitation Centers. Washington: Association of Rehabilitation Centers, 1967.

Galloway, J. R. & Kelso, R. R. Don't handcuff the aide. Rehabilitation Record, 1966, 7: 1–3.

Gordon, J. E. Project cause, the federal anti-poverty program and some implications of sub-professional training. American Psychologist, 1965, 334–343.

Hansen, D. A. Functions and effects of sub-professional personnel in counseling. *In* McGowan, J. F. (Ed.) Counselor Development in American Society. Columbia, Missouri: 1965.

Harvey, L. V. The use of non-professional auxiliary counselors in staffing a counseling service. Journal of Counseling Psychology, 1964, 4: 348–351.

Hensley, G. & Buck, D. P. (Eds.) Rehabilitation manpower in the west. Boulder: Western Interstate Commission for Higher Education, 1968.

Leslie, G. R. (Ed.) Supportive personnel in rehabilitation centers: Current practices and future needs. Washington: Association of Rehabilitation Centers, 1967.

Mase, D. J. Manpower utilization for the future. Journal of Rehabilitation, 1964, 30: 37–39.

McAlees, D. C. & Warren, S. L. Increasing the supply of qualified rehabilitation counseling personnel in state vocational rehabilitation agencies. Washington: U.S. Department of Health, Education and Welfare, Vocational Rehabilitation Administration, 1966.

Muthard, J. E., Dumas, N. S. & Salomone, P. R. (Eds.) The profession, functions, roles and practices of the rehabilitation counselor. Jacksonville, Florida: Convention Press, 1969.

Patterson, C. H. Counselor or coordinator? Journal of Rehabilitation, 1957, 23: 13–15.

Patterson, C. H. Rehabilitation counseling: A profession or a trade? Personnel and Guidance Journal, 1968, 46: 567–571.

Patterson, C. H. The rehabilitation counselor: A projection. Journal of Rehabilitation, 1966, 32: 31–49.

Pearl, A. & Riessman, F. New careers for the poor. New York: The Free Press, 1965.

Samler, J. (Ed.) Rehabilitation counselor-aide functions and relationships. A report of proceedings and recommendations, VRA Training Conference. College Park, Maryland: University of Maryland, 1966.

Savino, M. T. & Schlamp, F. T. The use of non-professional rehabilitation aides in decreasing rehospitalization. Journal of Rehabilitation, 1968, 34:28–31.

Schlossberg, N. K. Sub-professionals: To be or not to be. Counselor Education and Supervision, 1967, 6:108–113.

Smits, S. J. Rehabilitation Counselor Recruitment Study: Final Report. Washington: National Rehabilitation Association, 1964.

Teague, D. & Buck, D. (Eds.) Developing programs in the helping services: Field experience, methods courses, employment implications. Boulder: Western Interstate Commission for Higher Education, 1968.

Truax, C. B. The training of non-professional personnel in therapeutic interpersonal relationships. *In* Arkansas Rehabilitation Research and Training Center & Association of Rehabilitation Centers, Inc. (Conference cosponsors), Selection training, and utilization of supportive personnel in rehabilitation facilities. Hot Springs, Arkansas: Arkansas Rehabilitation Research and Training Center, 1966.

Truax, C. B. The use of supportive personnel in rehabilitation counseling: Process and outcome. *In* Leslie, G. R. (Ed.) Supportive Personnel in rehabilitation centers. Evanston, Illinois: Association of Rehabilitation Centers, 1967.

Truax, C. B. The effects of supportive personnel as counselor-aides in vocational rehabilitation. NRCA Professional Bulletin, 1968, 8, No. 4.

Whitten, E. B. Rehabilitation: A look ahead. Journal of Rehabilitation, 1966, 32:22–23.

Section IV

REHABILITATION COUNSELING RESEARCH

23 Editorial Introduction

The expansion of rehabilitation research, especially that which has focused on the rehabilitation counseling process, has paralleled the development of rehabilitation counseling training programs, both having their common origin in the Amendments to Public Law 565, which was enacted by Congress in 1954. In fact, several of the articles in this section are based on research projects that were funded by grants from the Social and Rehabilitation Services division of the Department of Health, Education, and Welfare. The first article, by Muthard and Salomone, summarizes a landmark study of the roles and functions of the rehabilitation counselor. Because of the length of the original monograph, which was published as a special issue of the *Rehabilitation Counseling Bulletin*, only the abstract, significant findings, and the last chapter are reprinted here. The primary significance of the investigation is that it was the first comprehensive analysis of the rehabilitation counselor's work activities. The study evolved from an earlier investigation by Jaques (1959).

Bozarth and Rubin present in succinct form the conclusions drawn from the results of a five-year nationwide field study of the rehabilitation counseling process. Two classes of variables were of primary concern: 1) counselor interview performance and 2) client psychological and vocational outcomes. Because the article is written in a straightforward manner, the conclusions and the authors' implications are not restated here; however, it should be noted that some of their conclusions are contradicted by other research, e.g., the article by Anthony on the interpersonal skill levels of rehabilitation personnel in Section V.

The next article, by Tinsley and Gaughan, reports the results of a follow-up study of almost 4,000 former rehabilitation clients. The investigators' major purpose was to assess the long-term impact of rehabilitation counseling on the vocational adjustment of clients. Their data supported the conclusion that rehabilitation counseling does have a beneficial effect on clients' work adjustment. In addition to providing objective support for the efficacy of rehabilitation counseling, this article, as well as the preceding one, demonstrates that scientific research can be conducted on the effectiveness of a highly complex social service system.

Kunce, Miller, and Cope summarize the results of their analyses of a data set of truly monumental proportions: almost 750,000 clients, who were served by 54 state-federal programs in 1968 and 1969, constitute the subject sample. However, it is important to point out that the unit of analysis was the state-federal program, not the client. Thus, the results of this investigation pertain to relationships between program characteristics and *average* client outcome statistics. One principal finding of the study was that rehabilitation rate and rehabilitant's salary are relatively independent aspects of overall program success; other results and conclusions are listed at the end of the article. A subsequent analysis of this data set by Flynn (1975), using a more sophisticated multivariate procedure, produced conclusions that were in substantial agreement with those of Kunce et al.

The article by Bolton reports comparisons among three groups of rehabilitation counselors who employed different verbal interaction styles in working with their clients. The results indicated that the three types of counselors—information providers, therapeutic counselors, and information exchangers—are characterized by different patterns of client service activity. In other words, they work with different kinds of clients, using different combinations of services, and are differentially successful with their clients. The results concerning the therapeutic counselors are of particular relevance to graduate programs in rehabilitation counseling. The interested reader is referred to two other articles in the series (Bolton, 1974; 1977).

Anthony and Carkhuff describe an investigation that was designed to assess the impact of graduate training in rehabilitation counseling on students' attitudes and interpersonal skills. Using comparison groups consisting of philosophy students and rehabilitation counseling faculty members, the authors concluded that "specific training in rehabilitation counseling has effects independent of graduate training in general." Another article by Anthony, which is included in the next section, extends the arguments and conclusions presented here.

The article by Winter summarizes data collected from senior psychology students and rehabilitation facility counselors that suggest that group decisions about client feasibility involve greater risk than decisions made by individuals. One implication of this finding, assuming that the generalization is warranted, is that more difficult clients would be accepted for rehabilitation services if decisions were made by teams rather than individuals.

The ultimate purpose of research in rehabilitation counseling is the improvement of services to disabled clients. While the past decade has seen a concentrated effort to enhance the utilization of rehabilitation research (see Bolton, 1975), most authorities would probably agree that the translation of research-based knowledge into improved rehabilitation services continues to be a slow, inefficient process. The final article in this section by Murphy is a review of the obstacles to the use of rehabilitation research. Awareness of the various problems is certainly the first step in their solution.

REFERENCES

Bolton, B. 1974. Three verbal interaction styles of rehabilitation counselors. Rehab. Couns. Bull. 18:34–40.

Bolton, B. (Ed.) 1975. Research utilization in rehabilitation. Rehab. Couns. Bull. (Special Issue) 19:353–448.

Bolton, B. 1977. Client psychological adjustment associated with three counseling styles. Rehab. Couns. Bull. 20:247–253.

Flynn, R. J. 1975. Determinants of rehabilitation rate: A causal analysis. Rehab. Couns. Bull. 18:181–191.

Jaques, M. E. 1959. Critical counseling behavior in rehabilitation settings. College of Education, University of Iowa, Iowa City, Iowa.

24 The Roles and Functions of the Rehabilitation Counselor

John E. Muthard
and Paul R. Salomone

ABSTRACT

Rehabilitation counselor (RC) roles and functions were studied to provide basic information concerning the work tasks and traits of rehabilitation counselors who work in state agencies and private rehabilitation facilities. A stratified random sample of 378 counselors completed the Rehabilitation Counselor Task Inventory and several standardized inventories and questionnaires. Educators, administrators, supervisors, and other professional rehabilitation workers answered the Abbreviated RC Task Inventory and other questionnaires.

Major findings include (1) Eight major duty factors describe RC role behaviors. A high degree of importance is attached by RCs to affective counseling, vocational counseling, and placement duties. (2) The rehabilitation counselor spends about one-third of his time in counseling and guidance activities; 25 per cent of his time is spent in reporting, recording, and performing clerical tasks. Generally, placement consumes only a small proportion (7 per cent) of the counselor's time. (3) A generic university curriculum for counselor preparation rather than specialist programs is supported by the data. Specific curriculum changes to reflect the counselor's actual job demands were suggested. (4) Counselors think few of the present RC tasks could or should be performed by support personnel and the RC aide was seen as a threat to traditional counselor functions. (5) Little relationship was found between counselor personality characteristics and the duties which the RC thought were important, desirable, or provided him satisfaction.

Significant Findings for the Rehabilitation Worker

1. Rehabilitation counselors (RCs) would delegate only the most routine and repetitive of their job tasks to support personnel such as counselor aides or trained clerks. However, counselors believe that other professional workers, such as social workers and placement counselors, can perform a substantial number of tasks which RCs do.

2. The views of counselors, counselor educators, and agency administrators-

This investigation was supported in part by a research grant (RD-1971-G) from the Social and Rehabilitation Service, Department of HEW, Washington, D.C.

Reprinted by permission from the October 1969 Special Issue of the *Rehabilitation Counseling Bulletin*, pp. iii–iv and 134–143.

supervisors concerning the desirable RC work role are dissimilar. Rehabilitation counselors experience job-related role strain (i.e., the discrepancy between role behaviors and role expectations) since agency personnel, educators, and significant others attach more importance to most counselor tasks than do the RCs.

3. Counselors in different rehabilitation settings have essentially the same job functions. However, compared to state agency counselors, RCs in facilities emphasize counseling and guidance activities more. Division of Vocational Rehabilitation counselors also spend substantially more time in rehabilitation planning activities than do facilities RCs.

4. University preparation of RCs should continue to focus on a general rehabilitation counseling curriculum rather than on programs in specialized training with certain disability groups.

5. The role behaviors of the RC can be described by eight job function factors. Affective counseling, vocational counseling, and placement duties are assigned highest importance by RCs.

6. No significant relationship was found between the job satisfaction of RCs and the extent to which counselors view their major job duties as important.

7. No significant relationship was found between counselor personality characteristics and the role behaviors of RCs.

8. Concerning the desirability of graduate preparation, a majority of counselors in all three settings believe an M.A. degree should be held by those doing affective counseling, group procedures, and test interpretation. On-the-job training was viewed as sufficient by a majority of RCs for such duties as medical referral and vocational counseling.

SUMMARY AND IMPLICATIONS

This study of rehabilitation counselor roles and functions, undertaken for the American Rehabilitation Counseling Association and the profession, was designed to provide basic information regarding the work of the RC.

Some of the questions studied include:

1. What functions are actually performed by RCs in various settings?

2. What are the perceptions of counselors, supervisors, administrators, counselor educators, and other professional rehabilitation workers of the current role of the RC?

3. What are the perceptions of counselors, supervisors, and administrators of the desirable role and functions of the RC?

4. What are the relations of setting and characteristics of counselors to (a) their actual functions, and (b) their conceptions of the desirable roles and functions of the RC?

5. What conceptions of the *future* roles and functions of the RC are held by leaders in the field of rehabilitation?

6. What are the implications of these data as seen by RCEs and vocational rehabilitation administrators for the preparation of RCs?

Among the developments in the past two decades which suggest the need for further study of the counselor's role are: (1) the substantial increase in the number of individuals served; (2) the widened spectrum of services developed to meet the needs of clients whose rehabilitation problems are seen as more complex and varied than those of earlier rehabilitation clients; (3) the development of new techniques, procedures, and knowledge through an extensive research and demonstration program; and (4) introduction of substantial numbers of university-prepared specialists in rehabilitation counseling both in state and private programs. Findings from this study are expected to provide a firmer basis for coping with critical personnel problems such as counselor selection, training, recruitment, retention, and utilization.

Methodology

The 378 RCs who volunteered to participate in the project were selected from a national roster developed for the study . Counselors were invited to participate to secure adequate representation with respect to type of agency, training level, experience level, and geographic area.

To obtain information about the RC's role and behaviors, a Rehabilitation Counselor Task Inventory was developed based upon a job analysis technique refined by the Personnel Research Laboratory of The United States Air Force at Lackland, Texas. For each of the 119 tasks, the counselor was asked to indicate if it *was* part of his job, the extent to which the task *should* be a part of his job, how satisfying he found it, with what proportion of clients the task was performed, what preparation he thought was necessary for the task, and who should perform it.

In addition to the TI, the Holland Vocational Preference Inventory, the Minnesota Importance Questionnaire, Modified Patterson Rehabilitation Counselor Response Exercise, a Counselor Preparation Survey, a scale measuring "Attitudes Toward Rehabilitation Counseling as a Profession," the Job Satisfaction Index, and the Inventory of Job Relationships were administered. These measures were used to test series of specific hypotheses regarding the relationship between counselor characteristics and counselor role behaviors. Counselors completed their inventories in groups of 15 to 30 at meetings held in large cities throughout the country. Data from rehabilitation counselor educators, agency administrators and supervisors, rehabilitation leaders, and other professional rehabilitation workers were secured by mailed questionnaires.

Results

Nature of the Rehabilitation Counselor's Job   Factor analyses of the RCs' responses to the TI indicate that the RC's position may be most parsimoniously described by eight major classes of role behaviors. Nearly all tasks had a factor loading of .30 or greater on one of the eight factors when responses to the Importance Scale were studied. The extent to which the factors accounted for the variability in RC job behavior is further shown from the fact that 80 percent of the tasks had factor loadings of more than .40. These findings suggest major work areas such as affective counseling, placement, etc., for which performance measures might be developed. With information regarding the relative importance of the duty factors, the findings also provide support for other implications regarding RC preparation for placement and psychological testing.

The tasks and duties to which a high degree of importance are attached by RCs fall in the following areas: placement and related activities; affective counseling; vocational counseling; and a combination of supervising, teaching, and group procedures tasks. Other less important factors are test administration, test interpretation, medical referral, and eligibility and case findings.

The way RC tasks clustered with respect to task importance, task desirability, and task satisfaction gives further credence to the possibility that, in the future, separate work roles might be established for coordinating tasks and functions and for counseling tasks and functions. A realignment of current counselor duties along these lines might enable agencies to utilize counselors differentially so that those with particular talents could make optimum use of them. That is, counselors with personality characteristics, preparation, skills, and interest in counseling tasks and functions might reasonably be asked to focus upon these areas. Individuals with backgrounds and interests better suited to the coordination role might be assigned that set of duties. Such a division would also change the manpower requirements for the rapidly expanding state-federal and private rehabilitation agency programs.

Coordinating roles would be especially suitable for many individuals switching to rehabilitation from other careers, e.g., second careerists such as retired military personnel. As experience in some agencies has already demonstrated, some tasks and duties in this general area can also be performed by "new careerists," also known as indigenous workers (Riessman, 1968). Such differentiation of function would better enable agencies sorely pressed to provide and secure sufficient manpower to staff the new programs of service from a broader range of potential personnel. Within the coordinating and case management areas there are clusters of duties which might be performed by individuals without collegiate backgrounds and certainly less than a master's degree in rehabilitation counseling. Such a division of labor also suggests the type of rehabilitation work which might be effectively carried on by individuals who lack the skill and talent to perform the counseling function. The use of support personnel raises the prospect of better utilization of the available talent for providing counseling services.

Rehabilitation Counselor Use of Time Counseling and guidance activities are the predominant areas in which the RC spends his time, but the data clearly show that he spends about two-thirds of his time performing other duties. That the combination of clerical work, recording, and reporting accounts for about 25 percent of the RC's time suggests that counselor skills may often be underutilized. Not only is it possible that additional clerical personnel would relieve the counselors of some tasks, but it is also possible that systematic application of caseload management procedures such as work simplification and operations research procedures may enable counselors to spend more time doing what must be done by the counselor.

Although placement is regarded as a relatively important duty, the summary data on Counselor Activity shows that it generally commands a small amount of RC time. Since counselors and administrators hold placement as a key goal for existing rehabilitation agencies, it is desirable to consider new ways to meet this goal. Differential involvement of RCs or arranging for new types of personnel to perform the placement duty is suggested by the study's findings. Also, if the placement activity of counselors can be shifted from finding jobs for clients to teaching clients how to find their own jobs, the counselor or support person might work most effectively with groups of clients.

Counselor Placement   Counselors should take into account their preferences and competencies in the basic duties of a counselor when choosing a work setting. They should then affiliate with that rehabilitation setting which seems most compatible. Rehabilitation counselors and graduates from programs in this field will find significantly different work patterns among rehabilitation agencies, particularly in the three major types studied. Although it is not known whether more selective counselor placement will lead to greater effectiveness, the study suggests that such matching may be associated with increased satisfaction.

As a specific procedure for implementing this suggestion, the Rehabilitation Counselor Task Inventory could be used by agencies and counselor job applicants, especially recent graduates of RCE programs, to systematically explore the extent to which the agencies' work pattern is compatible with the interest, competencies, and expectations of the applicant. If any agency had a basic TI profile for a particular type of counseling position or had several positions which varied in some way, the personcant could examine the nature of the fit between what the applicant is "suited for" and the available opportunities.

Counselor Preparation

University Programs   A generic university curriculum for RCs rather than a specialist program is supported by the similarity in the types of duty factors emerging from the studies of counselors from three major settings. The differences among settings in the relative emphasis given specific tasks and duties could be accommodated by specialized experiences in clinical practice along with some elective course work.

Evaluation of counselor performance by either objective or subjective measures should include indices covering the duties and tasks found to be of major importance in the study. Thus, such duties as affective counseling, placement, vocational counseling, group procedures, counseling-teaching, and medical consultation should have greater emphasis than test administration and interpretation, medical referral, and eligibility-case findings.

Counseling tasks and activities were found to be of predominant importance to the counselor's job, but it was also shown that he presently performs a wide range of other tasks in order to achieve the goals of his agency and to satisfy the needs of his clients. University programs for RC preparation should develop competencies associated with the major duties if the duty or task is such that it requires the integration of basic knowledges and skills provided by universities. Universities cannot, of course, be expected to provide vestibule training for any particular program of rehabilitation services. However, as the study shows, the professional aspects of the counselor's job go beyond the counseling function.

The differing role expectations and perceptions for the counselor's present job found among RCEs, administrators, supervisors, counselors, and leaders has significance for counselor educational programming. It is possible to view the differences between RCEs and agency head supervisors with considerable alarm and admonish the educators to realign their curricula with the real world. One might easily say that the educators need to adjust their expectations and their programs so as to provide optimal preparation for agency employment. Changes in this direction might indeed ameliorate some of the role strain experienced by counselors, especially the recently trained counselors.

A more temperate reaction might be that curricula for RCs probably need to change in some ways, but the agencies' conceptions of how RCs can be best used may also need modification. Within the general educational goals of the university there would seem to be latitude for enhancing the background of knowledge and competencies in such areas as placement and vocational counseling.

There is also the difference in point of view reflected by the phrases, "training for the job as it exists" as opposed to "preparing the rehabilitation counseling student for a profession." Persons with the latter view believe the university's job is to prepare individuals to enter an evolving profession with basic skills and knowledges which will enable them to cope with a wide range of problems and with the rapidly changing demands being placed upon them and their agency. The similarity between the degree of change in the counselor's job which RCEs think desirable and the amount of change which leaders anticipate for 1980 lends some credence to the "preparation for the future" argument of RCEs.

The substantial importance attached to rehabilitation planning and job placement duties by counselors in all settings suggests that relevant skills and knowledges of this type must be developed during some phase of the counselor's student career. To the extent that aspects of vocational and personnel psychology such as theories of vocational choice and research on work adjustment provide an academic base for effective work in these duties, such study would seem justified as part of the RC's M.A. program. Perhaps one approach to meeting this need would be to have a vocational psychology course which incorporated occupational information with job placement and vocational planning principles and knowledge. Specific provision for helping the student to understand relationships between this academic area and his clinical practice would, of course, also be desirable.

For the RC in the M.A. program, there seems to be no justification for including more than one or two courses concerned with psychological testing. This caution would particularly apply with respect to technique courses in testing such as individual mental testing. The relatively limited importance attached to test administration further suggests a new focus for the counselor's education in testing. Courses oriented toward the understanding and use of tests in vocational counseling rather than courses in clinical testing are the directions which the current practice of RCS suggests.

Adminstrators   and   Supervisors
Although administrators and supervisors were expected to value counselor preparation in accord with their own education and experience, these factors were not found to be related to four major skills and abilities factors. The supervisors and administrators did tend to associate the need for certain types of training with the degree to which they thought duties such as affective counseling, placement, and referral were desirable counselor duties.

Educators Comparisons between educators' estimates of their provisions for the development of task proficiency and their judgments of the desirability of RC tasks generally indicate that they think they provide for the development of task proficiencies at a level higher than the desirable importance they attach to RCS' tasks. A correlational analysis, however, showed that the RCES are definitely congruent in their judgments of what the counselor should do and what their programs provide for in skill development. In a similar fashion, the RC desirability scores were found to be significantly correlated with the RCES' estimates of task proficiency provided.

Although RCES are known to differ in their counseling orientations, it does not appear that this results in significant differences in the extent to which they provide for the development of RC task proficiency in their M.A. programs. Perhaps even more surprising was the fact that in the RCE group, differences in the counseling orientation measure (MPRCR exercise) were not associated with differences in the relative desirability of a large sample of counselor tasks.

Agency-Educator Relationships
The discrepancy between the educator's perception of what the counselor does and should do and what the RC reports he does and thinks he should do reflects a gap of understanding and knowledge. This could be detrimental to agency-university collaboration and may result in the reflection of attitudes which prejudice RC students against positions in the state-federal program. To say that improved understanding between agency and university is needed says nothing new, but the need for continued contact between RCES and agency heads merits mention even if somewhat redundant. It is through such experiences, associations, and discussions that agency leadership and counselors can see new opportunities for the improvement of client service through the suggestions of researchers and teachers. Through such discussions, educators can better understand the present and future needs of rehabilitation agencies and more intelligently guide their efforts to prepare students to meet the client's need for professional assistance. Such discussions may also lead toward increased acceptance, by both agency

staff and educators, of the changing needs and problems of clients as they are perceived by both groups. This fresh look may encourage and enable agencies and their representatives to provide different levels of personnel to satisfy the needs of different kinds of clients.

Role Strain Among Counselors

Today's RC appears to experience a substantial amount of role strain. His supervisors, administrators, and other professional rehabilitation workers all hold greater expectations for him in the performance of most tasks and duties. There is almost universal agreement that the counselor should do more vocational rehabilitation planning and placement. Many groups also think he should increase his efforts in group procedures or the administration of special tests, while agency heads would place more emphasis upon counselors cooperating with other rehabilitation personnel, and case reporting.

Counselors and their employers may move in a number of ways to ameliorate the degree to which role strain is experienced. One of these would be to enhance the mutual understanding between the counselors and their co-workers. This may be accomplished among agency staff through discussions directed toward clarification of counselor role, but it is more likely that the RC himself needs to take the lead in clarifying his role for his collaborators in the community.

The presence of role conflict or strain may have beneficial effects on the development of the field of rehabilitation counseling. As one participant in the research utilization conference held by the project suggested, "The

dynamics of professional growth and improved services could not exist for long without the tensions and confrontations that grow out of differential expectations concerning rehabilitation counselor role, function, and preparation."

Counselor Role and Counselor Characteristics

The lack of relationship between the extent to which RCs find satisfaction in counseling or placement duties and various measures of counselor personality suggest that some counselor stereotypes need to be reconsidered. The belief that the enterprising, energetic, realistic person would be well suited to placement would be one of these as well as the notion that a social service orientation or need for responsibility and autonomy might be associated with greater satisfaction with the counseling activities.

Personality characteristics of counselors were expected to be associated with the relative emphasis counselors placed upon various duties and also were expected to show that personality factors would be associated with what the counselor thought should be important on his job. Again, the negative results of this analysis provide no support for the view that self concept and personality are expressed in the manner in which the RC views his job. However, these findings do not rule out the possibility that personality factors may be related to other criteria variables such as quality of the client-counselor working relationship or the number of rehabilitation closures.

Salomone's (1968) findings with a sample of male DVR counselors suggest that within the total group there may be smaller groups defined by type of agency, sex, training, experience, etc., which do have identifiable personality attributes. The significant relationships he found between selected needs and work patterns suggest the need for further analysis and study of this question among RCs. For example, it is of some interest to know whether the master's degree counselors working in facilities are different in their orientations and needs from those working in state general agencies.

There appears to be a notable association between the extent to which RCs think training is required for such major duties as placement, affective counseling, group procedures, and eligibility-casefinding and the educational level of the counselor. That this relationship is most marked between educational level and affective counseling might readily be anticipated in terms of cognitive dissonance theory. That is, having had graduate preparation, the counselor places higher value on the pertinence of such preparation for a high status duty and thus avoids dissonance between his career choice and the value of activities central to his work. Similarly, the person who qualified for rehabilitation counseling through a graduate program may also generalize the value of graduate study to other activities which are significant elements of his job, but are not prestigious or directly linked to his schooling.

Facilities counselors, who tend to have more graduate preparation, also regard graduate preparation as more highly necessary for major aspects of the counselor's job than do state agency counselors. However, there appears to be substantial agreement among counselors from all three types of agencies that extensive educational preparation is desirable for affective counseling, group procedures, and test interpretation.

Support Personnel for Vocational Rehabilitation   The lack of any substantial consensus among RCs regarding which of present RC tasks counselor aides (CAS) might perform suggests that RCs do not expect aides to take over many RC duties. Rather, the aides are expected to be adjunctive workers who will assist with certain types of ancillary tasks—possibly those which are necessary for effective case management, but which do not require extended training or experience. This result also suggests that the CA can be expected to be a threat to the RC and should be carefully introduced into rehabilitation settings as a person who complements the counselor's work rather than as a trainee for the RC position.

The present RCs see counselor aides as being suitable for performing only a limited number of RC tasks. These opinions may be restricted to aides who would have less than collegiate preparation rather than to persons with two or four years of college background. The possibility of rehabilitation specialists with college backgrounds working side by side with RCs may be an approach to meeting the demand for more and broader services to more clients. Such specialists may not be prepared to incorporate specialized knowledge regarding vocational adjustment or personal adjustment into the counseling process, but they would have or could develop basic approaches for helping clients mobilize their personal resources and make effective use of the available resources of the agency and the community. Specialists at this level would also be compatible with staff patterns and employment practices which the agencies now follow or have used in the past.

The opinions held by RCs regarding tasks which should be performed by them or by other professional workers may certainly be expected to influence their acceptance of other rehabilitation workers and CAS as collaborators in the vocational rehabilitation process. Counselors definitely think tasks involving client eligibility, vocational counseling, rehabilitation planning, and referral to other agencies and resources should be reserved for RCs. Counselors, especially those with graduate education, think graduate preparation is necessary for the other tasks and duties. It appears that counselor acceptance of new specialists or CAS will require a change in the counselor's view of what is proper for various rehabilitation workers to do. The counselor is ready to accept the contribution of specialists in such areas as psychological testing and placement, but he does not regard the CA as an individual who would be able to assume many of his tasks and responsibilities. Incorporating support personnel, CAS, and "new careerists" into the vocational rehabilitation program will probably meet the least resistance if these workers are assigned relatively new roles or duties which the counselor has

generally neglected in the past or if the new person is provided with a specialist role such as that of placement specialist.

Some of the aspirations of this study have been fulfilled and others have not. It provides further knowledge about the structure of the RC's job. Information about the relative importance of the RC's duties and tasks provides some guidance to those concerned with counselor preparation and utilization. It presents some encouraging findings such as the general congruence between what RCEs think should be changed in the counselor's job and what rehabilitation leaders expect to change by 1980. It includes discouraging findings such as the lack of relationships between RC personal traits and the emphases they place upon their duties. The study also introduces another research instrument to the rehabilitation counseling community. Finally, the problems, methods, results, and implications of this study may serve to stimulate other investigators to further study the changing roles and functions of the rehabilitation counselor.

REFERENCES

Riessman, F. New careers development center, vocational rehabilitation—a partner in new careers. New Careers Newsletter, 1968 (Fall), 2, No. 4.

Salomone, P. R. Rehabilitation counselor job behavior and vocational personality: needs and work style. Unpublished doctoral dissertation, University of Iowa, 1968.

25 Empirical Observations of Rehabilitation Counselor Performance and Outcome
Some Implications

Jerold D. Bozarth
and Stanford E. Rubin

A nationwide field study of the rehabilitation counseling process was undertaken by the members of the Council of State Directors in collaboration with the faculty of the Arkansas Rehabilitation Research and Training Center. This study took as its objective the ferreting out of information associated with the following questions: How do we measure the success of a rehabilitation program? Is vocational adjustment the only goal of the rehabilitation process, or should personal-social functioning be considered? Are vocational and personal adjustment interdependent processes, or can one occur without the other? In general, what are the major treatment factors contributing to a successful outcome for clients?

The Counselor-Client Interaction Project lasted approximately five years. It involved the collection of extensive information from 160 rehabilitation counselors and 1,000 clients in 12 states. The independent counselor variables were derived from audio recordings of counselor-client interviews and questionnaire information collected from the counselors. The following four categories of variables resulted: (a) demographic (e.g., age, education, experience); (b) self-report (e.g., perceptions of the relative importance of various counseling skills and activities); (c) interpersonal skills (i.e., Carkhuff's [1969] empathy, respect, and genuineness dimensions); and (d) subrole behavior (such as information-seeking/specific, confrontation, and information-giving/structuring (Richardson & Rubin 1973)). Four categories of dependent client variables were assessed: (a) psychological adjustment (i.e., Tennessee Self-Concept Questionnaire and Mini-Mult); (b) rehabilitation gain (i.e., employment potential and social

Details concerning the conclusions presented in this article are reported in the following monograph, available on request: Bozarth, J. D.; Rubin, S. E.; Krauft, C. C.; Richardson, B. K.; & Bolton, B. Client-counselor interaction, patterns of service, and client outcome: Overview of project, conclusions, and implications. *Arkansas Studies in Vocational Rehabilitation*, Monograph XIX. Fayetteville, Ark.: Arkansas Rehabilitation Research and Training Center, 1974. The project was supported by SRS Grants No. 12-P-55219 and No. 16-56812 to the Center.

Reprinted by permission from the September 1975 *Rehabilitation Counseling Bulletin*, pp. 294–298.

adaptability); (c) R-300 report (i.e., closure status, work status, and salary), and (d) six-month follow-up report (i.e., work status, salary, and work satisfaction).

The purpose of this article is to summarize the major conclusions of this project and outline some of its tentative implications. Several considerations should be kept in mind as these conclusions and implications are presented. First, the study was restricted to counselor interview behavior; thus, activities the counselor performs for the client such as job finding and placement are omitted from consideration. Second, relatively little variability existed among the tape-rated counselor variables—three interpersonal skills and twelve subroles—reducing the possibility of effective differential client change. Third, the measures of psychological adjustment and rehabilitation gain were self-reported, not objectively evaluated. Fourth, many of the difficulties and problems encountered illustrate the limitations of large-scale field research studies. Finally, the Project is the first nationwide study of the actual counseling behavior of vocational rehabilitation field counselors.

The conclusions of this study are based on those statistically significant findings that occurred at least twice throughout the analyses and were not contradicted by any results in the opposite direction.

COUNSELOR WORK ROLE

Conclusion I

Counselors are not a homogeneous group performing in a unitary manner.

Three distinct interaction styles were identified and labeled as information providers, therapeutic counselors, and information exchangers. Training, job function, and verbal interaction were related to these three interaction styles.

Conclusion II

Therapeutic counselors and information providers have a higher proportion of psychologically disabled clients rehabilitated than do information exchangers.

Conclusion III

Rehabilitation counselors do spend the majority of their job roles engaged in information-seeking, information-giving, and advice-giving behaviors.

Even though counselors tend to fall within the three different interaction styles, they generally spend most of their client contact interview behaviors using the three subroles cited above. This might result from the general agency definition of the job role of the rehabilitation counselor.

Conclusion IV

Certain subrole functions are related to more successful outcomes with certain groups of people.

Specific subrole behaviors were related to positive and to negative change of different types, depending on client age and sex. For example, relatively greater use of the information-giving/administering subrole tended to be related to positive psychological change and higher earnings at follow-up for females, but it was associated with negative psychological change and lower earnings at follow-up for males.

Implications

The following are the role conclusions and implications of counselor work arrived at from the results.

1. Counselors could be differentially assigned to clients in ways that would maximize the use of their interaction styles.

2. The assignment of psychologically disabled clients to particular counselors may improve the efficiency of the rehabilitation process.

3. Administrative role definitions, reward incentives, and emphases on performance could, in many instances, be altered to permit greater freedom for the less often used subrole behaviors to predominate with certain clients.

4. Administrators could change their emphases and counselors their interview behavior to take client goals, age, and education more into consideration as they are related to desired outcome.

COUNSELOR INTERPERSONAL SKILLS LEVELS

Conclusion I

Counselors do function at acceptable levels on the interpersonal skills dimensions.

The counselors were at least as high on levels of empathy, respect, and genuineness dimensions as many other professional groups, including experienced psychotherapists in private practice (Mitchell, Truax, Bozarth & Krauft 1973). They were found to function on the average at slightly above the minimal level of facilitative interpersonal functioning on the Carkhuff rating scales (i.e., a rating of three). This conclusion is contradictory to previous research with rehabilitation counselors and, like most of the conclusions, needs to be further investigated.

Conclusion II

The higher levels of the interpersonal skills, even though falling on the operational scale definition of minimally facilitative, tended to be related to higher vocational gain at closure, higher monthly earnings at follow-up, positive psychological change 10 months or more following intake, and greater job satisfaction at follow-up.

Conclusion III

Empathy relationships were variable and interacted with age and sex.

For clients over age 35 higher empathy was related to positive psychological change, higher earnings at follow-up, and greater job satisfaction. For males, higher empathy was associated with positive psychological change and greater job satisfaction at follow-up, whereas for females higher empathy was associated with negative psychological change and less job satisfaction.

Conclusion IV

Lower empathy and respect are associated with less vocational gain and a lower proportion of clients on jobs for the psychologically disabled.

Implications

The following interpersonal skills results were arrived at:

1. Counselors might increase their levels of functioning in interpersonal skills by having their major job task in rehabilitation interviews altered. They are performing as a group at a minimally facilitative level, even though job performance involves rational, cognitive subrole work behaviors, and is not primarily relationship focused.

2. Counselors might be amenable to increasing their levels of interpersonal skills by intensive, concentrated training, which should pay dividends in the form of increased client benefits on multiple criteria.

3. The assignment of older male clients to more empathic rehabilitation counselors should facilitate greater client benefits.

4. Higher levels of counselor empathy and respect appear especially important when working with the psychologically disabled client, thus suggesting the possible value of selective assignment of this client group.

GENERAL CHANGE FEATURES

Conclusion I

Client psychological change and vocational benefits appear to be associated with the work of rehabilitation counselors with their clients.

Conclusion II

Vocational change and client-reported psychological change emerge as independent dimensions.

Conclusion III

Case service expenditure appears to be positively related to greater vocational success of clients at closure.

Implications

The following statements are implications of general change features:

1. Counselor awareness of psychological components is important. Training related to psychological components ought to continue and perhaps be expanded, especially for counselors who work with particular groups.

2. Psychological change goals are worthy rehabilitation objectives in and of themselves.

3. Major monetary outlays for physical restoration and training may pay worthwhile dividends.

SUMMARY

We have presented some of the major, tentative implications of rehabilitation counselor performance based on this one study. As is true of most research, more questions have been generated here than answered.

Generally, this study suggests that we (a) allow the work role to be more flexible—consider review and revision of work rewards and counseling emphases; (b) insert adequate interpersonal skills training—it pays off; (c) begin to move toward differential assignments of clients to counselors; and (d) consider psychological change per se as a possible rehabilitation goal.

Overall, rehabilitation counseling looks excitingly positive. Change is being effected on multiple criteria; counselors appear to be functioning at adequate interpersonal skills levels; changes not commonly associated with rehabilitation procedures are taking place; and agencies and counselors are willing to embark on self-examination.

The profession compares favorably from nearly any view with other social action agencies; its willingness and effort to continue self-examination can only indicate further growth and improved effectiveness.

REFERENCES

Carkhuff, R. R. Helping and human relations: A primer for lay and professional helpers. Vol. 1 Selection and training. New York: Holt, Rinehart & Winston, 1969.

Mitchell, K. M.; Truax, C. B.; Bozarth, J. D.; & Krauft, C. C. Antecedents to psychotherapeutic outcome (Final Report, NIMH Grant No. MH 12306). Fayetteville, Ark.: Arkansas Rehabilitation Research and Training Center, 1973.

Richardson, B. K., & Rubin, S. E. Analysis of rehabilitation counselor subrole behavior. Rehabilitation Counseling Bulletin, 1973, 17(1):47–57.

26 A Cross-Sectional Analysis of the Impact of Rehabilitation Counseling

Howard E. A. Tinsley
and Suzanne M. Gaughen

Substantial evidence has accumulated which indicates that rehabilitation programs enable handicapped persons to regain some degree of lost physical functioning and to achieve vocational adjustment in the face of residual disability (Hefferin & Katz 1971). This general result has been repeatedly demonstrated for general populations of clients (Fox, Miller & Lawrence 1967; Levi 1964; McPhee & Magerby 1960; Michigan Department of Education 1972; Schletzer et al. 1958; Tinsley et al. 1969) and for selected disability groups such as handicapped college students (Condon 1957; Hetlinger 1963; Reed & Cantoni 1966), psychiatric patients (Kunce & Worley 1970; Olshansky 1973; Olshansky, Grob & Ekdahl 1960; Sterling, Miles & Miskimins 1967; Weinberg 1964), cardiac patients (Goldberg & Spector 1965), and drug addicts (Banganz 1966).

Relatively little research, however, has been addressed to the question of whether rehabilitation services have a lasting impact on the work adjustment of the client. In the only investigations relevant to this question (of which we are aware), Fox, Miller, and Lawrence (1967) reported a 15 percent increase in the unemployment rate over a three- to five-year period, and McPhee and Magerby (1960) reported a 25 percent increase in the unemployment rate over a four- to eight-year period. The evidence suggests, therefore, that the impact of rehabilitation counseling on the vocational adjustment of the client may be temporary for a sizeable proportion of those receiving such services. More substantial evidence regarding this possibility is highly desirable. Accordingly, this research was intended to answer the following questions: What proportion of those rehabilitation clients judged rehabilitated at termination maintains a satisfactory vocational adjustment? Does the proportion of former clients judged as having a satisfactory vocational adjustment decrease over time?

METHOD

Data Collection

Information regarding the personal characteristics and vocational adjustment of the former clients at referral, closure, and follow-up was obtained from the records of the Division of

Reprinted by permission from the March 1975 *Rehabilitation Counseling Bulletin*, pp. 147–153.

Vocational Rehabilitation (DVR) and from a follow-up questionnaire completed by the subjects. *Referral* indicates the time period beginning when the subject first requested services from DVR and ending when DVR officially accepted the former client for services. *Closure* refers to the time when the subject's case was officially closed by DVR. *Follow-up* refers to the time when the subject completed the follow-up questionnaire. The information obtained from DVR records was relevant only to the referral and closure time periods.

The Minnesota Survey of Employment Experiences, a printed questionnaire designed for use with former rehabilitation counseling clients, was used as the follow-up instrument in this research. The topics covered in the survey included the client's (a) work experiences prior to acceptance for rehabilitation counseling and subsequent to case closure, (b) current vocational adjustment, and (c) satisfaction with current employment.

The Minnesota survey was mailed to a sample of 6,435 former clients of the Minnesota Division of Vocational Rehabilitation (DVR) one to five years after the official closure of their case. A total of 4,912 (76 percent) former clients returned the survey or provided information by telephone. Information pertinent to the issues under consideration in this investigation was obtained from 3,977 (62 percent) respondents.

Analysis

The subjects were classified into four groups according to the length of time which had elapsed between closure and follow-up. The groups are hereinafter referred to as follow-up groups 1, 2, 3,. and 4, indicating the groups which were evaluated one, two, three, and four years after case closure, respectively. The status of the four groups was compared at referral, closure, and follow-up using chi-square analysis and analysis of variance. The comparison of the four groups at referral was relevant in determining whether there were significant differences in the precounseling characteristics of the follow-up groups; the analyses of the closure data were relevant in determining whether there were significant differences in the end-of-counseling vocational adjustment of the follow-up groups. Comparison of the referral and closure data indicated the impact of rehabilitation counseling and thereby established the baseline against which the long-term impact of rehabilitation counseling was evaluated. The four groups were compared at follow-up to determine whether there were significant differences in their postcounseling vocational adjustment.

Because of the large sample of subjects under study, numerically inconsequential differences having no practical significance may achieve statistical significance. This problem was dealt with in two ways. First, the .01 level of significance was chosen as the critical probability level. Second, omega-squared or Goodman and Kruskal's index of symmetrical predictive association was computed, as appropriate, when statistically significant differences were observed. These indexes provide an indication of the strength of association between the independent variable (group membership) and the dependent variable (work adjustment). (See Hays 1963, pp. 381–384 and 604–606 for a more detailed discussion of these indexes.) Values of .05 or less were interpreted as indicating that the statistically significant difference was of little practical significance.

Because of the wide variety of specific occupations held by the respondents, each occupation was coded according to the *Dictionary of Occupational Titles* (*DOT*—U.S. Department of Labor 1965) coding system. Occupations were then grouped according to their first digit *DOT* code. Subsequent occupational analyses were performed on these occupational groups.

Subjects

Few statistically significant differences were observed among the four follow-up groups at referral or closure, and none of the statistically significant differences were judged to be of practical significance. The variables analyzed included the work status and usual job before seeking services from DVR; work status, job, earnings, and job satisfaction at referral; work status, source of support, mobility, major disability, and public assistance at acceptance; and job, mobility, and public assistance at closure. In the total sample of 3,977 respondents, approximately 70 percent were male, the mean age was 27.3 years, and the mean number of years of school completed was 10.8. Only 29 percent of of the respondents were mar-

ried, and they had an average of three children. A sizeable minority (46 percent) of the respondents lived in rural areas of the state.

RESULTS

Immediate Effect of Rehabilitation

The status of the follow-up groups at referral was compared to their status at closure in order to ascertain the immediate effect of rehabilitation counseling. A substantial majority (80 percent) of the subjects had been employed at one time or another prior to their referral to DVR, but slightly less than 30 percent were employed at referral and 17 percent at acceptance. (Housewives and unpaid family workers were counted as employed, but students were regarded as unemployed.) At closure, 89 percent of the respondents were employed, an increase of 59 percent in the rate of employment from referral to closure.

At referral the clients were primarily employed in miscellaneous (26.5 percent), service (22 percent), clerical and sales (14.5 percent), or farming, fishing, forestry, and related occupations (11 percent). At closure the greatest number of clients was employed in clerical and sales (22 percent), service (19 percent), professional and managerial (18 percent), and miscellaneous occupations (11 percent). The percentage of persons employed in professional-managerial and clerical-sales occupations increased 12 percent and 7 percent, respectively, from referral to closure. Decreases of

15 percent and 5 percent were observed in the percentages of persons employed in miscellaneous and fishing, farming, forestry, and related occupations, respectively, for the same time period. At acceptance, 10 percent of the respondents indicated they were receiving public assistance, whereas only 4 percent were receiving public assistance at closure.

Long-Term Impact of Rehabilitation

Of central interest in this investigation was the question of whether rehabilitation counseling has a temporary or lasting impact on the work adjustment of the recipient. The finding that the follow-up groups differed in terms of their work adjustment at follow-up would support the conclusion that the impact of rehabilitation counseling is temporary. On the other hand, the failure to find significant differences among the groups at follow-up is consistent with the conclusion that rehabilitation counseling has a lasting impact on the client.

The groups differed significantly at follow-up in terms of the proportion employed in the various *DOT* occupational groups, but a .02 value was found for Goodman and Kruskal's index of symmetrical predictive association, indicating the result was of little practical significance. In brief, a greater number of persons from follow-up group 1 were employed in professional and managerial occupations, whereas a disproportionate number of respondents in follow-up group 4 held service occupations.

The follow-up groups did not differ significantly on any of the other quantitative or qualitative indicators of work adjustment. Approximately 67 percent of all respondents were employed at follow-up, an increase of 37 percent over the employment rate at referral. The employment rate was 65.5 percent, 70.8 percent, 64 percent, and 68 percent for follow-up groups 1 through 4, respectively, and the employed respondents worked an average of 41.2, 41.2, 41.5 and 41.7 hours per week. Only 9 percent of all employed respondents worked less than 35 hours a week. A majority of the respondents indicated that their handicap did not prevent them from doing a good job (mean = 3.6, 3.8, 3.8, and 3.7 for groups 1 through 4, respectively, on a 5-point scale) and that working at their jobs did not make their handicap worse (mean = 3.3, 3.3, 3.4, and 3.2, respectively, for groups 1 through 4 on a 5-point scale). More than 82 percent of all employed respondents reported that their job made their handicap much better, a little better, or neither better nor worse. Finally, the four groups had means of 63.6, 62.5, 61.8 and 61.9 (groups 1 through 4, respectively) on general job satisfaction.

DISCUSSION

The data are in accordance with the previously cited research, which indicates that rehabilitation programs are successful in helping handicapped individuals attain work adjustment. The increase of 59 percent in the employment rate from referral to closure attests to the efficacy of rehabilitation counseling. Moreover, there was a noticeable shift away from occupations classified in the *DOT* as miscellaneous and farming, fishing, forestry, and related occupations toward the professional-managerial and clerical-sales occupations. Even in the manual trades there was a slight trend away from the processing and structural work occupations toward the machine trades and bench work. One result of rehabilitation counseling, therefore, seems to be a marked increase in the employment rate and a shift toward occupations which make fewer physical demands on the client.

These gains are largely maintained at follow-up. Although the employment rate drops some, it is still markedly higher than the employment rate at referral and acceptance, and over 90 percent of the employed former clients are working full time. In addition, the tendency for former clients to be more frequently employed in less physically demanding occupations is maintained. Qualitatively, the respondents reported that working at their jobs did not make their handicaps worse, that their handicaps usually did not interfere with their doing a good job, and that they were satisfied with their jobs.

Of more importance to this investigation is the question of whether there is progressive deterioration in the work adjustment of former rehabilitation clients. The data clearly indicate that such is not the case. Although there were random fluctuations in the employment rate, it is clear that those clients who had been out of counseling the longest were employed as frequently, worked as many hours per week, and were as satisfied with their jobs as were those clients who had been

in counseling more recently. The same is true with regard to the qualitative indicators of work adjustment. Taken as a group, then, the former clients seemed to have as good a work adjustment four years after rehabilitation as they did one year after rehabilitation. Whatever deterioration occurs in the work adjustment of rehabilitated former clients seems largely confined to the first year.

One interesting question which cannot be answered from the data is whether those former clients who were unemployed one year after case closure will also be unemployed four years after case closure. Is there an approximate 35 percent who are more-or-less steadily unemployed after rehabilitation counseling, or is there a large number who are employed at some points after case closure and unemployed at other points after closure? An answer to this question requires longitudinal follow-up data which are presently unavailable.

The results of this research, then, support the conclusion that rehabilitation counseling has a lasting impact on the work adjustment of the client. Although these results are encouraging, further research is clearly desirable.

REFERENCES

Baganz, P. C. Problems associated with the vocational rehabilitation of drug addicts. Rehabilitation Counseling Bulletin, 1966, 10(1):18–22.

Condon, M. E., Ten year survey of physically handicapped students at the City College of New York. Personnel and Guidance Journal, 1957, 36(4):268–271.

Fox, S.; Miller, G. A.; & Lawrence, R. The rehabilitant: A follow-up study. Rehabilitation Counseling Bulletin, 1967, 10(2):99–107.

Goldberg, R. T., & Spector, H. T. Rehabilitation of patients after cardiac surgery: A follow-up study. Archives of Physical Medicine and Rehabilitation, 1965, 46(5):374–377.

Hays, W. L. Statistics for psychologists. New York: Holt, Rinehart, & Winston, 1963.

Hefferin, E. A., & Katz, A. Issues and orientations in the evaluation of rehabilitation programs: A review article. Rehabilitation Literature, 1971, 32(4):98–107.

Hetlinger, D. F. Physically handicapped college graduates. Vocational Guidance Quarterly, 1963, 11(2), 85.

Kunce, J. T., & Worley, B. Simplified prediction of occupational adjustment of distressed clients. Journal of Counseling Psychology, 1970, 17(4):326–330.

Levi, L. Rehabilitation of severely handicapped patients in Sweden: Methods and medical, social, and economic results. Archives of Physical Medicine and Rehabilitation, 1964, 45(9):454–459.

McPhee, W., & Magerby, F. Success and failure in vocational rehabilitation. Personnel and Guidance Journal, 1960, 38(6):497–499.

Michigan Department of Education, Vocational Rehabilitation Service. Two years later: A follow-up study of cases closed by the Michigan Vocational Rehabilitation Service in fiscal year 1970, 1972. (Mimeographed)

Olshansky, S. A five year follow-up of psychiatrically disabled clients. Rehabilitation Literature, 1973, 34(1):15–16.

Olshansky, S.; Grob, S.; & Ekdahl, M. Survey of employment experiences of patients discharged from three state mental hospitals during period 1951–1953. Mental Hygiene, 1960, 44(4):510–522.

Reed, A. E., & Cantoni, L. J. Fifty-three handicapped college graduates. Rehabilitation Counseling Bulletin, 1966, 10(2):63–69.

Schletzer, V. M.; Davis, R. V.; England, G. W.; & Lofquist, L. H. A follow-up study of placement success. Minnesota Studies in Vocational Rehabilitation, 1958, 3.

Sterling, J. W.; Miles, D. G.; & Miskimins, R. W. The mental health and manpower project: Research and demonstration in psychiatric rehabilitation. Rehabilitation Counseling Bulletin, 1967, 11(1):11–16.

Tinsley, H. E. A.; Warnken, R. G.; Weiss, D. J.; Dawis, R. V.; & Lofquist, L. H. A follow-up survey of former clients of the Minnesota Division of Vocational Rehabilitation. Minnesota Studies in Vocational Rehabilitation, 1969, 26.

U.S. Department of Labor, United States Employment Service. Dictionary of Occupational Titles. Washington: U.S. Government Printing Office, 1965.

Weinberg, J. L. The contribution of workshop experience in the vocational rehabilitation of post-hospitalized schizophrenic patients. Rehabilitation Counseling Bulletin, 1964, 8(1):58–59.

27 Macro Data Analysis and Rehabilitation Program Evaluation

Joseph T. Kunce,
Douglas E. Miller,
and Corrine S. Cope

Evaluation of rehabilitation programs is generally carried out in a single setting such as a workshop, hospital, or agency. The process typically involves the identification of client characteristics, critical program variables, and relevant outcome criteria, and the determination of the relationships among these variables. Few studies have been conducted outside of a limited institutional setting. One such study, the Psychiatric Evaluation Project, used data from a number of Veterans Administration hospitals, permitting analysis of relationships difficult to evaluate in a single setting, e.g., the size of a hospital (patient load) to patient turnover (Davis 1964). Another large-sample approach to program evaluation is the use of already available census-type data. For example, identification of characteristics of a psychologically healthy community was sought by studying the relationship of the size of 75 communities to indications of social pathology (Galle, Gove, McPherson & Miller 1972).

The applicability of a macro data analysis for evaluation of the relationships of rehabilitation program characteristics and outcomes is investigated in this study. State-federal vocational rehabilitation agencies collect data yearly on all state programs, including information on client characteristics, program operations (financing, personnel, etc.), and client outcomes. This data is collected nationally and from it descriptive statistical tables, charts, and publications are prepared. Selected information from these materials provides the data for this research.

METHOD

Subjects

The state-federal rehabilitation programs of 54 states and U.S. territories were considered as subjects for this study. The characteristics of the subjects were selected from available statistical summary information for the general and blind combined caseloads

This research was sponsored in part by Social Rehabilitation Service Grant 15-P-55245/7-06, Department of Health, Education and Welfare. Special thanks is given to Nathan Lesowitz, Chief, Statistical Analyses and Systems Branch, Rehabilitation Service Administration, for his assistance in the preparation of this study.

Reprinted by permission from the March 1974 *Rehabilitation Counseling Bulletin*, pp. 132–140.

for each program for fiscal years 1968 and 1969. The total data for this study are based on 680,415 cases for 1968 and 781,614 cases for 1969.

The 1968 and 1969 *State Data Books* (U.S. Department of Health, Education and Welfare 1968 and 1969) for federal-state programs of vocational rehabilitation and the 1968 and 1969 *State Vocational Rehabilitation Agency Program Data Books* (U.S. Department of Health, Education and Welfare 1968, 1969) served as the sources of information. When blind and general caseloads were provided by separate agencies, the data were compiled together. Thus, the data reflect each state's entire effort.

Variables

The program variables used in this investigation were assigned to one of three categories: input, process, or output. A wide array of variables was available, necessitating preselection of those that were of special interest to rehabilitation program operation. Three of the 12 selected factors or variables could be categorized as input, 6 as process, and 3 as output.

Input Variables The three input variables were the following: (a) the number of active rehabilitation cases per 100,000 state population, (b) the state per capita expenditures (state monies) for vocational rehabilitation including both federal and state Section 2 monies, and (c) the state agency rehabilitant caseload feasibility. Scores for caseload feasibility were determined for each agency from selected caseload characteristics of rehabilitated clients. These scores were obtained by using a variation of the simplified statistical procedure proposed by Kunce and Worley (1970) and subsequently applied and cross-validated on all clients ($n = 10,034$) from two state agencies (Kunce & Miller 1972). For the present study, each agency was assigned a caseload feasibility score based upon the total number of affirmative responses (scored 1) to the eight variables shown in Table 1.

Process Variables The six process variables included (a) the number of

Table 1. Agency Rehabilitation Feasibility

Variable	Item[1]
1. Education	Less than 35% of clients have an 8th grade education or less
2. Earnings	22% or more clients have earnings at acceptance
3. Weekly salary	Average per client $12.00 or more at acceptance
4. Age	Average client 27 years old or younger
5. Independence	Less than 12% of clients on welfare
6. Responsibility	More than 40% of clients have a dependent
7. Health	Less than 12% of clients are applications for OASI
8. Race	Less than 22% of clients are nonwhite

Note: Source of data *State Data Book* (1968, pp. 10–13). Rules were determined by above or below the national average for each variable. Similar procedures were applied for the 1969 data.
    [1] Score 1 if affirmative.

months in active status (vocational rehabilitation status 10 or higher); (b) the average total cost of case services (based on total number of clients receiving services with cost to a state agency); (c) the percentage of state expenditures for counseling and placement activities; and the percentage of state Section 2 monies spent for (d) workshops, (e) client maintenance, and (f) client training.

Output Variables The three output variables included (a) the average total cost per successful rehabilitation (Section 2 monies), (b) the number of successful rehabilitations per 100,000 state population, and (c) the average weekly salary of a successful rehabilitant at closure.

Statistical Procedures

The interrelationships of the 12 variables for the 54 rehabilitation programs were determined for fiscal year 1968 and again for 1969. Pearson product-moment correlations were computed using the Biomedical Computer Program 03D (Dixon 1968).

RESULTS

The interrelationships of the input, process, and output variables are presented in Table 2. This table shows the correlations obtained separately for years 1968 and 1969. In addition, those correlations that were significant at the .10 level or higher ($r = .23$) for two consecutive years are italicized to facilitate identification of consistent and meaningful relationships. (The probability of two such correlations occurring successively at the .10 level for two samples

could be considered to be equal to or less than .01.) In the following discussion, the numbers refer to the variables' rank as listed in Table 2.

Input Variables

The input variable, number of cases served per 100,000 population (3), was consistently related to 5 of the other 11 program variables. First, the number of cases (3) was positively and significantly related ($p < .001$) to available state monies (2) for each of the two years ($r = .83$ and .64) and to the rehabilitation rate (11) ($r = .92$ and .89). Second, the number of cases correlated negatively with percentage of monies spent for training (8) ($r = -.26$ and $-.26$), the rehabilitant's salary (12) ($r = -.29$ and $-.34$), and the cost per rehabilitation (10) ($r = -.43$ and $-.38$).

The relationships of the input variable, available state monies (2), to the other program variables were similar to those for the number of cases input variable. The input variable, caseload feasibility (1), showed a pattern of relationships markedly different from the other two input measures. For example, caseload feasibility (1) was positively related to percentage of funds spent for training (8) ($r = .26$ and .27) and to rehabilitant's salary (12) ($r = .48$ and .42). In contrast, the relationships of the other two input variables (state monies [2] and number of cases [3]) were negatively related to the training and salary variables.

Process Variables

The six process variables showed few consistent relationships among themselves (except that training [8] was

Table 2. Correlations of Program Evaluation Variables

Variable	Year	Input				Process					Outcome	
		2	3	4	5	6	7	8	9	10	11	12
INPUT												
1. Caseload feasibility	1969	−.16	−.10	.13	.05	−.03	.05	**.26**[1]	−.05	.14	−.16	**.48**[4]
	1968	−.24[1]	.01	.00	−.02	−.31	−.21	**.27**[2]	−.15	−.29[2]	−.13	**.42**[4]
2. State per capita expenditure	1969		**.83**[4]	−.23[1]	−.10	**.23**[1]	−.11	−**.47**[4]	.07	−.04	**.82**[4]	−**.28**[2]
	1968		**.64**[4]	−.08	.05	**.50**[4]	−.06	−**.51**[4]	−.10	.28[2]	**.62**[4]	−**.46**[4]
3. Cases per 100,000 population	1969			−.08	−.15	.12	−.23[1]	−**.26**[1]	.10	−**.43**[4]	**.92**[4]	−**.29**[2]
	1968			−.06	−.14	.23[1]	−.18	−**.26**[1]	.18	−**.38**[3]	**.89**[4]	−**.34**[2]
PROCESS												
4. Months in active caseload	1969				.09	−.07	.05	**.40**[3]	−.09	**.31**[2]	−**.37**[3]	.10
	1968				.13	−.04	.18	**.43**[3]	.06	**.36**[3]	−**.23**[1]	.23[1]
5. Cost of case services	1969					−.12	.09	−.01	−.23	−.03	−.15	.01
	1968					.00	.26[1]	.06	−.07	.22	−.05	−.10

190

		(1)	(2)	(3)	(4)	(5)
6. Percent funds for workshops	1969	.23[1]	−.30[2]	.02	.21	−.32[2]
	1968	.05	−.41[3]	.24[1]	.29[2]	−.42[3]
7. Percent funds for maintenance	1969		−.08	.26[1]	−.27[2]	.15
	1968		−.02	.35[3]	−.15	−.05
8. Percent funds for training	1969			.02	−.38[3]	.55[4]
	1968			−.10	−.21	.52[4]
9. Percent funds for counseling and placement	1969			.03	.04	.15
	1968			−.05	.17	.21
OUTPUT						
10. Cost per rehabilitation	1969				−.56[4]	.30[2]
	1968				−.39[3]	.06
11. Rehabilitation rate per 100,000	1969					−.39[3]
	1968					−.39[3]
12. Rehabilitant's salary	1969					
	1968					

[1] p < .10.
[2] p < .05.
[3] p < .01.
[4] p < .001.

positively related to months in active caseload status [4] and negatively related to funds expended for workshops [6]). These process variables did show several consistent and significant relationships to output variables. Both the months in active caseload (4) and percentage of funds spent for maintenance (7) related to the total cost per rehabilitation (10). The months in active caseload (4) correlated negatively to the rehabilitation rate (11). Finally, the percentage of funds spent for workshops (6) was negatively related and the percent of funds spent for training (8) positively related to the rehabilitant's salary (12).

Output Variables

As the rehabilitation rate (11) went up, total cost per rehabilitation (10) went down ($r = -.56$ and $-.39$). Furthermore, as rehabilitation rate increased, rehabilitant's salary (12) decreased ($r = -.39$ and $-.39$). The other significant relationships of the outcome variables to the process and input variables have been described in the previous paragraphs.

DISCUSSION

Both the high levels of rehabilitation rate and rehabilitant's salary are desirable program outcomes. Yet, the results suggest that these outcomes may be incompatible with each other. Such an incompatiblity is highlighted by the opposite relationship that the two output variables (the rehabilitation rate and rehabilitant's salary) have to the number of cases served. Where more clients are served, the rehabilitation rate is higher but rehabilitant's salary is lower. Conversely, when fewer clients are served a higher placement level (rehabilitant's salary) is achieved. Parenthetically, it is noted that volume, as measured by number of cases per 100,000, is associated with lower rehabilitation cost.

The inverse relationship between rehabilitation rate and rehabilitant's salary has special implications for program evaluation. Many programs that look good on one of these outcome variables will look bad on the other one. This finding does not necessarily imply that programs high or low on either of these variables are good or bad. However, the results do strongly support a position that the two kinds of programs have different resources and strategies. Those agencies with high rates tend to have more financial resources, work with more clients, rely more on workshops, and keep clients in the caseload for a shorter period of time. Those with lower rates tend to deal with fewer clients, be more selective in accepting clients, keep them in the program for a longer period of time, and provide them more training. Therefore, examination and evaluation of a program on the basis of only one criterion could lead to erroneous conclusions about program effectiveness.

Further inspection of the data revealed possible regional differences on several of the variables. The most obvious differences were rehabilitation rate and rehabilitant's salary. A number of state programs in the southeastern part of the United States have above average rehabilitation rates and below average rehabilitant's salary for the two consecutive years: Alabama, Florida, Georgia, Kentucky, Mississippi, North Carolina, Rhode Island, South Carolina, Virginia, and West Virginia. Many of the programs in the western states had below average rates but above average rehabilitant's salary: Arizona, California, Hawaii, Idaho, Kansas, Minnesota, Nebraska, Nevada, South Dakota, and Washington.

As expected, caseload feasibility related significantly to job salary but, contrary to our expectations, caseload feasibility apparently did not affect rehabilitation rate. One way to achieve a high rehabilitation rate in spite of a difficult client caseload was described in a recent report (Voor 1971). The report, in effect, recommends: work with many, not a few; be a salesman—play the odds (10 successes out of 100 contacts is twice as good as 5 success out of 10 contacts in the same period of time); don't keep clients in the caseload long; don't get bogged down in client-centered or other therapeutic strategies. Although the merits of such a salesmanship approach could be readily debated, a major defense might be that many clients who would otherwise do nothing may need only a little help to get started.

The results pose a question as to whether training or caseload feasibility is the primary factor that influences an agency's job placement level. Some insight into this question can be gleaned statistically by computing a correlation between training and rehabilitant's salary while holding caseload feasibility constant. The partial correlation obtained for 1968 was $r=.51$ $(p<.01)$ and for 1969, $r=.47$ $(p<.01)$. These results

indicate that training may be as helpful to the disadvantaged client as it is to the non-disadvantaged client in increasing subsequent salary level.

The importance of a satisfactory rehabilitation rate should not be overlooked. The significant correlation between rehabilitation rate and state appropriations suggests that demonstration of agency success, as measured by rehabilitation rate, may be used as convincing evidence for securing legislative appropriations. In other words, if more cases are served and more "rehabs" are accomplished, more monies may be made available.

CONCLUSIONS

A correlational analysis of macro data using state agency program summary information for 54 rehabilitation programs showed several consistent and meaningful relationships among input, process, and output variables over a two-year interval. Some of the more important findings and conclusions are:

1. Rehabilitation rate and rehabilitant's salary represent two distinctly different measures of program outcome and are inversely related to each other.

2. Agencies are more likely to achieve higher rehabilitation rates if they serve larger numbers of cases, have sufficient financial resources, spend proportionally more money on workshops and less on training and maintenance, and keep clients a shorter time in active service status.

3. Agencies are more likely to place clients in higher paying jobs if they work with fewer, but more select, clients; have limited resources in terms

of state money; and tend to spend more of their money on training than on workshops.

4. Indications of caseload feasibility can be obtained from those client characteristics that relate to general employer-hiring practices (previous education, prior employment, etc.).

5. Agencies in the southeastern United States have higher rehabilitation rates but lower rehabilitant's salary in contrast to those in the western states.

6. The percentage of money spent for training significantly increases rehabilitant's salary regardless of the agency's caseload difficulty. The use of training, however, tends to reduce client turnover and may result in a lower rehabilitation rate.

7. The percentage of monies allotted for counseling and training tend to favorably influence final salary.

8. In the evaluation of program effectiveness, consideration should be given to several output measures, since programs may be unfairly evaluated using a single criterion.

REFERENCES

Davis, J. E. Empirical dimensions of psychiatric hospital effectiveness. *In* Psychiatric evaluation project: Factors in mental hospital effectiveness, Intramural Report 64-5. Washington, D.C.: Veterans Administration Hospital, 1964. Pp. 19–36.

Dixon, W. J. (Ed.) Biomedical computer programs. Berkeley, Calif.: University of California Press, 1968. Pp. 60–66.

Galle, O. R.; Gove, W. R.; McPherson, J. M.; & Miller, J. Population density and pathology: What are the relations for man? Science, 1972, 170:23–30.

Kunce, J. T., & Miller, D. E. Simplified prediction: A follow-up study. Journal of Counseling Psychology, 1972, 19:505–508.

Kunce, J. T., & Worley, B. Simplified prediction of occupational adjustment of distressed clients. Journal of Counseling Psychology, 1970, 17:326–330.

Social Rehabilitation Service. State data books. Washington, D.C.: Department of Health, Education and Welfare, Rehabilitation Service Administration, 1969.

Social Rehabilitation Service. State Vocational Rehabilitation Agency program data books. Washington, D.C.: Department of Health, Education and Welfare, Rehabilitation Service Administration, 1969.

Voor, J. L. Short term rehabilitation of social security disability insurance applicants. (Final report) Lexington, Ky.: Department of Education, Bureau of Rehabilitation Services, Commonwealth of Kentucky, 1971.

28 Case Performance Characteristics Associated with Three Counseling Styles

Brian Bolton

A previous research study (Bolton 1974) isolated three verbal interaction styles that rehabilitation counselors employ in their interviews with clients: *information providers* give general administrative information, specific details about services, and information tailored to the client's needs; *therapeutic counselors* listen, explore, reflect, and provide support to their clients; and *information exchangers* solicit information from clients, provide educational and occupational information, discuss various topics, and offer advice.

The validity of this empirically derived typology of rehabilitation counselors' verbal-interaction styles was supported by data regarding professional development and counseling practice. Information providers drove twice as many miles per month, reported the highest percentage of successful closures, had the lowest undergraduate GPAs, and were predominantly client-centered or eclectic in counseling orientation. Therapeutic counselors had the highest proportion reporting supervised practica and internships, considered the communication of ideas among co-workers to be a relatively unimportant job function, were most apt to use research findings to modify counselor performance, had the highest undergraduate GPAs, and were predominantly client-centered or eclectic in counseling orientation. Information exchangers rated themselves most proficient in dealing with information, had the lowest proportion reporting supervised practica and internships, considered the communication of ideas among coworkers to be an important job function, were predominantly rational-cognitive in counseling orientation, and reported the highest proportion of counseling activity the preceding week.

These findings provided evidence suggestive of relationships among rehabilitation counselor training, orientation, and job function, and the style of verbal interaction that counselors use in their actual counseling function. However, it should be stressed that this conclusion was based on analyses of counselor data only; the research ques-

Preparation of this report was supported by SRS Grants No. 16-P-56812/6-07 and No. 12-P-155219 to the Arkansas Rehabilitation Research and Training Center. Appreciation is expressed to Jim Duncan, Diane Graham, Patty King, and Allan Shub for assistance with the analysis of data.

Reprinted by permission from the March 1976 *Rehabilitation Counseling Bulletin*, pp. 464–468.

tion of major importance to the assessment of the construct validity of the three counseling styles concerns their differential impact on rehabilitation clients. Accordingly, the purpose of the investigation reported in this article was to compare the three groups of counselors from the previous study, using R-300 data from a sample of 207 clients who had received services and were closed in statuses 26, 28, or 30.

METHOD

Samples

Fifty-four rehabilitation counselors and 207 clients they served while participating in a nationwide investigation of the rehabilitation counseling process made up the research groups for this study. Of the counselors, 87 percent were male, average age was 38 years, 85 percent were married, 24 percent were disabled, 56 percent held a master's degree, and average experience in rehabilitation was 5 years.

Clients had the following characteristics: 50 percent were male, the average age was 32 years, 30 percent were single and 31 percent were married, 41 percent were mentally disabled, 48 percent were high school graduates, and 84 percent were not working at the time of acceptance for services.

Instrumentation

The 3 groups of clients who received services from the information providers, therapeutic counselors, and information exchangers (90, 71, and 46 clients, respectively) was compared on 32 standard variables derived from the client R-300 report. The 32 variables fall into 3 categories; (a) client characteristics (sex, age, number of dependents, referral source, Social Security Disability Insurance [SSDI] status, and so forth); (b) case services (diagnosis, restoration, vocational, cost, and so forth); and (c) client outcome (closure status, weekly earnings, and the like). Chi-square and analysis-of-variance tests were used to evaluate the statistical significance of the differences among the 3 groups on each of the 32 variables.

RESULTS

Eleven of the 32 comparisons among the 3 groups of clients were statistically significant at the .10 level. These 11 case performance correlates of the 3 counseling styles are summarized in Table 1. The case of performance correlates indicate the differential modes of operation and the relative effectiveness of the counseling styles.

The information providers worked with the least difficult clients: fewer clients were not working at acceptance (77%) and reported no earnings (82%), and fewer were mentally disabled (36%). These counselors worked with fewer clients in the "no services with cost" category (24%), authorized less vocational training (9%) and fewer "other" services (29%), and spent the least amount of money per client ($330) while achieving the highest rate of successful closures (89%). In summary, the information providers served the least difficult clients, with fewer vocational and supplementary services, at

Table 1. Case Performance Correlates of Three Counseling Styles

Correlate	Information Providers %	Therapeutic Counselors %	Information Exchangers %	p
Client characteristics				
Work status: Not working	76.7	91.6	84.8	.001
Weekly earnings: None	82.2	94.4	89.1	.06
Disability				
Mental	35.6	49.3	39.1	.09
Orthopedic	22.2	16.9	34.8	
Marital status: Single	28.9	22.5	45.6	.03
Case services*				
Vocational training	8.9	18.3	28.3	.01
On-the-job training	7.8	15.5	2.2	.05
Maintenance	27.8	42.2	10.9	.002
Other services	28.9	46.5	50.0	.02
No services with *cost*	24.4	50.7	45.6	.002
Client outcome				
Successful (26) closure	88.9	76.1	71.7	.03

* Mean total cost: Information providers $330, therapeutic counselors $663, information exchangers $546 ($p < .04$).

the lowest cost, and produced the highest success rate.

The therapeutic counselors served the most difficult clients: more clients were not working (92%) and had no earnings (94%), and almost one-half of their clients were mentally disabled (49%). More clients were assisted with maintenance (42%) and placed in on-the-job training (16%), at the highest average cost per client ($663). The rate of successful closures was intermediate for this group (76%). In summary, the therapeutic counselors served the most difficult clients, using more maintenance and OJT services, with the greatest expenditures per case, and achieved an intermediate success rate. This group also had the lowest counselor/client caseload ratio—21 counsel-

ors closed 71 clients—suggesting a more intensive counseling relationship.

The information exchangers worked with clients who were intermediate in difficulty: 85 percent of the clients were not working at acceptance and 89 percent had no earnings; 39 percent were mentally disabled. These counselors worked with more single clients (46%), using more vocational training (28%), more supplementary services (50%), and less maintenance (11%) and on-the-job training (2%). They authorized an intermediate level of case expenditures ($546) and produced the lowest successful closure rate (72%). In summary, the 12 information exchangers served moderately difficult clients, with more vocational and supplementary services, at an intermediate cost per client, and were the least successful.

DISCUSSION

The three composite profiles constructed from the case performance correlates of the three counseling styles are clearly consistent with the earlier interpretations based on counselor verbal interview behavior and data regarding professional development and rehabilitation counseling practice. Because the original investigation, in which the three styles were isolated, and the current validation study are nonexperimental in design, it was not possible to control relevant situational variables. Three major classes of uncontrolled variables are non-interview counselor behaviors, state agency procedures and policies, and economic and labor market conditions. Data reported previously indicate that the counselors in this study differed considerably in the extent to which they used professional consultation, sought job placement opportunities for their clients, and other functions of that nature (Rubin, Bolton & Richardson 1973, pp. 35–36). The variability in rehabilitation practices among state agencies has been thoroughly documented by Truax, Lawlis, and Bozarth (1969). Finally, the large geographical variance in economic and labor market conditions is reflected in monthly government reports. The reality of the typology of counseling styles is greatly enhanced when it is realized that the differences between the three styles must be substantial in order to emerge through so much uncontrolled and potentially confounding variance!

Despite the inherent limitations of nonexperimental field research studies, the results of the current investigation add considerable support to the previously stated conclusions regarding the antecedents of and the counselor characteristics associated with the three counseling styles. The pattern is clearest for the therapeutic counselors. They are products of academic training programs (high GPA, supervised counseling practicum and internship, experience in tape recording interviews, inclined to use research findings, and client-centered or eclectic counseling orientation), and their counseling performance, as reflected in the client service data summarized in this report, is consistent with the expectations of rehabilitation counselor educators. Very little evidence exists to support the academicians' claim that graduate education that emphasizes therapeutic counseling skills prepares more effective rehabilitation counselors (Miller & Bozarth 1975). In fact, the results of this study, which suggest that therapeutic counselors deal with more difficult clients and achieve a respectable success rate, may be the first to provide solid, objective evidence.

Note—In the article (Bolton 1974) which reported the isolation of three verbal interaction styles, Figure 1 on page 38 contains an error which has confused several readers. The profiles for styles 2 and 3 should be reversed beginning with subrole L-CE.

REFERENCES

Bolton, B. Three verbal interaction styles of rehabilitation counselors. Rehabilitation Counseling Bulletin, 1974, 18:34–40.

Miller, L., & Bozarth, J. What are the effects of graduate school training programs in rehabilitation counseling: Some plain talk. (CRCE Task Force Report on Graduate Education.) Iowa City: University of Iowa, Department of Counselor Education, 1975.

Rubin, S.; Bolton, B.; & Richardson, B. Empirically derived rehabilitation counselor subgroups and their biographical correlates. Counselor-Client Interaction Project Monographs, No. 6. Fayetteville, Ark.; Arkansas Rehabilitation Research and Training Center, 1973.

Truax, C.; Lawlis, G. F.; & Bozarth, J. Uniformity and differential rehabilitation practices in the state-federal vocational rehabilitation program. (Third Report.) Fayetteville, Ark.: Arkansas Rehabilitation Research and Training Center, 1969.

29 Effects of Training on Rehabilitation Counselor Trainee Functioning

William A. Anthony
and Robert R. Carkhuff

As a relatively new field, rehabilitation counseling is presently in the throes of developing an identity (Krause, 1965), and considerable disagreement exists concerning the roles and functions of the rehabilitation counselor. Should he be primarily a counselor or a coordinator (Goldin, 1966; Patterson, 1968)? Should his training and practice be oriented toward solving psychological or vocational problems (Gellman, 1966; Olshansky & Hart, 1967)? Should he specialize in particular areas of functioning (Warren, 1959)? Numerous surveys have been conducted and committees formed to consider the professional concerns, duties, and role conflicts of the rehabilitation counselor (American Rehabilitation Counseling Association, 1967; Bronson, Butler, Thoreson, & Wright, 1967; Hall & Warren, 1956; Jaques, 1959; Olshansky & Hart, 1967). These concerns have quite naturally permeated the area of rehabilitation counselor training.

Despite this wealth of surveys and airing of opinion on the problems inherent in the role and training of the rehabilitation counselor, very little research has been carried out to consider the efficacy of counselor training. The research that has been done on the effects of training has been confined almost exclusively to the area of counselor personality characteristics (Patterson, 1967a). While of interest, this research is of little practical value because as yet the personality characteristics of the counselor (measured by current psychological tests) have not been shown to relate to counseling outcome. The growing need for more practical research in the area of rehabilitation counselor training is emphasized by the fact that once a rehabilitation student graduates and becomes a practicing member of his profession, his performance with clients is seldom evaluated effectively (Muthard & Miller. 1964).

In an attempt to meet this need, this study was designed to measure the effects of one rehabilitation counselor training program on several areas of functioning that have been empirically or theoretically related to counseling outcome. Specifically, the following

The authors wish to acknowledge all of the subjects who gave their time to this investigation. In addition, the contributions of the raters (John Cannon, James Drasgow, Ted Friel, Dan Kratochvil, Richard Pierce, and B. Todd Holder) are gratefully acknowledged.

Reprinted by permission from the June 1970 *Rehabilitation Counseling Bulletin*, pp. 333–342.

four indexes of functioning—based on extensive research evidence—were assessed:

1. *Attitude toward disabled persons* (using a scale developed by Yuker, Block, and Campbell, 1960), which is positively related to (a) close personal contact with disabled persons and (b) the work performance of nondisabled persons functioning in helping relationships with disabled persons (Anthony, 1969; Yuker, Block, & Young, 1966).

2. *Level of communication of the facilitative dimensions* (empathy, respect, concreteness, genuineness, and self-disclosure), which is positively related to (a) indexes of client process movement and (b) a variety of outcome indexes of constructive client change or gain (Carkhuff, 1969a; Carkhuff & Berenson, 1967; Truax & Carkhuff, 1967).

3. *Level of client self-exploration*, which is (a) an index of counselor behavior in the respect that it is dependent in part upon counselor level of functioning (Truax & Carkhuff, 1965) and (b) related to indexes of constructive client change or gain (Carkhuff, 1969a; Carkhuff & Berenson, 1967; Truax & Carkhuff, 1967).

4. *Level of discrimination*, which has been found to be a necessary although not sufficient condition of effective communication (Carkhuff, Kratochvil, & Friel, 1968).

In each instance it is hypothesized that advanced trainees would demonstrate significantly higher levels of functioning than beginning trainees, and that rehabilitation trainees would demonstrate significantly higher levels of functioning than a control group of graduate students over the same time period. In addition, with regard to indexes 2, 3, and 4 on which the rehabilitation faculty members were assessed, it was hypothesized that the rehabilitation trainees would move in the direction of their trainers (Carkhuff, 1967).

METHOD

Subjects

A sample of 32 graduate students was randomly selected from four larger groups of students (first and fourth semester rehabilitation counseling students and first and fourth semester philosophy students) to make four groups of eight students each. Seven faculty members of the rehabilitation counseling department, four of whom had doctorates, comprised a fifth group.

The rehabilitation counseling program studied was large and well established, specifically designed to train counselors to help individuals with "physical, emotional, or social disabilities. . . ." The program conceptualized this help as given primarily through the development of a "a close counseling relationship with the handicapped client." The two-year master's level students are required to complete a research-oriented project.

Procedure

All 39 subjects were cast in the helping role twice, once with a physically disabled client and once with a physically normal college student, and were simply told to "be as helpful as possible." Five individuals served as clients: a physically disabled young adult male and four male college students. The physically disabled client saw all 32 students and dealt with real-life vocational problems; each of the four normal college student-clients was seen by eight counselors (two students from each of the four groups) and discussed real-life personal problems. The physically disabled client was seen by seven faculty members, but because of scheduling difficulties the normal clients were not evenly distributed among the faculty members. One normal client saw three faculty members, two saw two faculty members, and one saw none.

Every interview was taped and three excerpts from each interview were rated to obtain the counselor's communication level and the client's depth of self-exploration, using the same 5-point rating scales (with 5 the best, 1 the worst, and 3 minimally facilitative) employed in other training studies (Carkhuff, Kratochvil, & Friel, 1968). Three pairs of raters who had demonstrated moderate to high level communication (2.5 and higher overall) and high discrimination in previous studies were employed. The Pearson rate-rerate reliabilities for each rater were high, ranging from .77 to .99, with a mean of .92. Pearson inter-rater reliabilities between the two raters in each pair were also high, ranging from .69 to .96, with a mean of .87.

Following the interviews, each subject listened to a discrimination tape consisting of 16 client stimulus ex-

---

The facilitator is a person who is living effectively himself and who discloses himself in a genuine and constructive fashion in response to others. He communicates an accurate empathic understanding and a respect for all the feelings of other persons and guides discussions with those persons into specific feelings and experiences. He communicates confidence in what he is doing and is spontaneous and intense. In addition, while he is open and flexible in his relationships with others, in his commitment to the welfare of the other person he is quite capable of active, assertive, and even confronting behavior when it is appropriate.

You will hear a number of excerpts taken from therapy sessions. Rate each excerpt using the continuum below.

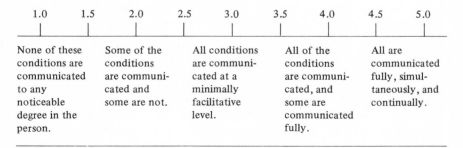

Figure 1. Gross ratings of facilitative interpersonal functioning.

pressions (Carkhuff, 1969a) followed by four alternative counselor responses role-played to illustrate different levels of functioning. The subjects were given a gross ratings form (see Figure 1) and asked to rate the counselor responses. A discrimination score was obtained by determining the absolute deviation of the subjects' ratings from the consensus ratings of experts (Carkhuff, 1969a; 1969b). The faculty did not respond to the ATDP. All students filled out the ATDP prior to any interviews.

RESULTS

Table 1 presents the overall means and standard deviations for each measure. Analyses of variance were computed for the overall effects on each measure, while simple t-tests were used to test each specific hypothesis.

Attitude Toward Disabled Persons

The overall analysis of variance indicated that rehabilitation students generally had more favorable attitudes than philosophy students ($F=9.61, p<.01$). While first semester rehabilitation students were not found to have significantly more positive attitudes than first semester philosophy students, fourth semester rehabilitation students had more favorable attitudes than first semester rehabilitation students ($t = 2.20, p<.05$) and fourth semester philosophy students ($t = 2.62, p < .05$).

Communication Level

Identical to the pattern of results obtained on the ATDP, there were no significant differences between first semester rehabilitation students and

first semester philosophy students. But fourth semester rehabilitation students functioned at significantly higher levels of communication than both first semester rehabilitation students ($t = 4.78, p < .001$) and fourth semester philosophy students ($t = 4.81, p < .001$). Except for first semester philosophy students who communicated at significantly higher levels with a physically normal college student than with a physically disabled student ($t = 4.33, p < .001$), all groups of students functioned at essentially the same level of communication with both types of clients. The rehabilitation faculty functioned at a level between the first and fourth semester rehabilitation students, not significantly different from either.

Client Self-Exploration

First semester rehabilitation students did not involve their clients in a significantly greater depth of self-exploration than first semester philosophy students, nor did fourth semester rehabilitation students involve their clients in a greater depth of self-exploration than first semester rehabilitation students. On the other hand, fourth semester rehabilitation students' clients did obtain a greater depth of self-exploration than the clients of fourth semester philosophy students ($t = 2.54, p < .05$). The physically disabled client's self-exploration was significantly lower than that of the physically normal clients ($F = 12.36, p < .01$). Although all groups tended to involve the physically normal clients in a greater depth of self-exploration, only the first semester philosophy students involved their physically normal clients in a signifi-

Table 1. Means and Standard Deviations on the Indexes of Attitudes, Communication, Client Self-Exploration, and Discrimination

Subjects	Attitude score*		Overall Communication**				Overall Client Self-Exploration**				Discrimination (Deviation Score)***	
			Normal		Disabled		Normal		Disabled			
	M	SD	M	SD	M	SD	M	SD	M	SD	M	SD
Philosophy												
1st Semester (N = 8)	101.0	20.9	1.8	.5	1.4	.4	2.0	.4	1.8	.6	82.1	10.1
4th Semester (N = 8)	111.3	22.8	1.2	.1	1.4	.3	2.0	.2	1.6	.4	85.8	16.1
Rehabilitation												
1st Semester (N = 8)	118.2	18.1	1.4	.3	1.3	.2	2.0	.4	1.9	.5	77.1	20.2
4th Semester (N = 8)	137.8	17.6	1.8	.3	1.9	.2	2.4	.4	2.0	.2	51.4	10.7
Faculty (N = 7)			1.6	.6	1.6	.5	2.0	.5	2.0	.2	34.5	3.4

* The higher the score the more favorable the attitude.
** Overall average level of conditions.
*** The higher the deviation score the poorer the discrimination.

cantly greater depth of self-exploration than their physically disabled client ($t = 2.91, p < .05$). Similar to the results on communication, there were no significant differences in the levels of client self-exploration elicited by faculty and first and fourth semester rehabilitation students.

Discrimination Level

Once again, while first semester rehabilitation students were not significantly better discriminators than first semester philosophy students, fourth semester rehabilitation students discriminated better than both first semester rehabilitation students ($t = 3.17, p < .01$) and fourth semester philosophy students ($t = 5.06, p < .001$). Significant differences between faculty and first and fourth semester rehabilitation students ($F = 19.74, p < .001$) is accounted for largely by the faculty's ability to discriminate better than both the fourth semester rehabilitation students ($t = 4.02, p < .01$) and first semester rehabilitation students ($t = 5.45, p < .001$), in conjunction with the above-mentioned differences between first and fourth semester rehabilitation students.

Correlational Analyses

Of eight correlations computed, six reached significance in a positive direction. The ATDP correlated significantly with client self-exploration (r $= .37, p < .05$) and discrimination (r $= .51, p < .01$) but not with communication (r $= .31$, NS). Communication did correlate significantly with client self-exploration (r $= .52, p < .01$) and discrimination (r $= .32, p < .05$), but

self-exploration was not significantly correlated with discrimination (r $= .27$, NS). A positive correlation was obtained between the subjects' level of communication with the two types of clients (r $= .62, p < .01$), as well as the depth of self-exploration of the subjects' two different clients (r $= .53, p < .01$).

DISCUSSION

On each of the four measures (attitudes, communication, client self-exploration, and discrimination), the first semester rehabilitation students performed at levels commensurate with and not significantly different from first semester philosophy students. Current selection practices based primarily on past academic performance (American Psychological Association, 1963; Patterson, 1962) apparently yield, when compared to other beginning graduate students in the helping professions (Carkhuff, Piaget & Pierce, 1968; Carkhuff, Kratochvil, & Friel, 1968) and base-rate data on the general population (Carkhuff & Berenson, 1967), essentially unselected students on indexes relevant to rehabilitation counseling. In addition, no evidence relates grades to indexes of functioning in the helping role (Allen, 1967; Bergin & Solomon, 1963; Carkhuff, Piaget, & Pierce, 1968).

On all but one of the four measures of functioning (client self-exploration), the fourth semester rehabilitation trainees functioned significantly higher than the first semester trainees. In comparison with data obtained on trainees in other helping profession programs, the graduates of this rehabilitation counselor training program function at a similar level of communication. That is, while this program initially received trainees who functioned at a poorer level, they improved over training to the level where trainees in other programs deteriorated (Bergin & Solomon, 1963; Carkhuff, Kratochvil, & Friel, 1968). Thus, at the conclusion of the training, the trainees in psychology and rehabilitation counseling function at approximately the same level (approximately level 2 overall).

On every one of the four measures, the fourth semester rehabilitation trainees functioned better than fourth semester philosophy trainees. In conjunction with other results, the implication is that specific training in rehabilitation counseling has effects independent of graduate training in general. These positive results, however, do not warrant the conclusion that rehabilitation training produces effective counselors. On the two measures (communication and client self-exploration) empirically related to indexes of client gain, the fourth semester rehabilitation trainees and their clients were functioning at less than minimally facilitative levels.

The corollary hypotheses predicting that students would converge on the level of functioning of their teachers yielded only one measure where the faculty was functioning at significantly higher levels than first semester trainees. On the discrimination index, the convergence of the students on their teacher's level of functioning was quite evident; yet even with the improvement over training, the fourth semester trainees did not attain the high level of discrimination of the faculty.

On communication, however, the results were more complex. The faculty's level of functioning fell between, and was not significantly different from, first and fourth semester trainees. The gain in the rehabilitation trainees' level of communication may be jointly a function of the faculty's relatively higher communication, combined with significantly higher discrimination. Rehabilitation trainers, it appears, are not chosen because of their excellence in communication level; rather they likely become trainers because of their excellence in discrimination, a skill that is reinforced in training, thus further increasing the discrepancy between communication and discrimination.

SUMMARY

Rehabilitation counseling, as a relatively new specialty within the rather new profession of counseling, is perhaps more flexible, innovative, and open to self-examination than more established helping professions. Rehabilitation educators have recently suggested that their selection procedures be revised so that, in addition to past academic performance, candidates selected should possess ". . . the potential for developing an effective counseling relationship" (American Rehabilitation Counseling Association, 1967, p. 164). At least one authority (Patterson, 1967b) has tentatively suggested that the selection of counseling students should be based on ratings of students' level of facilitative conditions. However, selection of students on their ability to communicate has far-reaching implications for their trainers. If the trainees are to function effectively in the helping role, the trainers themselves must be selected on the basis of their ability to communicate.

REFERENCES

Allen, T. W. Effectiveness of counselor trainees as a function of psychological openness. Journal of Counseling Psychology, 1967, 14:35–40.

American Psychological Association, Division of Counseling. The role of psychology in the preparation of rehabilitation counselors. Report of the Division 17 Ad Hoc Committee, 1963.

American Rehabilitation Counseling Association. The professional preparation of rehabilitation counselors. Draft of a statement of policy. Rehabilitation Counseling Bulletin, 1967, 10:163–167.

Anthony, W. A. The effect of contact on an individual's attitude toward disabled persons. Rehabilitation Counseling Bulletin, 1969, 12:168–171.

Bergin, A., & Solomon, S. Personality and performance correlates of empathic understanding in psychotherapy. American Psychologist, 1963, 18:393.

Bronson, W. H., Butler, A. J., Thoreson, R. W., & Wright, G. N. A factor analytic study of the rehabilitation counselor role: dimensions of professional concern. Rehabilitation Counseling Bulletin, 1967, 11:87–97.

Carkhuff, R. R. Toward a comprehensive model of facilitative interpersonal processes. Journal of Counseling Psychology, 1967, 14:67–72.

Carkhuff, R. R. Helping and human relationships: a primer for lay and professional helpers. New York: Holt, Rinehart & Winston, 1969. (a)

Carkhuff, R. R. Helper communication as a function of helpee affect and content. Journal of Counseling Psychology, 1969, 16:126–131. (b)

Carkhuff, R. R., & Berenson, B. G. Beyond counseling and therapy. New York: Holt, Rinehart & Winston, 1967.

Carkhuff, R. R., Kratochvil, D., & Friel, T. The effects of professional training: communication and discrimination of facilitative conditions. Journal of Counseling Psychology, 1968, 15:68–74.

Carkhuff, R. R., Piaget, G., & Pierce, R. The development of skills in interpersonal functioning. Counselor Education and Supervision, 1968, 7:102–106.

Gellman, W. New perspectives in rehabilitation. American Psychological Association Bulletin, Division 22, 1966, 13:40–47.

Goldin, G. J. Some rehabilitation counselor attitudes toward their professional role. Rehabilitation Literature, 1966, 27:360–364.

Hall, J. H., & Warren, S. L. (Eds.) Rehabilitation counselor preparation. Washington, D.C.,: National Rehabilitation Association and Vocational Guidance Association, 1956.

Jaques, M. E. Critical counseling behavior in rehabilitation settings. Iowa City: College of Education, State University of Iowa, 1959.

Krause, E. Structured strain in a marginal profession: rehabilitation counseling. Journal of Health and Human Behavior, 1965, 6:55–62.

Muthard, J. E., & Miller, L. A. Criteria for rehabilitation counselor performance in state vocational rehabilitation agencies. Journal of Counseling Psychology, 1964, 11:123–128.

Olshansky, S., & Hart, W. R. Psychologists in vocational rehabilitation or vocational rehabilitation counselors? Journal of Rehabilitation, 1967, 33 (2):28–29.

Patterson, C. H. Selection of rehabilitation counseling students. Personnel and Guidance Journal, 1962, 41:318–324.

Patterson, C. H. Effects of counselor education on personality. Journal of Counseling Psychology, 1967, 14:444–448. (a)

Patterson, C. H. The selection of counselors. Paper presented at Conference on Research Problems in Counseling, Washington University, St. Louis, Missouri, 1967. (b)

Patterson, C. H. Rehabilitation counseling: a profession or a trade? Personnel and Guidance Journal, 1968, 46:567–571.

Truax, C. B., & Carkhuff, R. R. The experimental manipulation of therapeutic conditions. Journal of Consulting Psychology, 1965, 29:119–124.

Truax, C. B., & Carkhuff, R. R. Toward effective counseling and psychotherapy. Chicago: Aldine, 1967.

Warren, S. L. The rehabilitation counselor today: what, where, and why? Journal of Rehabilitation, 1959, 25 (5):7–9.

Yuker, H. E., Block, J. R., & Campbell, W. J. A scale to measure attitudes toward disabled persons: Human Resources study no. 5. Albertson, N.Y.: Human Resources Center, 1960.

Yuker, H. E., Block, J. R., & Young, J. H. The measurement of attitudes toward disabled persons: Human Resources study no. 7. Albertson, N.Y.: Human Resources Center, 1966.

30 The Rehabilitation Team

A Catalyst to Risky Rehabilitation Decisions?

Marlene S. Winter

The literature on rehabilitation reflects the concept of the team effort as a vital, pervasive element in the success or failure of a rehabilitation plan. During the early 1950s, frequent references were made to the importance of the rehabilitation team and the dynamic aspects of interrelationships among its members (Lofquist 1957). In view of the many positive attributes of the so-called "team approach," there appears to be one issue that has not been fully explored: Might rehabilitation decisions made by a team, rather than by one individual, be more risk oriented? Could team decisions ultimately lead to the acceptance of more clients for rehabilitation services, particularly to the acceptance of those individuals whose disabilities have been viewed for years as too severe? In order to explore these questions, we must first review the general studies that have been done on risk taking and investigate the role of groups in risky decision making. The results of these studies will then be applied in a speculative manner to current modes of decision making in a rehabilitation setting.

A review of psychological research identifies risk taking as a rela-tively recent subject of investigation in the area of psychology. Although existence of such a construct has probably been alluded to for years, risk taking per se has been recognized as a topic for formal investigation only within the past ten to fifteen years, receiving its greatest emphasis as an outgrowth of the major empirical investigations on decision making (Dishart 1964; Edwards 1955; Edwards, Lindman & Phillips 1965; Pruitt 1962).

RISK TAKING

Risk taking, in the popular sense of the term, usually refers to some type of gambling activity, such as race track betting, card games, and lotteries, where the elements of uncertainty and potential monetary gain or loss are usually involved. However, many ordinary life situations also exemplify risk-taking activities, and it is in such activities of daily living—economic decisions, vocational choice, physical dangers attendant to driving an automobile or even crossing a street—that elements of risk are perhaps most prevalent, though consciously unacknowledged. In a review of major research on risk

Reprinted by permission from the June 1976 *Rehabilitation Counseling Bulletin*, pp. 580–586.

taking, Kogan and Wallach (1967, p. 114) have aptly described the insensitivity of most individuals to elements of risk in the daily life experience: "Despite the alleged sensitivity of the layman to matters of risk, he probably will ignore a wide variety of common life situations with inherent risk-taking elements, possibly for the reason that it is quite unsettling to admit that particular actions are taken with less than total certainty regarding eventual outcomes."

From the psychologist's point of view, risk taking refers to behavior in situations where there is a desired goal and a lack of certainty that it can be attained. Risk-taking situations may require a choice between more or less desirable goals, with the former having a lower probability of attainment than the latter. A further possible characteristic of risk-taking situations involves the threat of negative consequences for failure, where individuals may find themselves in a worse situation after the decision has been made.

GROUP FUNCTIONING
AND RISK TAKING

Wallach, Kogan, and Bem (1962, 1964) have carried out studies of group functioning and risk taking over the past fifteen years. Prior to their work, it was believed that decisions made by a group would be equivalent to the average of individual decisions. Thus, if ten people made individual or independent decisions about a risky situation, the group decision would be viewed simply as the average or mean of the individual decisions. Another view upheld the notion that group discussion leads to increased conservatism in relation to the average of the prior individual decisions. A third and perhaps least accepted view pointed to increased risk taking in relation to the average of the prior decisisons of the group members working separately.

Contrary to the then prevailing views, Wallach, Kogan, and Bem (1962), utilizing the Choice Dilemmas Scale, found what they termed the "risky shift" phenomenon in group decision making. They also concluded that persons with stronger individual risk-taking proclivities tended to become more influential in the group than persons who were more conservative and that the shift toward the risky decision is generally maintained by individual group members. Additional research suggested, as one explanation for the risky shift in group decision making, that group members draw support from each other and begin to feel that responsibility rests with the group, thereby warranting greater risk taking.

In a group situation, discussion has been found to be a critical element in the group-induced risky shift. Kogan and Wallach (1967) have indicated that direct verbal confrontation offers the possibility of affective interdependencies, which lead individuals to feel linked to some extent in a common fate.

METHOD

In an investigation of the risky-shift phenomenon as it might appear in rehabilitation decision making, I administered the Rehabilitation Counseling Judgment Scale (RCJS) (Moran,

Table 1. Rehabilitation Decisions (after Group Discussion to Consensus) on the Rehabilitation Counseling Judgment Scale

Item	1968	1969	1970	1971	1972	1973	1974	1975		O^c	E^d	D^e	$\dfrac{D^2}{E}$	Chi-square
Group Decisions														
I[a]	3	3	6	6	4	2	6	1	=	31	21	10	4.76	9.52*
II[b]	1	1	0	1	2	2	1	3	=	11	21	−10	4.76	
Total Groups	4	4	6	7	6	4	7	4	=	42				

[a] Group decisions indicating more risk than the average of individual decisions.
[b] Group decisions indicating more conservatism than the average of individual decisions.
[c] Observed cumulative results for 42 groups.
[d] Expected frequencies (if chance governed the occurrence of risky vs. conservative outcomes).
[e] Observed minus expected frequencies.
* Results are significant: 1 df, $p < .005$.

211

Winter & Newman 1972) to under-graduate senior psychology majors enrolled in a rehabilitation seminar. The RCJS is a semiprojective scale with descriptions of twelve rehabilitation referral situations. Included in each item is a description of a disabled person, a rehabilitation plan requiring services from a multiple-service rehabilitation agency, and an alternative to the requested plan.

Respondents to the scale are asked to indicate their opinions regarding the probability of success of the requested rehabilitation plan by estimating the number of chances out of 100 that services rendered will eventuate in the rehabilitation objective. This subjective response is made on an 11-point scale in which probabilities range from 0 to 100. When probabilities close to 0 are chosen, the respondents indicate that they perceive the requested plan as unlikely to achieve the desired rehabilitation objective. Probabilities close to 100 reflect the opinion that the requested services will result in successful rehabilitation. Next, respondents are instructed to indicate the degree to which they would agree with a decision to accept the client for the requested case services. This response is made on a 5-point scale that ranges from "strongly agree" to "strongly disagree." The risk-taking measure is derived from the sum of differences between probability estimates and level of acceptance for each of the twelve items on the RCJS.

Over a period of 8 years the RCJS was administered to a total of 183 senior rehabilitation students. The number of students participating in the rehabilitation seminar varied from year to year (see Table 1). Within a particular academic year, students in the course were instructed to complete the RCJS independently, following which answer sheets were collected and shuffled. Students were then assigned to groups based on a random selection of names that appeared on the shuffled answer sheets. Except for the small size of groups from the class of 1968, the size of most groups usually varied from four to six members, depending on the number of students enrolled in the seminar during any one particular academic year. The scores of individual members were computed and then averaged for each group. The mean of individual scores was then compared with the group score. To obtain this group score, students assigned to the groups were instructed to discuss thoroughly the rehabilitation situations presented in the RCJS and then to arrive at a group consensus regarding (a) estimates of success probabilities for the rehabilitation applicants whose cases are discussed in the scale and (b) the group decision regarding acceptance of that client for rehabilitation services. The group score was then compared with the mean of individual scores.

RESULTS

From 1968 to 1975, a total of 42 groups were tested. As shown in Table 1, in 31 of 42 groups the risky shift was evident (i.e., the group decision was more risky than the average of the prior decisions of individual group members who responded separately). In keeping with the pioneering investigations of Kogan and Wallach (1967) relative to the effects of group interaction on decision making, any of the following three outcomes could have been observed: (a) no effect (i.e., the group decision would correspond directly to the mean of individual decisions), (b) greater conservatism, or (c) risky decision making.

An analysis of the data relative to the three previous possibilities indicated that group interaction did have some effect on participants and on the types of decisions made when they engaged in group discussion (chi square = 35.28; $df = 2; p < .001$). Had chance been the significant factor in the observed outcomes of group decisions, equal numbers of groups would have made conservative and risky group decisions that were no different from the means of individual decisions. However, this latter occurrence was never observed. In addition, an analysis of data relative to risky versus conservative decisions would have yielded equal numbers of groups that were conservative as well as risk oriented. Again, results gave credibility to the existence of the risky shift phenomenon (chi square = 9.52; $df = 1; p < .005$). Although the data are not conclusive, they do strongly suggest that group interaction may be a vehicle for decisions that are more risk oriented.

Another element of investigated group interaction involved the influence exerted by individuals with stronger individual risk-taking proclivities. To test this, group members were asked at the end of group discussions to indicate whom they considered to be the most persuasive or influential member of their group. In approximately 64

percent of the cases, the risk-oriented individuals were designated as the most influential by their peers. Further attention was then given to those groups in which the risky shift did not appear. It was found that here participants who were least risk oriented in their individual responses were, in fact, designated as most influential by peers. This latter finding simply points to the importance of personality variables and the dynamic interrelationship that may take place in group situations.

WORKSHOP ON GROUP INTERACTION

In the spring of 1974, I presented several inservice workshops for counselors at the Vocational Rehabilitation Center of Allegheny County. One of these was devoted to a discussion of the effects of group interaction on counselor decision making. At the beginning of the session, the RCJS was individually administered to thirteen counselors. Answer sheets were numbered from 1 to 13, as ultimately those counselors with an odd number would be assigned to one discussion group, while counselors with even-numbered answer sheets would be assigned to another. On independent completion of the scale, counselors were assigned to a group in keeping with the numbers on their answer sheets. Groups were instructed to spend five minutes discussing each of the twelve clients whose cases were presented in the RCJS; they were then to arrive at a group decision relative to probability estimates of the client's potential for success with a particular rehabilitation plan, and they were to make a decision regarding the degree of acceptance or rejection of the client for the rehabilitation plan as outlined.

After more than one hour of discussion, all counselors met to report group results. Although it was not my express purpose to test for the existence of the risky shift phenomenon, interestingly, in both groups, decisions made by the group were more risk oriented than the mean of individual decisions. This exercise did lend support to the findings reported above, in which senior psychology majors enrolled in a rehabilitation seminar were tested. Even more significant is the fact that the people participating in the workshop were practicing counselors, a majority of whom held master's degrees in rehabilitation counseling.

CONCLUSIONS

In applying the above findings speculatively to the functioning of the rehabilitation team in rehabilitation decision making, several points stand out. Although the above data are limited, they do suggest that a group decision may be more risk oriented. In cases where ambivalence exists about acceptance or rejection of an applicant by state offices of vocational rehabilitation, more clients, particularly more difficult clients, might be accepted for services if decisions were made by teams rather than by individuals. That great numbers of potential clients have been denied services has been borne out by Dishart (1964). In addition, various members of a team may have different conceptions of eligibility, which may, as a result of group discussion, lead to more liberal decisions about providing services, particularly to those clients who are initially considered to be poor rehabilitation prospects.

Some of the trends in the rehabilitation field involve efforts aimed at the rehabilitation of individuals whose physical, emotional, or mental disabilities had previously been considered too serious. The severe nature of a disability had at times precluded any efforts to provide services that would ultimately enable the individual to live independently or semiindependently in the community rather than in an institution. If more individuals working in a team were involved in making decisions about the disposition of such clients, more clients who were previously rejected for rehabilitation services would be accepted, thus enabling them to sever the ties of dependency they now have to the institution. Individuals who in the past were said to be too severely disabled may now be viewed in a different, more optimistic light.

Group decisions of a risky nature, risky in terms of increased tendencies to elect rehabilitation plans that at first might appear minimally feasible, may even serve to enhance the efforts of these decision makers as they work with their clients. For example, when the team makes a decision to accept the client for services, responsibility for carrying out the rehabilitation plan rests more firmly with every single member of that team. Since each team member has contributed to the decision to work with the client, individual as well as group efforts on the part of team members should be increased. When decisions are made by teams, the group members may feel linked together in a common interest, namely the ultimate fate of their clients. In addition, group discussion and decision making may enable individual members of the group to draw support and security from one another as they provide services for the severely disabled clients, whose general physical and psycho-social conditions present a challenge to rehabilitation workers.

REFERENCES

Dishart, M. (Project Director). A national study of 84,699 applicants for services from state vocational rehabilitation agencies in the United States. Washington, D.C.: Department of Health, Education, and Welfare, Office of Vocational Rehabilitation, 1964.

Edwards, W. The prediction of decisions among bets. Journal of Experimental Psychology, 1955, 51:210–214.

Edwards, W.; Lindman, H.; & Phillips, L. D. Emerging technologies for making decisions. In T. M. Newcomb (Ed.), New directions in psychology II. New York: Holt, Rinehart & Winston, 1965, Pp. 259–325.

Kogan, N., & Wallach, M. A. Risk-taking as a function of the situation, the person, and the group. In T. M. Newcomb (Ed.), New directions in psychology III. New York: Holt, Rinehart & Winston, 1967. Pp. 113–278.

Lofquist, L. H. Vocational counseling with the physically disabled. New York: Appleton-Century-Crofts, 1957.

Moran, M. F.; Winter, M. S.; & Newman, J. A scale for measuring the risk-taking variable in rehabilitation counselor decision-making. Rehabilitation Counseling Bulletin, 1972, 15:211–219.

Pruitt, D. G. Patterns and level of risk in gambling decisions. Psychological Review, 1962, 69:187–201.

Wallach, M. A.; Kogan, N.; & Bem, D. J. Group influence on individual risk-taking. Journal of Abnormal and Social Psychology, 1962, 65:75–86.

Wallach, M. A.; Kogan, N.; & Bem, D. J. Diffusion of responsibility and level of risk-taking in groups. Journal of Abnormal and Social Psychology, 1964, 68:263–274.

31 Problems in Research Utilization

A Review

Stephen T. Murphy

The field of rehabilitation has demonstrated in its writings and by its activities a strong commitment to research and the practical utilization of research findings. Dumas, Butler, and Wright (1968) contend that professional development is synonomous with counselor proficiency, since rehabilitation counselors cannot provide effective services to their clients without adequate and continuing professional development. Further, the authors note that counselor proficiency is based in part on the availability of research relevant to professional responsibilities and on the communication and implementation of this knowledge. Associates of the Human Interaction Research Institute (1965) point out that progress in the field of rehabilitation is a function not only of the development of new knowledge and procedures, but also of the "prompt, effective, and imaginative application of such innovations to everyday life." Rogers (1971) states the belief that "until innovations are put into practice, they represent an unrealized public investment. . . . Until the practice of vocational rehabilitation is improved by such utilization, the research process is not complete" (p. 249).

The activities of national rehabilitation leaders have also reflected this strong commitment to research and the application of research results to counselor practice. In 1954 the Vocational Rehabilitation Amendments (83rd Congress, 1954) provided for a national program of research in which federal funds were made available for projects holding promise of making substantial contributions "to the solution of vocational rehabilitation programs common to all or several states" (PL 565, Sect. 4, p. 4). In 1965 the VRA noted that the goals of the Research and Development (R & D) Grant Program were "to discover new principles and concepts basic to the understanding of the rehabilitation process and to use such knowledge for the invention and demonstration of improved devices or procedures in vocational rehabilitation" (p. 1). Rogers (1971, p. 250) has enumerated a number of other professional activities, conferences, and task forces that have been initiated to heighten the efficiency of research utilization efforts.

Counselor educators, administrators, and researchers have discovered that counselors are generally unreceptive to research findings and

Reprinted by permission from the December 1975 *Rehabilitation Counseling Bulletin*, pp. 365–376.

frequently consider research to be generally irrelevant and alien to their professional goals (Crocker & Muthard 1972; Dumas 1971; Dumas & Muthard 1970a; Dumas, Butler & Wright 1968; Glaser 1965; Glaser & Marks 1966; Newman 1968; Trotter, Wright, & Butler 1968; and Wright, Smits, Butler, & Thoreson 1968). Apparently this commitment to research referred to previously is not shared by the great numbers of practicing counselors who make up the majority of professionals in the field.

The purpose of this review article is to examine the reasons that have been given for the low rate of research utilization among practicing counselors and to explore some of the proposed solutions to this problem. Although this topic has received much attention in literature in the field, a large proportion of the writing is fragmented, and no attempt has been made to bring it together in any cohesive way.

PERSPECTIVE ON METHODS OF DISSEMINATING RESEARCH

Although it has been claimed that heightened methods of dissemination will not guarantee increased use of research information (Crocker & Muthard 1972), many writers advocate the use of more imaginative, concise, and personal techniques of transmitting research results in order to increase practitioners' interest in research and heighten its use. Rusalem and O'Connor (1965) feel that the manner in which research information is transmitted is a fundamental obstacle to its wider use. The authors predict that research production will outstrip the field communication resources, and they call for the establishment of a rehabilitation journal and monograph series dealing primarily with research findings in order to facilitate the flow of information.

Overs and Trotter (1968) concur with Usdane (1967), who feels that the large and diverse audience to which the field of rehabilitation addresses itself requires the use of a national information service, "using automated data equipment to collect, store, analyze, retrieve, and disseminate information." Usdane contends that the utilization of research results is closely tied to the competent dissemination of such information in a form that increasingly burdened practitioners may take advantage of. Dumas (1969) feels that the field "needs, wants and will eventually have" its own information system but warns that such an endeavor requires that expert utilization techniques be available.

Glaser (1965) and Salomone (1970) advocate the use of well-planned research utilization conferences in which specific innovations are discussed and possibly observed by researchers and potential consumers. Salomone proposes two primary goals for such a conference: first, to disseminate research results to individuals "who are able, willing and likely to use the research" and "secondly . . . to tap the creative capacities of individuals who may aid the research project director in discovering and understanding the implications of his project." Both Usdane (1967) and Salomone (1970) believe that such a conference will facilitate the use of the research being demonstrated.

One of the underlying assumptions of such an approach has been the contention that journals, in their present form, are inadequate, undynamic, and too limited to be an efficient transmitter of information or an effective instrument of research utilization (Trotter, Wright, & Butler 1968; Glaser & Marks 1966; Overs & Trotter 1968; Rusalem & O'Connor 1965; Usdane 1966). However, as Dumas and Muthard (1970) point out, "journals are likely to be a professional's most accessible source of research results."

Crocker and Muthard (1972) have suggested several factors that may account for the difficulty that rehabilitation personnel have in staying abreast of current developments in the field: "the wide range of content encompassed; the high rate of production from funded research and demonstration activities; and the lack of special systems for information transfer and utilization of research activities." In an attempt to determine the impact and the usefulness of the bibliography and subject index of "Rehabilitation Research and Demonstration Projects 1955–70," prepared by Dumas and Muthard (1970b) the authors of the publication designed a follow-up study to determine how frequently the index was used, by whom, and for what purposes. They conclude that it has been used frequently by many professionals for a wide variety of purposes, a fact that demonstrates its real value for rehabilitation personnel.

Rogers (1967, 1971) has been one of the most prolific writers in the area of research, dissemination, and utilization. In 1967 he presented a conceptualization of research dissemination in the field of rehabilitation. He based it on a body of communication research called "diffusion of innovations," which is concerned with the "communication of an innovation from some source to members of a social system over time." The crucial elements in this dissemination system consist of a source to members of a social system cation, and receivers.

Rogers recommends that the following steps be taken to improve methods of communicating research:
1. Establish better communication links between the source and the potential adopters.
2. Determine the relative effectiveness of the demonstration method.
3. Encourage vocational rehabilitation personnel to become better consumers of research results.
4. Establish an information retrieval system for relevant research results.
5. Bring vocational rehabilitation researchers and administrators into the world of the counselor upon occasion.

LACK OF COMMUNICATION

A number of authors have contended that there is a lack of communication between researchers and practitioners, frequently reflected in the publication of literature that is considered irrelevant by practitioners. This situation was noted early by Graham (1961), who calls for these two groups to improve their patterns of communicating. Overs and Trotter (1968) relate their belief that the low rate of research may be due to the fact that "practicing professionals see research as not offering solutions to the problems they face." The authors note that many professionals are distrustful of research findings and tend to place greater emphasis upon knowledge derived from their clinical experience. They also state that in the real world of the practitioner, occasionally research has to be disregarded because it deals with trivia or conflicts with "accepted clinical wisdom." Usdane (1967) points out that one of the major problems faced by researchers is that practitioners often view them as an "alien breed" and therefore are not receptive to research ideas and innovations.

Dumas and Muthard (1970) found in polling 860 ARCA members for their reading interests that 48 percent felt that journal articles needed to be expanded and improved. Some counselors specifically advocated more meaningful articles directed toward counselor needs. The authors feel that enrichment of the journals with articles of maximum consumer interest will affect positively the rate of research utilization.

Bozarth (1971) views the problems of research dissemination and utilization jointly, noting that studies have been completed that (a) are not being given to practitioners, (b) are not being used by practitioners and administrators, and (c) are not being used fast enough. The author states that research dissemination-utilization consists of three components, the transmitter, the medium, and the receiver, and that each contributes to the problem of low research use. The transmitter or researcher frequently conducts research that will not directly or rapidly affect counselor practice.

Bozarth concludes that there is a "vast communication gap between the transmitter and the receiver, a gap fostered by both and often confounded . . . by difficulty in the use of appropriate media." He proposes the following solutions for improvement of communication in the research dissemination-utilization process:

1. The transmitter should direct his attention toward applied as well as basic research.
2. SRS should provide more opportunity and money for monographs, speed up the printing process, and provide RRRI and R & T Centers with lists of appropriate audiences in rehabilitation.
3. Research utilization specialists might help practitioners by providing on-site information and interpretations of current research material.
4. Receivers should make more of an effort to read the brief research reports.
5. Receiver and transmitter should become known to each other as people and try to understand each other's attitudes better.

In order to encourage a more cooperative atmosphere between researchers and practitioners and to combat some of the criticism directed at current research, several authors proposed conjoint research efforts. Soloff (1972) and Glaser and Marks (1966) support the full participation of agency personnel in the planning and implementation of any agency innovation, and Mase (1961) advocates the initiation of research units featuring the collaboration of local DVR staffs and university personnel. In such a venture, Kunce (1969) stresses the importance of using clear, differentiated research goals that would be initiated according to the complexity of their evaluative mission. Kunce also stresses the use of simple record-keeping systems for all programs being evaluated. Thus, program effectiveness would be documented and specific problem areas uncovered by the research would be identified.

According to Bolton (1971), the attitude that research is irrelevant to practice is not entirely unwarranted, but rather is symptomatic of the gulf that exists between practitioners and researchers. In order to overcome this gulf, the author proposes that practitioners and researchers collaborate on research endeavors with each professional assuming the role to which he or she is best suited. Obermann, Smits, and Curtiss (1965) also advocate such a model of collaboration and suggest that counselors assume specific responsibilities for (a) suggestion of research ideas, (b) participation in research activities, and (c) the utilization of research results.

In their well-known investigation Glaser (1965) and Glaser and Marks (1966) attempt to stimulate new attitudes and interactions within a rehabilitation organization through the use of an outside consultant. Their purpose is to "reduce organizational and institutional resistance to change." The results indicate that such consultative service helps selected agencies to become significantly more receptive to both internal and external communication than are matched controls.

An illustration of the difficulty between educator-researcher and practitioners has been manifested in a recent exchange between Loscocco and Goldman (1972) in which Loscocco, a practicing counselor, accuses Goldman and other educators of discouraging the publication of material that is "truly reflective of counseling activity." Goldman responds by stating that "perhaps some of the more practically oriented material, which Loscocco advocates publishing, more rightly belongs in divisional journals . . . and other less formal kinds of journals" and that the more relevant material should "cut across the specialty lines" and be "of more general interest."

LACK OF HIGH-QUALITY RESEARCH AND RESEARCH FACILITIES

The lack of high-quality research and research facilities has been cited as an obstacle to practitioner utilization of research results (Graham 1961; Mase 1961; Soloff 1972). Soloff believes that planned research utilization requires new social institutions in order to attain the level of efficiency being sought.

A number of writers have pointed out that the quality of rehabilitation research is notoriously variable. Kauppi and Brummer (1970) have characterized the state of research in rehabilitation as "dismal," noting that "if a counselor does hope to use the literature in his own professional growth, he finds little of value. Ninety-five percent of the articles published in rehabilitation literature should best be ignored; if the flaws in sampling, methodology, logic and reporting are overlooked, their conclusions will be misleading."

Trotter, Wright, and Butler (1968) apparently agree that high-quality research is needed in rehabilitation, noting further that "a means for conveying the adequacy and limitations of research is essential to research reporting." The authors believe that the findings of VRA-sponsored R & D projects are often difficult to use because the final reports follow no prescribed format and differ in quality and coverage. They suggest that perhaps this situation exists because rehabilitation project directors come from such varied backgrounds and their levels of research sophistication differ greatly.

Presumably no one would advocate using information that was derived from research containing serious technical flaws. If rehabilitation research is poorly conducted, and if practitioners are able to note such shortcomings, the reason for the lack of counselor enthusiasm toward research material should be apparent.

UNDESIRABLE RESEARCH REPORT CHARACTERISTICS

The unreadability of research material has been a source of considerable criticism among researchers and practitioners. Soloff (1972) recommends that writers pay close attention to clarity of communication when introducing new information; and he notes that careful, simple writing is important, especially since such presentations are often directed at populations who are diverse in their definitions of words and in their frames of reference. Dumas (1969) contends, however, that professional terminology is a bottleneck to the development of a meaningful information system; the author presumably feels that the solution lies more in "an improved understanding of how individuals communicate and the underlying structure of language" than in merely heightened efforts on the part of writers and researchers to achieve clarity and preciseness.

Specific criticism has been directed at particular research-report characteristics that a number of writers felt are to blame for the lack of enthusiastic counselor response. In addition to technical quality, which has been addressed in the preceding section, two research-report characteristics have received prominent mention in the literature: length and format.

Halpert (1966), Overs and Trotter (1968), and Trotter, Wright and Butler (1968) point out that insufficient time to read research material has been cited as a critical problem among practicing rehabilitation counselors. As Halpert states, "practitioners often find it easier to learn by looking, listening and talking than by reading." It is felt that briefer, more organized research articles will save the practitioner considerable time (Dumas, Butler & Wright 1968; Wright, Smits, Butler, & Thoreson 1968). Presumably the shorter time needed will increase counselors' receptivity to reading research material. Thus, Wright and Butler (1968) believe that their study, which concludes that "abstracts of R & D final reports convey content and research adequacy information as well as the final reports themselves," has profound implications for the field of rehabilitation.

The format of the report, or the manner in which it is presented, has been cited as a frequent obstacle to receptivity. Usdane (1967) contends that the utilization of research results is closely tied with their competent dissemination in a form that counselors may take advantage of. Goldin, Margolin, and Stotsky (1969) believe that one of the major variables affecting the use of rehabilitation research is the clarity and attractiveness with which results are presented. Overs and Trotter (1968) say that research findings should be translated from research terminology into English. Glaser (1965) and Glaser and Marks (1966) state that research material should be "brief, readable and attractively presented."

PRACTITIONERS' LACK OF EVALUATIVE SKILLS

Certainly a critical part of the research utilization process is the ability to understand and evaluate what is being said by the researcher and to judge whether it is supported by the available data. Many rehabilitation professionals, however, have noted that more research material is usable than is being used, and that practicing counselors may not possess the necessary technical skills to differentiate between good and bad research. However, it should be noted that in the only empirical study conducted on this topic, Trotter, Wright, and Butler (1968) demonstrate that rehabilitation practitioners are able to assess communication of research adequacy and content as well as rehabilitation counselor educators and researchers. It may be concluded, therefore, that either practitioners are competent judges of research adequacy or that neither counselors nor counselor educators are able to properly evaluate research material.

Salomone (1970) and Goldin, Margolin and Stotsky (1969) contend that for maximum effectiveness of seminars, workshops, journals, and research briefs, counselors should be provided education and training in research procedures and methods designed to teach them "to analyze and judge critically the quality of research results, and to estimate how useful these results may be to their everyday practice" (Salomone 1970). Rogers (1971) notes that counselors who encounter difficulties in their practice and seek additional information often do not know how much credibility to place in the available literature (p. 249). He also suggests that researchers and practitioners differ on a number of important dimensions, such as education and technical expertise (p. 259), which adversely affects the quality of their communication. One way he advocates alleviating what he describes as this "heterophilious" situation is by initiating a "series of inservice training institutes designed to increase counselor competence in how to understand research reports'' and in recognizing promising vocational rehabilitation innovations (pp. 260–261).

Cherns (1969) defines several types of research, noting that primarily two types, operational and action research, lend themselves to practical utilization. He further contends that in order to maximize the likelihood that this research material will be used, an individual capable of understanding such analytic material must be specifically trained for the task.

Kauppi and Brummer (1970) feel that counselor education programs should bear a major responsibility for the lack of technical skills among practitioners. The authors state that ''in most students' past work, research has been taught in ways that enhance its separateness from practice, as though it has no relevance except to researchers. . . . Further, the assumption is usually made that the best way to teach research is to teach people to do it . . . (which) is clearly invalid in training counselors who should use research, but whose doing will be limited.''

Dembo (1969) takes sharp issue with professionals who feel that the way to increase counselor receptivity to research material and its ultimate use is by changing article format rather than practitioner expertise. She relates that simplification of research information could decrease its utilization value, and she states that counselors should not be pampered or spoon-fed, but rather trained and helped to understand, appreciate, and utilize research findings in their original format.

In an attempt to test empirically the effect of article length, format, and technical quality on counselors' receptivity, Murphy (1973) composed articles of differing length (long, short), format (traditional, nontraditional), and quality (high, low). Practicing school and rehabilitation counselors were asked to rate articles of varied characteristics. The author found, contrary to much literature in the field, that none of these variables had a consistent effect upon counselor receptivity. It was also found that neither counselor age, sex, years of experience, nor credit hours of statistics or research methodology affected receptivity. The findings also suggest that although counselors are able to differentiate between some articles on the basis of technical quality, their knowledge is superficial and too limited to distinguish subtle differences in design.

LACK OF THEORETICAL FRAMEWORK

The lack of a meaningful theoretical framework within both the specific area of research utilization and the general area of rehabilitation have been singled out as major impediments to the increased use of research. Rogers (1971) suggested that research users need a body of skills and techniques based upon theory that focuses on getting research used and on processes that build on practitioners' readiness to receive new ideas and information. In their study, Glaser and Marks (1966) note their feeling that research utilization is only one dimension of the broader phenomenon of change which confronts most agencies and organizations.

Although Goldberg (1969) views rehabilitation research as a specialization "in that it presupposes a knowledge and sensitivity to the problems of adaptation to disability and handicap," Newman (1968) and McDaniel (1965) claim that the paucity of consistent theory within the general field of rehabilitation is a major obstacle to more extensive use of research material. The authors feel that an important function of good theory is to give meaning to research findings and provide a basis for evaluation of their relevance. Newman points out that, lacking the reference point of theory, "research findings tend to become perplexing if not meaningless."

CONCLUSION

This review has attempted to collate and summarize many of the problems that reportedly have hindered research utilization efforts in rehabilitation. The vast majority of the problems cited are based primarily on personal experience and/or subjective observation. As insightful as such conclusions may be, they are sorely deficient in explaining the process of research utilization, since they lack a meaningful conceptual context.

Currently, there are neither theoretical paradigms nor well-accepted definitions of the research utilization process. In order to evaluate properly the impact of the problems cited on research utilization, researchers must direct more inquiry into the process itself. The writings of Bozarth (1971),

Cherns (1969), Rogers (1971), and Salomone (1970) have made a start in expanding our understanding of research utilization. Although these efforts fall far short of theoretical formulations, they have provided the field with some testable hypotheses and general models. I feel that future research efforts should focus on examining of such hypotheses empirically and modifying and building upon these models.

In order to conduct such research, there is an obvious need to develop a specific method of defining and measuring research utilization. Although several writers have measured utilization (Glaser 1965) or related concepts (Murphy 1973), such efforts have been limited. Without additional attempts to operationalize such concepts, inquiry into this area will continue to be impoverished.

In calling for more empirical investigation, I feel that problems in research utilization are not unrelated. In view of the paucity of knowledge about research utilization, it appears self-defeating to offer solutions to each problem individually. I feel that the most far-reaching solutions will be developed only after we have gained more insight into the process of research utilization and are able to view such problems in a theoretical context.

REFERENCES

Bolton, B. Research in deafness: some implications for education and rehabilitation. Rehabilitation Research and Practical Review, 1971, 3(1):1–4.

Bozarth, J. D. Some problems in applied research. Rehabilitation Research and Practical Review, 1970, 2(1):21–26.

Bozarth, J. D. Research dissemination and utilization. Rehabilitation Research and Practical Review, 1971, 2(2):51–58.

Cherns, A. Social research and its diffusion. Human Relations, 1969, 22(3):209–218.

Crocker, L. M., & Muthard, J. E. Evaluating the usefulness of an informational tool for rehabilitation workers, Rehabilitation Research and Practical Review, 1972, 3(2):1–6.

Dembo, T. Statement at the Research Utilization Conference, October, 1968, at Springfield College, Springfield, Massachusetts. In Goldin, G. J.; Margolin, K. N.; & Stotsky, B. A., (Eds.), The utilization of rehabilitation research. Boston: New England Regional Institute, Northeastern University, Monograph No. 6, 1969.

Dumas, N. S. On the development of a rehabilitation information system—some practical considerations. Journal of Rehabilitation, 1969, 35(2):22–24.

Dumas, N. S. Optimizing the utilization of professional literature for rehabilitation personnel: three jobs and three journals. Rehabilitation Counseling Bulletin, 1971, 15(1):19–24.

Dumas, N. S.; Butler, A. J.; & Wright, G. N. Counselor perceptions of professional development. In Wright, G. N. (Ed.), Wisconsin Studies in Vocational Rehabilitation, Series I, Monograph IV. Madison, Wisconsin: Regional Rehabilitation Research Institute, 1968.

Dumas, N. S., & Muthard, J. E. The consumer in the scientific and technical information market: managing the flow of literature in a professional journal. Rehabilitation Counseling Bulletin, 1970, 14(1):5–13. (a)

Dumas, N. S., & Muthard, J. E. Rehabilitation research and demonstration projects 1955–1970. Gainesville, Fla.: Regional Rehabilitation Research Institute, University of Florida, 1970. (b)

Eighty-Third Congress. S. 2759. Amendments to the Vocational Rehabilitation Act, Public Law 565. Washington, D.C.: U.S. Government Printing Office, 1954.

Glaser, E. M. Utilization of applicable research and demonstration results. Journal of Counseling Psychology, 1965, 12(2): 201–205.

Glaser, E. M. & Marks, J. B. Putting research to use. Rehabilitation Record, 1966, 7(6):6–10.

Goldberg, R. T. Rehabilitation research as a specialization. Rehabilitation Literature, 1969, 30:66–70.

Goldin, G. J.; Margolin, K. N.; & Stotsky, B. A. The utilization of rehabilitation research. Boston: New England Regional Institute, Northeastern University, Monograph No. 6, 1969.

Graham, M. D.. Social research in rehabilitation, or one researcher's Camelot. Rehabilitation Literature, 1961, 22:130–138.

Halpert, H. P. Communications as a basic tool in promoting utilization of research findings. Community Mental Health Journal, 1966, 2(3):231–236.

Human Interaction Research Institute. Utilization of applicable research and demonstration results, progress report. Los Angeles: The institute, 1965.

Kauppi, D. W., & Brummer, E. Goals and curricular modifications to provide training in research for masters degree students in rehabilitation counseling. Unpublished manuscript, State University of New York at Buffalo, 1970.

Kunce, J. T. Social research: nusiance or necessity? Paper presented at Research Utilization Conference on Rehabilitation in Poverty Settings, In Northeastern studies in vocational rehabilitation, Boston: Northeastern University, 1969.

Loscocco, L., & Goldman, L. Feedback: an exchange of letters. Personnel and Guidance Journal, 1972, 50(10):779–783.

Mase, D. J. (ed.). The development of research in vocational rehabilitation. Proceedings of a Conference on Research in State Program Development, Final Report. Gainesville: University of Florida, College of Health Related Services, 1961.

McDaniel, J. W. Rehabilitation research in state agencies. Rehabilitation Literature, 1965, 26:66–70.

Murphy, S. T. The effect of particular research report characteristics upon coun-

226   Murphy

selor receptivity to research material. Unpublished doctoral dissertation, State University of New York at Buffalo, 1973.

Newman, J. Readings lists, rehabilitation & ragbags. Rehabilitation Counseling Bulletin, 1968, 12(4):308–311.

Obermann, C. E.; Smits, S. J.; & Curtiss, J. W. The rehabilitation counselor and research. NRCA Professional Bulletin, 1965, 5(2):1–3.

Overs, R. P., & Trotter, A. B. Disseminating and using research reports. Rehabilitation Counseling Bulletin, 1968, 12(1):14–22.

Rogers, E.M. The diffusion of vocational rehabilitation innovations. Communication, dissemination and utilization of research information. Washington, D.C.: Social and Rehabilitation Service, 1967.

Rogers, E. M. Research utilization. In Neff, W. S. (Ed.). Rehabilitation psychology. Washington, D.C.: American Psychological Association, Inc., 1971, 248–264.

Rusalem, H., & O'Connor, J. An assessment of publication outlets for rehabilitation counseling research articles. Rehabilitation Counseling Bulletin, 1965, 8(4): 125–129.

Salomone, P. R. The research implementation process: some reflections and suggestions. Rehabilitation Counseling Bulletin, 1970, 13(1):349–354.

Soloff, A. The utilization of research. Rehabilitation Literature, 1972, 33(3):66–71.

Trotter, A. B.; Wright, G. N.; & Butler, A. J. Research media. In Wright, G. N. (Ed.). Wisconsin Studies in Vocational Rehabilitation, Series I, Monograph V. Madison, Wisconsin: Regional Rehabilitation Research Institute, 1968.

Usdane, W. D. Problems and progress in the dissemination and utilization of vocational rehabilitation research findings by the practicing counselor. Paper presented at Educators—Directors Conference on Communication, Dissemination, and Utilization of Rehabilitation Research Information, Miami, Florida, December 1966.

Wright, G. N.; Smits, S. J.; Butler, G. N.; & Thoresen, R. W. A survey of counselor perceptions, In Wright, G. N. (Ed.), Wisconsin Studies in Vocational Rehabilitation, Series I, Monograph II. Madison, Wisconsin: Regional Rehabilitation Institute, 1968.

Section V

REHABILITATION COUNSELOR EDUCATION

32 Editorial Introduction

Concomitant with the emergence of rehabilitation counseling as an independent helping profession has been the rapid expansion of graduate training programs in rehabilitation counseling. At the present time there are in excess of 100 master's degree-granting programs, with approximately 40 of them having received accreditation by the Council on Rehabilitation Education (see the last article in Section I). Although there is some uniformity in all rehabilitation counselor programs, there are numerous variations on the common theme. One notable recent development is undergraduate education in rehabilitation (Steger, 1974). The purpose of the first selection in this section is to outline the official ARCA position regarding the common requirements and standards for rehabilitation counselor preparation.

In the second article, Anthony advocates a strong position on the importance of human relations skills in rehabilitation counseling. He argues that if the counselor is not functioning at a higher level on interpersonal communication dimensions such as empathy, respect, genuineness, etc., than the client is, then the client cannot benefit from the counseling relationship. After summarizing data from several studies, Anthony concludes that "rehabilitation counselors do not possess the skills needed to function as effective counselors." He then recommends an optimal educational program that integrates contact with physically disabled persons and human relations skills training into the traditional academic program. The reader may be interested in Bolton's (1973) brief reply to some of Anthony's conclusions and the subsequent response by Anthony (1974).

In the next article Anthony, Slowkowski, and Bendix describe in detail the evaluation of a psychosocial aspects of disability course that was developed following Anthony's recommendation in the previous article. The focus of this approach to course development is the setting of observable, behavioral goals toward which students' progress can be measured. The results of their evaluation suggest that the authors were successful in providing a series of experiences that did indeed change the students' behavior in several areas of functioning. Interestingly, this article also provoked a response (Diamonti and Murphy, 1977) and another rejoinder (Anthony et al., 1977).

Steger outlines and discusses in general terms the competency-based instruction (CBI) model that was illustrated in the Anthony et al. article above. The CBI approach to curriculum development is characterized by an emphasis on the specification of demonstrable knowledge and performance standards. Once the behavioral objectives have been determined, students' performance is systematically observed or measured until minimum levels of competency are demonstrated. As Steger points out, the CBI model is appealing in its apparent simplicity, but, in fact, it requires an extensive amount of time and effort to implement. If adopted in its entirety, the CBI model would entail the complete restructuring of traditional rehabilitation counseling training programs. Not unexpectedly, the CBI approach has its detractors; obviously, the criticisms of Diamonti and Murphy (1977) apply to this article as well as to that of Anthony et al.

In conjunction with supervision of rehabilitation counseling students in field placements, Slaney makes some observations that have implications for the professional preparation of rehabilitation counselors. His experience suggests that many students view psychotherapy with their clients as the desirable and prestigious form of interaction, while they regard vocational counseling, job placement, etc. as less interesting and important. Slaney distinguishes between counseling approaches that are oriented to changing the clients' personalities and those that focus on the maximum use of clients' strengths and assets. The article concludes with several suggestions for dealing with the myth of "real" counseling in rehabilitation education programs.

The last two articles describe educational programs that are specifically addressed to the needs of severely disabled clients. Walker, Clark, and Sawyer outline a short program that was designed to prepare rehabilitation practitioners to discuss sexual adjustment and functioning with clients possessing severely handicapping conditions. In the concluding article in this section, Kauppi discusses the promises and problems of continuing education programs for employed rehabilitation counselors as a vehicle for enhancing their effectiveness in serving severely disabled clients.

REFERENCES

Anthony, W. A. 1974. Human relations training and rehabilitation counseling: Further implications. Rehabil. Couns. Bull. 17:171–175.

Anthony, W. A., Dell Orto, A. E., Lasky, R. G., Power, P. W., Shrey, D. E., and Spaniol, L. J. 1977. The realities of competency-based rehabilitation counselor education. Rehabil. Couns. Bull. 21:58–62.

Bolton, B. 1973. Reply to Anthony. Rehabil. Couns. Bull. 17:4–5.

Diamonti, M. C., and Murphy, S. T. 1977. Behavioral objectives and rehabilitation counselor education: A critique. Rehabil. Couns. Bull. 21:51–57.

Steger, J. M. 1974. A multidisciplinary model for undergraduate education in rehabilitation. Rehabil. Couns. Bull. 18:12–20.

33 A Statement of Policy on the Professional Preparation of Rehabilitation Counselors

This statement, by the American Rehabilitation Counseling Association, is one of a series prepared to supplement the American Personnel and Guidance Association policy statement on the preparation and role of counselors. ARCA's statement elaborates upon the APGA statement, emphasizing special preparation required for the professional rehabilitation counselor. This revision takes into consideration the broadening scope of rehabilitation counseling and the recognition afforded professional rehabilitation counselor preparation through the newly established program accreditation process.

These standards are concerned with the preparation of counselors who are employed in such public and private vocational rehabilitation agencies as State Divisions of Bureaus of Vocational Rehabilitation, agencies for the visually handicapped, rehabilitation centers and workshops, rehabilitation units in mental health facilities, correctional institutions, drug and alcohol programs, and any other organizations whose services to handicapped people emphasize rehabilitation philosophy and principles.

Clients of such agencies are usually adolescents or adults who are handicapped either by physical, mental, social, or emotional disabilities that often have major socio-cultural and psychological ramifications and who, thereby, are usually in need of general counseling services as well as services specific to vocational placement. Although the focus is, typically, upon the optimal vocational development and placement of the client, the concern of the agency and of the rehabilitation counselor is with the individual's total development and functioning as a contributing member of society.

The functions of a counselor in such agencies vary according to the mandates under which the agency operates and the characteristics of the clientele. Although these functions may vary in nature, their ultimate objective is the same—to mobilize both client and environmental resources to meet client objectives. The role of the counselor, however, is the same from agency to agency. The role of the professional rehabilitation counselor is, primarily, to utilize one-to-one and group counseling procedures to bring about improved personal, educational, vocational,

October, 1974 Revision. Submitted by the ARCA Professional Preparation and Standards Committee: Robert L. Masson, Chairman, Donald Linkowski, Alice Randolph, and John Steger.

and social adjustment. This policy statement is directed at the preparation of people to engage in this role at a professional level.

As the APGA Policy Statement emphasizes, the counselor is a professional person and, as such, is expected to demonstrate expertness necessarily involving independent judgment in his areas of competence. He accepts and performs his work in consonance with a professional code of ethics as exemplified in the APGA Code of Ethics. His proper expectation is that his work setting and work atmosphere will enable him to function as a professional person at a professional level. The professionally educated rehabilitation counselor will expect to receive technical supervision, but this must come from those professionally qualified through training and experience. The nature of rehabilitation counseling, finally, frequently requires professional relationships with others in counseling, related disciplines, and community agencies, in order to assure that the total needs of clients are met.

A statement of Professional Preparation and Standards from a professional organization must necessarily serve the broad interests of the professional community. Such a statement should not constrain or discourage the application of research and demonstration findings and should possess inherent durability to survive the daily successes, failures, and conflicts associated with dynamic professional growth.

I.   Statement of Objectives—A statement on professional preparation and standards in rehabilitation counselor education should:

   A.   Promote concern for quality in the establishment and review of professional education programs in rehabilitation counseling that in turn will lead to better services for people with handicaps.

   B.   Encourage self-study and improvement of rehabilitation counseling programs to ensure the maintenance of competencies relevant to the professional field.

   C.   Help to meet manpower needs of agencies providing rehabilitation services by ensuring that graduates have been instructed in the skills and knowledge necessary for delivering vocational rehabilitation services to disabled and disadvantaged people.

   D.   Protect the needs and rights of students who wish to acquire the knowledge and skills requisite for obtaining adequate employment as counselors in the vocational rehabilitation field and who wish to continue their professional development as the field evolves.

   E.   Offer an articulated standard of professional education in vocational rehabilitation counseling through which mutual respect and cooperation with programs in other helping professions can be fostered.

II.   Objectives of Professional Education in the Field—The objective of graduate education is to prepare the individual for entering upon a lifelong profession, not for a specific job or position. Therefore, a rehabilitation counselor education program should:

A. Provide students with basic education in rehabilitation counseling and promote the knowledge and skills necessary to provide adequate vocational rehabilitation services to handicapped people.

B. Foster in the learner the development of habits of scholarship and professionalism, a commitment to respecting individual human values, support of high ethical standards and personal integrity, and maintenance of an objective and inquiring attitude.

C. Foster the development of practitioners, educators, and researchers through a program of academic study, clinical training, continuing education, and consultation that will lead to effective practice in the field.

D. Promote the advancement of knowledge and skill in the field of rehabilitation counseling by conducting research and demonstration activities and facilitating the incorporation of new and improved practices in the education process and, where possible, in the field through continuing education and consultation.

III. Standards for the Academic Program—An adequate curriculum of rehabilitation counselor preparation should meet the following requirements:

A. The curriculum should be relevant to the field of vocational rehabilitation and should allow a student to acquire a professional orientation and identification.

B. Stated competencies in the curriculum should take into consideration client needs related to the vocational rehabilitation process.

C. The program of study should provide a balance between broad rehabilitation principles and special topic areas so that a graduate can meet the competency requirements for membership in a recognized professional organization in the rehabilitation counseling field and professional certification by the National Commission on Rehabilitation Counseling Certification.

D. Curriculum evaluation procedures should provide for adequate feedback by students, alumni, clients, supervisors, and employers.

E. The overall curriculum should provide a solid foundation in the rehabilitation processes while providing flexibility sufficient to accomodate and encourage individual personal growth and the pursuit of special interests.

F. Courses in the rehabilitation counseling curriculum should be designed and scheduled so as to move the student from a more generic helping profession base to greater specialization in rehabilitation; from elementary knowledge and skill levels to more complex functions in keeping with sound principles of learning.

G. Paramount in this preparation is the development of an understanding of the philosophy, the theory, and the psychological, sociological, and economic principles that constitute the foundations of counseling.

Techniques and skills are operating means of applying the principles built upon these foundations.

H. The curriculum should include the following elements, which are shared with all counselors:
1. The foundations of human behavior and dynamics of behavior change;
2. Social, cultural, and economic factors influencing individuals and groups, particularly in their economic and occupational aspects;
3. Professional studies in counseling:
    a. Philosophic and assumptive bases in counseling.
    b. Counseling theory and practice.
    c. Group approaches to counseling.
    d. Psychological and vocational appraisal by means of tests and other methods of evaluation and measurement, including the requisite statistics.
    e. The psychology and sociology of vocational development, including economic and environmental factors influencing vocational choices, as well as techniques for facilitating job placement and followup.
    f. Techniques for understanding and utilizing research findings.

I. The curriculum should include the following elements, which are specific to rehabilitation counselors:
1. An understanding of the goals, functions, and services of rehabilitation agencies.
2. Knowledge of psychological aspects of disability, including personal, family, social, and vocational problems, and concomitant techniques to facilitate adequate client adjustment.
3. Knowledge of the medical aspects of rehabilitation.
4. Knowledge and understanding of the differential impact of disability on standard counseling, testing, and placement procedures.
5. Specific in-depth preparation in disability areas as required by the student's selection of a field placement setting and eventual employment goals.
6. Knowledge of coordinating and decision-making techniques in order to analyze and evaluate client problems and formulate and carry out appropriate rehabilitation plans and programs.
7. Knowledge of legislative programs critical to the provision of services to handicapped clients and the attitude and skills necessary to promote the concept of client advocacy as recognized by professional groups and promoted by federal and state legislation.

J. There should be opportunities, both formal and informal, for the student to develop in self-awareness and understanding, including opportunity for personal counseling.

K. Specific criteria for evaluating student performance in skills required for providing adequate client services should be established and articulated.

L. If competencies, rather than or in addition to courses, are established, the specific level at which competency is to be demonstrated should be clear to the student.

IV. Standards for Supervised Experience—An adequate program of rehabilitation counselor education should provide a graduated series of experiences for the student.

A. In the earlier stages of the program, opportunities for observation (audio-video tapes, films, direct) should be provided. Laboratory experience in interviewing and testing should also be an integral aspect of the training prior to the assignment of complete responsibility of a client to a trainee. In addition, pre-practicum field assignments with rehabilitation agencies may provide students with relevant information about the structure and function of agencies and the nature of the client population.

B. Rehabilitation counseling program faculty should, in cooperation with rehabilitation agencies, establish methods of ensuring adequate counseling and casework supervision as well as ensuring that student learning experiences are designed to maximize learning opportunities within the prescribed time frame.

C. Rehabilitation settings should be initially and periodically evaluated to ensure that the total program of services available to clients, the frequency and quality of supervisory contacts, and the specific in-depth student learning experiences are meeting the training objectives of the program.

D. Practicum experience in counseling should be provided. This experience should meet the following requirements:

1. It should be meaningfully integrated with the didactic training. The experience should be intensive, concentrated, and under close supervision.

2. This experience should consist of work with a number and variety of clients.

3. It is important that the student carry a number of clients for several contacts over a period of time.

4. Close and direct (at least one hour per week) supervision should be provided, including some first-hand observation of the student, either through monitoring or through taped interviews. University supervisors should be counselors, preferably trained to the doctoral level, with experience in counseling beyond that acquired in practicum.

5. Because growth in counseling requires time, the practicum should extend over a period of at least one quarter or semester and/or until

specific pre-established competencies are demonstrated by the student.

6. The practicum setting should be conducive to maintenance and progress of the counseling relationship.

E. An internship should be provided. Internship is a supervised experience in a rehabilitation work setting. It should meet the following requirements:

1. The internship may be in a single rehabilitation agency or in more than one agency—it may be on a block or on a concurrent basis—it may be paid or unpaid experience. Regardless of the nature of the experience, it should be looked upon as much more than observation or orientation. It must consist of concentrated periods of time in the agency setting so that the student can fully demonstrate the professional and work-related competencies that are established as goals for the placement experience. For the inexperienced student, a minimum of 480 clock hours in an agency is suggested as a guide to ensure sufficient time to prepare for and demonstrate appropriate competencies.

2. The agency must provide adequate facilities, equipment, and materials for the student to function at a professional level.

3. The agency must provide day-to-day supervision by a supervisor qualified by education and experience.

4. The educational institution maintains contact with the student and provides supervision aimed at assisting the student to integrate his academic training with agency programs and requirements. University supervisors should have experience related to the agency in which the student is placed.

5. Practicum instructors and internship supervisors should be assured of adequate time for individual instruction.

6. Internship settings should be selected in terms of their adequacy in providing the kind and quality of experience required by the student.

V. Standards for Faculty in Relation to Professional, Academic, and Community Service Activities

A. A rehabilitation counseling program faculty should be adequate to meet the needs of the program in terms of academic background, interest areas, and academic rank and tenure status.

B. The program administration and faculty should strive toward an optimal student-faculty ratio consistent with the goals of the program and with consideration given to full and part-time student enrollments, continuing education activities, and other academic and professional responsibilities of the program.

C.   The program faculty should demonstrate, to the extent their backgrounds, training, and work environments allow, strong leadership roles in rehabilitation, including participation in professional organizations at national, regional, and local levels, production of research and/or scholarly papers in the rehabilitation field, contribution to the review and formulation of rehabilitation legislation and administrative policies at various levels of government, and general contribution to the field of practice in the form of direct practice, consultative services, and programs of continuing education.

D.   Rehabilitation counseling program faculty should take an active role in facilitating the employment of program graduates through the preparation of appropriate letters of reference, coordinating job availability information, and conducting other employment-related activities.

E.   Program faculty should observe and model appropriate professional behavior with strict adherence to ethical standards for conducting and publishing research, providing counseling and/or testing services to clients, and with students in both teaching and advising roles.

VI. Standards for Student Recruitment and Retention

A.   An education institution should have a program of recruitment and selection that will ensure the selection of candidates:

1.   Possessing an appropriate undergraduate background;
2.   Capable of successful academic performance at the graduate level;
3.   Having the potential for developing an effective counseling relationship;
4.   Possessing characteristics indicative of professional growth; and,
5.   Expressing a strong commitment to the field of rehabilitation.

The nature of graduate preparation in rehabilitation counseling is primarily psychological and a background of undergraduate work in the behavioral sciences appears to be desirable. Students with work in psychology, sociology, anthropology, statistics, and tests and measurements or an undergraduate rehabilitation education degree are in a position to pursue a more advanced or accelerated program of rehabilitation counselor preparation at the graduate level.

B.   The selection of graduate students in rehabilitation counseling should include a process of continuous evaluation throughout the student's program to eliminate those candidates not demonstrating the requisite characteristics for becoming effective counselors. Rehabilitation counselor education programs are responsible for the continuous evaluation of their selection and retention procedures.

C.   Admissions requirements and screening procedures should be explicitly stated with sufficient flexibility to take into consideration the diverse academic interests, personal needs, and career goals of rehabilitation counseling applicants.

D. Opportunities should be provided for an equitable representation of students with handicaps and students from minority group backgrounds in a rehabilitation counseling program.

VII. Standards for Student Rights and Responsibilities

A. A rehabilitation counseling program should provide an opportunity for students to discuss their perception of the program and give specific feedback regarding the content of courses and the method of instruction.

B. The rehabilitation counseling faculty should, to the extent possible, create a total professional environment by involving students in relevant professional activities and by encouraging students to affiliate with rehabilitation organizations.

C. The resources available within the rehabilitation counseling program and the faculty should, as far as possible, facilitate the graduation of qualified students and the elimination of students whose interests and/or competency levels preclude success in the rehabilitation field.

D. A rehabilitation counseling program should provide, in conjunction with college and university administration, appropriate appeal procedures to facilitate the just review of decisions regarding grading, dismissal, and related student matters in keeping with the concept of due process.

E. Rehabilitation counseling program faculties have an obligation to the student, as well as to the client-consumer and the profession, to periodically conduct a curriculum evaluation designed to gather data regarding the effectiveness and relevance of the competency areas taught, and to make appropriate curriculum modifications based on these data.

REFERENCES

American Rehabilitation Counseling Association. 1968. The Professional Preparation of Rehabilitation Counselors. Rehabil. Couns. Bull. September, 12:29–35.
Council on Rehabilitation Education, Inc. 1974. Manual on Accreditation.

34 Human Relations Skills and Training

Implications for Rehabilitation Counseling

William A. Anthony

Recent research in the areas of counseling process and outcome has shown that the counselor's level of human relations skills accounts for a significant amount of therapeutic progress in his clients. These human relations skills have been called the facilitative and action-oriented conditions, and even more specifically labeled as empathy, respect, concreteness, genuineness, immediacy, and confrontation. The extensive research supporting the therapeutic effectiveness of these counselor communicated skills has been summarized periodically (Berenson 1973; Carkhuff 1969a, 1969b, 1971; Carkhuff & Berenson 1967; Truax & Carkhuff 1967).

Additional studies have found that not only is it possible to reliably measure a counselor's ability to communicate these conditions, but also the client's level of functioning on these skills can be determined (Carkhuff & Berenson 1967). Based on this finding, Carkhuff and Berenson (1967) have proposed and subsequently researched (Carkhuff 1969a, 1969b, 1971) a model for understanding and predicting the effectiveness or ineffectiveness of counseling.

COUNSELING MODEL

Very simply, the Carkhuff-Berenson model[1] suggests that the human relations skills of both clients and counselors can be rated on a 5-point scale (see Table 1). Using this scale developed by Carkhuff (1969a), the human relations skills of any person (counselor, client, parent, teacher, etc.) can be observed and rated by casting the person in the helper role with another individual and giving the helper the mental set to be as helpful as possible.

In general, their model of counseling dictates that persons functioning at higher levels of human relations skills can help persons functioning at lower skill levels. Thus, in order for counseling to have a positive effect, a discrepancy in functioning must exist with the counselor communicating at a higher level than his client. For example, clients functioning at level 2 can only be helped by counselors functioning above level 2. Furthermore, the counselor's level will limit the amount of growth in his client. For example, a client functioning at level 1 will not achieve a level of functioning beyond his level 2 helper.

---

[1]Readers who wish a complete description of the model should consult Carkhuff and Berenson (1967) and Carkhuff (1969b).

Reprinted by permission from the March 1973 *Rehabilitation Counseling Bulletin*, pp. 180–188.

Table 1. Gross Ratings of Human Relations Skills

Statement:

The helper is a person who is living effectively himself and who discloses himself in a genuine and constructive fashion in response to others. He communicates an accurate empathic understanding and a respect for all of the feelings of other persons and guides discussions with those persons into specific feelings and experiences. He communicates confidence in what he is doing and is spontaneous and intense. In addition, while he is open and flexible in his relationships with others, in his commitment to the welfare of the other person he is quite capable of active, assertive, and even confronting behavior when it is appropriate.

Ratings:	Level
None of these conditions is communicated to any noticeable degree in the person.	1.0
Some of the conditions are communicated and some are not.	2.0
All conditions are communicated at a minimally facilitative level.	3.0
All of the conditions are communicated, and some are communicated fully.	4.0
All are communicated fully, simultaneously, and continually.	5.0

Client populations typically function between levels 1 and 3. Thus, a counselor who functions in the low ranges (levels 1 and 2) offers little prospect for gain to his clients, while the higher level helper offers much prospect for constructive client change.

It should be mentioned that variables other than level of human relations skills also can exert a positive influence on a client. For example, effective programs (such as those developed from learning theory) have been able to bring about constructive client change. However, evidence suggests that the effectiveness of any program is enhanced if the individuals who are running the program are themselves functioning at high levels of interpersonal skills (Aspy 1969; Carkhuff 1971; Mickelson & Stevic 1971; Vitalo 1970).

RELEVANT REHABILITATION RESEARCH

The field of rehabilitation is different from some of the more established helping professions in one important way: It is much more open to evaluating its training and counseling efforts. As a result, a number of studies have assessed the skillfulness with which various groups of professionals, graduate students, and subprofessionals function in one traditional rehabilitation role—helping a physically disabled person.

These research studies have measured the human relations skills of these groups in a variety of ways, including written responses to taped excerpts of physically disabled clients' statements, taped interviews of actual counseling sessions with a physically disabled client, and taped interviews with physically disabled standard clients. The results presented in Table 2 indicate that the level of human relations skills ranges from a low of 1.3 for nursing aides and beginning rehabilitation students to a high of 2.1 for advanced rehabilitation students.

Note that a sample of physically disabled clients was found to be functioning at 1.8, a level commensurate with the advanced rehabilitation students and professionals who counsel them and higher than the level of functioning of the subprofessionals with whom they come in contact. While not a high level of functioning, the physically disabled clients' level is somewhat higher than the level of human relations skills of other client groups. For example, the level of human relations skills for counseling center clients has been reported as 1.6

Table 2. Level of Human Relations Skill with Physically Disabled Clients

Population	N	Mean	Reference
Professionals			
Rehabilitation educators	7	1.6	Anthony & Carkhuff (1970)
Rehabilitation counselors	12	1.6	Kenney & Anthony (1972)
Rehabilitation counselors	22	1.7	Equinozzi (1969)
Master's level psychologists and social workers	10	1.7	Kenney & Anthony (1972)
Students			
Advanced rehabilitation students	8	1.9	Anthony & Carkhuff (1970)
Advanced rehabilitation students	8	2.1	Rubacher & Woods (1969)
Advanced rehabilitation students	8	1.5	Rubacher & Woods (1969)
Beginning rehabilitation students	8	1.3	Anthony & Carkhuff (1970)
Beginning rehabilitation students	23	1.4	Grand & Stockin (1970)
Graduate students in a non-helping profession	16	1.4	Anthony & Carkhuff (1970)
Subprofessionals			
Subprofessionals at a rehabilitation center	12	1.7	Crisler & Porter (1969)
Nursing aides	23	1.3	Anthony & Wain (1971a)
Clients			
Physically disabled clients (DVR)	30	1.8	Morris (1970)

(Pagell, Carkhuff, Berenson 1967), for psychiatric patients as 1.1 to 1.3 (Pierce & Drasgow 1969; Vitalo 1971), and for parents of emotionally disturbed children as 1.5 (Carkhuff & Bierman 1970).

While factors other than level of human relations skills undoubtedly do play a role in a person's psychological adjustment, and while many other ways to measure psychological adjustment also exist, evidence has been accumulating that a person's level of human relations skills is a meaningful measure of his psychological adjustment. Research studies have found level of human relations skills to be related to a variety of measures of psychological adjustment, including a paper and pencil test of self-actualization (Foulds 1969), high school grade point average, and a self-reported list of achievements (Frankel 1969), and ratings of "acceptance of disability" (Anthony 1973).

IMPLICATIONS

First, it appears that physically disabled clients are functioning at a slightly higher level of human relations skills than psychiatrically disabled clients. This finding is consistent with the fact that the physically disabled person usually becomes a client for reasons different from the psychiatric client. Typically, the physically disabled person becomes a client because of financial or physical dependence and not necessarily because of emotional or interpersonal difficulties. Yet because of the physically disabled person's financial or physical dependence, he may be encouraged to evaluate himself and enter into a quasi-therapy relationship when that was neither his intent nor his need.

However, based on the Carkhuff-Berenson model, the counselor with whom the physically disabled client may be forced to interact can offer him little or no effective counseling, and at times may be destructive. The implication of the model and related research for the agencies and hospitals who serve the physically disabled person through medical, financial, educational, and vocational assistance is clear: They should not conceive of their role as providing psychotherapy for the physically disabled client. The physically disabled person's financial and physical dependence should not be exploited by the agency to seduce him into a counseling relationship from which he stands to profit very little.

In the light of the research data summarized in Table 2, the issue of whether or not a rehabilitation counselor should function as a counselor or coordinator can be reexamined. The data seems to consistently indicate that rehabilitation counselors do not possess the skills needed to function as effective counselors. Whether or not their training provides them with unique coordinating skills is not known, but it would appear that the demands of society and the financial and physical needs of their clients require the rehabilitation counselor to at least function in a coordinating capacity. If, as Patterson (1968) has stated, rehabilitation counselors do not really wish to function as counselors, it may be because they feel they have not been trained to be effective counselors.

Other research studies (Engelkes & Roberts 1970; Truax & Lister 1970) have reported on the inability of rehabilitation counselors to have a more constructive impact on their clients than other master's level professionals or rehabilitation subprofessionals. These results are consistent with the Carkhuff-Berenson model and the data presented in this study which shows that rehabilitation professionals, other professionals, and subprofessionals (excluding nurses aides) all function at approximately the same level of human relations skills. As counselors in the traditional sense of the word, all groups are equally trained (untrained?).

HUMAN RELATIONS TRAINING

The implication of the data for the physically disabled client who must for financial reasons become a client is also clear: He should "take the money and run." In this client-counselor relationship it is highly probable that the client is functioning at a level of human relations skills that is similar to or higher than the counselor's.

While it appears that many professionals and subprofessionals (rehabilitation and otherwise) are not functioning at a high enough level of human relations skills to be able to have a constructive impact on the physically disabled client, this does not have to be the case. Carkhuff (1969a, 1969b, 1971) has developed a proven systematic human relations training program, capable of improving a person's human

relations skills. Just as the model dictates that individuals who function at higher levels of human relations skills can effectively help persons functioning at a lower skill level, these more skilled individuals can also train the individuals with lesser skills to function at a higher level.

This type of training program has demonstrated its ability to improve the human relations skills of various groups in their interactions with physically disabled individuals, including graduate students in a helping profession (Anthony 1971), rehabilitation subprofessionals (Crisler & Porter 1969), and nurses aides (Anthony & Wain 1971a). It is suggested here that not only should rehabilitation counseling students be systematically trained in these skills, but as Patterson (1967) has previously stated, they should also be selected on their present ability to communicate these human relations skills. Recent research studies have developed selection indices capable of predicting beyond a chance level those individuals most able to profit from a human relations training group (Anthony & Wain 1971b; Carkhuff 1969a, 1969b, 1971).

Results of still other research which has investigated one specific human relations skill (confrontation) seem to have implications for the training of rehabilitation counselors. Briefly, the skill of confrontation involves the ability of the counselor to honestly communicate to the client any incongruities which he perceives in his client—incongruities which in the case of the physically disabled client may have been precipitated or complicated by the presence of a physical handicap (Anthony 1970). By itself, confrontation is of negligible value, but when employed by a person functioning at high levels of empathy, respect, etc., confrontation can have a potent effect. A severely handicapped woman has described the dearth of such high level functioning people thusly: "There are, at least to my present knowledge, very few people who are sufficiently mature, stable, yet sensitive . . . and who are also willing to be fully honest" [Sutherland, 1968, p. 29].

The research into confrontation has indicated that counselors trained in rehabilitation are hesitant to confront a physically disabled client (Anthony 1970; Kenney & Anthony 1972). However, even counselors trained in human relations skills, including confrontation, appear equally as reluctant to employ confrontation with a physically disabled client (Anthony 1971). This lack of confrontation occurred even though the written history of the physically disabled client given to the counselors prior to their attempt at helping described several areas where confrontation would seem to have been appropriate.

The group trained in human relations skills, while able to function at a minimally facilitative level with a physically disabled client, were not able to be completely honest. Lacking extensive contact and knowledge about physical disabilities, their effectiveness with this particular type of client was somewhat reduced.

Thus, it would appear that if we are to train counselors who are willing and able to function at the highest level of human relations skills with a physically disabled client, the training approach must be two-pronged, combining education and contact with the physically disabled with human relations skills training. Each separately is a necessary but not completely sufficient source of training effect.

SUMMARY

The implications flowing from the Carkhuff-Berenson model and existing rehabilitation research into human relations skills and training suggest that the rehabilitation student, and ultimately his clients, could benefit from human relations training. It should be mentioned that no data have been presented indicating that present rehabilitation courses need to be deleted. Instead, the implication is that human relations training should become integrated within the traditional academic emphasis of rehabilitation training.

While the present review can be considered critical of the present status of rehabilitation training, it appears that master's level rehabilitation practitioners, contrary to the beliefs of McArthur (1970), are not functioning at a significantly lower skill level than doctoral practitioners. What does appear to be unique to the field of rehabilitation is its relative openness to self-evaluation. How much rehabilitation educators wish to be guided by the results of the research remains to be seen.

REFERENCES

Anthony, W. A. The physically disabled client and facilitative confrontation.

Journal of Rehabilitation, 1970, 36(3):22–23.

Anthony, W. A. A methodological investigation of the "minimally facilitative level of interpersonal functioning." Journal of Clinical Psychology, 1971, 27:156–157.

Anthony, W. A. The relationship between human relations skills and an index of psychological adjustment. Journal of Counseling Psychology, 1973, in press.

Anthony, W. A., & Carkhuff, R. R. The effects of rehabilitation counselor training upon trainee functioning. Rehabilitation Counseling Bulletin, 1970, 13:333–342.

Anthony, W. A., & Wain, H. J. An investigation of the outcome of empathy training for medical corpsmen. Psychological Aspects of Physical Disability, 1971, 18:86–88. (a)

Anthony, W. A., & Wain, H. J. Two methods of selecting prospective helpers. Journal of Counseling Psychology, 1971, 18:155–156. (b)

Aspy, D. The effect of teacher-offered conditions of empathy, positive regard and congruence upon student achievement. Florida Journal of Educational Research, 1969, 11:39–48.

Berenson, B. Confrontation in counseling and life. Champaign, Ill.: Research Press, 1973, in press.

Carkhuff, R. R. Helping and human relations: A primer for lay and professional helpers. Vol. I. Selection and training. New York: Holt, Rinehart & Winston, 1969. (a)

Carkhuff, R. R. Helping and human relations: A primer for lay and professional helpers. Vol. II. Practice and research. New York: Holt, Rinehart & Winston, 1969. (b)

Carkhuff, R. R.. The development of human resources. New York: Holt, Rinehart & Winston, 1971.

Carkhuff, R. R., & Berenson, B. G. Beyond counseling and therapy. New York: Holt, Rinehart & Winston, 1967.

Carkhuff, R. R., & Bierman, R. Training as a preferred mode of treatment of parents of emotionally disturbed children. Journal of Counseling Psychology, 1970, 17:157–161.

Crisler, J. R., & Porter, T. L. The effects and utility of training and using subprofessional rehabilitation personnel as group facilitators. Georgia Division of Vocational Rehabilitation, Project 629. Athens, Georgia: University of Georgia 1969.

Engelkes, J. R., & Roberts, R. R. Rehabilitation counselors' level of training and job performance. Journal of Counseling Psychology, 1970, 17:522–526.

Equinozzi, A. M. The process of rehabilitation counseling: Relationship of the facilitative conditions to cases closed rehabilitated. Unpublished doctoral dissertation, State University of New York at Buffalo, 1969.

Foulds, M. L. Self-actualization and the communication of facilitative conditions during counseling. Journal of Counseling Psychology, 1969, 16:132–136.

Frankel, S. D. Variables related to moderate and low discriminators and communicators. In R. R. Carkhuff (Ed.), Helping and human relations: Vol. II. New York: Holt, Rinehart & Winston, 1969. Pp 312.

Grand, S. A., & Stockin, B. C. The effects of group therapy on rehabilitation counselor trainee's empathy. Rehabilitation Counseling Bulletin, 1970. 14:36–41.

Kenney, J. P., & Anthony, W. A. The impact of experience and training in rehabilitation on the counseling relationship with a physically disabled client. Rehabilitation Research and Practice Review, 1972, 3(2):31–34.

McArthur, C. C. Comment on "Effectiveness of counselors and counselor aides." Journal of Counseling Psychology, 1970, 17:335–336.

Mickelson, D. J., & Stevic, R. R. Differential effects of facilitative and nonfacilitative behavioral counselors. Journal of Counseling Psychology, 1971, 18:314–319.

Morris, J. A. Empathic communication and acceptance of disability in rehabilitation clients. Unpublished master's thesis, George Washington University, 1971.

Pagell, W.; Carkhuff, R. R.; & Berenson, B. G. The predicted differential effects of high and low functioning counselors upon the level of client functioning. Journal of Clinical Psychology, 1967, 23:510–512.

Patterson, C. H. The selection of counselors. Papers presented at Conference on Research Problems in Counseling, Washington University, St. Louis, Missouri, 1967.

Patterson, C. H. Rehabilitation counseling: A profession or a trade? Personnel and Guidance Journal, 1968, 46:567–571.

Pierce, R., & Drasgow, J. Teaching facilitative interpersonal functioning to psychiatric inpatients. Journal of Counseling Psychology, 1969, 16:295–298.

Rubacher, R., & Woods, J. E. Therapeutic functioning level of students in two graduate rehabilitation counseling programs. Rehabilitation Counseling Bulletin, 1969, 13:184–189.

Sutherland, P. A. On the need of the severely handicapped to feel that they are human. Journal of Rehabilitation, 1968, 34(5):28–30.

Truax, C. B., & Carkhuff, R. R. Toward effective counseling and psychotherapy. Chicago: Aldine, 1967.

Truax, C. B., & Lister, J. Effectiveness of counselors and counselors aides. Journal of Counseling Psychology, 1970, 17:331–334.

Vitalo, R. L. Effects of facilitative interpersonal functioning in a conditioning paradigm. Journal of Counseling Psychology, 1970 17:141–144.

Vitalo, R. L. Teaching improved interpersonal functioning as a preferred mode of treatment. Journal of Clinical Psychology, 1971, 27:166–170.

35 Developing the Specific Skills and Knowledge of the Rehabilitation Counselor

William A. Anthony,
Peter Slowkowski,
and Lois Bendix

Rehabilitation counselor education, like most of the relatively older helping professions, has relied rather heavily on the teaching of concepts and theories. Rehabilitation counseling students have traditionally learned and been evaluated in such content areas as vocational development theory, counseling theory, and personality theory, and on various concepts related to medicine and psychological aspects of disability.

However, an applied profession such as rehabilitation counseling must be defined by more than just its theoretical expertise; it must also be defined by its mastery of a specific set of skills and facts, which, when combined with its theoretical component, make up a distinctive profession identified by a unique set of skills and knowledge. To achieve this end, rehabilitation course work must present a balance between theory and skills.

A recent article (Anthony 1974) focused on the need for rehabilitation educators to restructure some of the traditional rehabilitation course work to teach and evaluate more than just the accumulation of theoretical concepts.

In order to achieve this more balanced approach, we must develop new and different goals for some of the traditional rehabilitation courses. In particular, an attempt must be made to set specific, observable goals that can be used to measure objectively whether the course changed any of the students' physical, intellectual, and emotional skills. Not only does this setting of observable goals allow objective assessment of the value of the course; it also facilitates more systematic programming of the course to ensure the achievement of these observable course goals.

The present article is an evaluation of the experimental restructuring of a traditional rehabilitation counseling course, Psychosocial Aspects of Physical Disability. The three goals of the experimental version of the course were to change (a) what students do in interactions with persons who are physically disabled, (b) what they know about such interactions, and (c) how they feel about persons with physical disabilities. Each of these goals was defined so that changes in what students

Reprinted by permission from the March 1976 *Rehabilitation Counseling Bulletin*, pp. 456–462.

do, know, and feel with respect to disabled persons could be effectively documented.

MEASUREMENT
OF COURSE WORK OUTCOME

Changes in what students do in their interactions with physically disabled persons were assessed by casting each student in the helping role with a disabled client and then measuring the level of human relations skills achieved by the student. Also, as a further check of the students' human relations skills, each student wrote answers to 25 written problem statements made by a physically disabled client (Anthony 1973b). All ratings were made by trained raters using the Carkhuff five-point scale of overall facilitative interpersonal functioning (Carkhuff 1969).

Changes in what students knew about interacting with disabled persons were assessed in two ways. One method had each student rate the level of human relations skills of 60 written helper responses to the same 15 written problem statements. The students' ability to determine what constitutes a helpful response to a person with a physical disability could then be assessed by comparing his or her ratings to the ratings of experts. The knowledge dimension was also assessed by an 18-item multiple choice test designed to measure knowledge of how best to interact with persons with various physical disabilities. An example of an item follows.

If you are seated next to a visually handicapped person who is using a

seeing-eye dog you should (1) let the dog sniff your hand so the dog is comfortable in your presence; (2) pet the dog so the dog knows you will be friendly to him; (3) speak to the dog in a soft voice; (4) ignore the dog; (5) do 1, 2, and 3.

Changes in how students felt about persons with a physical disability were measured by means of the Attitude Toward Disabled Persons Scale (ATDP) (Yuker, Block & Young 1966). The ATDP test measures the degree to which the respondent perceives disabled persons as different from nondisabled persons (i.e., different in the sense of being "inferior" or "disadvantaged").

COURSE CONTENT

To the best of the instructor's ability, the course work was structured so as to change what the students were able to do, know, and feel about persons with a physical disability. The four major components of the course were as follows:

1. Ten hours of systematic human relations training as developed by Carkhuff (1971, 1972). Consonant with the overall goals of the course, there were two modifications in the training procedure: One of the cotrainers was blind, and students were asked to explore their experiences and feelings concerning persons with a physical disability while other group members practiced their human relations skills on them.

2. Persons with disabilities served as guest lecturers. They agreed on the correct answer to the test items relating

to knowledge about how to interact with persons with physical disabilities. The content of their lectures consistently covered the following three points: (a) barriers facing persons with a physical disability, (b) how they themselves are trying to overcome these barriers, and (c) how nondisabled persons can either help or hinder their efforts.

3. Each student was taught the skills of program development (Carkhuff 1974) and was required to construct a new program "in the interests of a person(s) with a physical disability." Some of the more notable programs that were constructed included an orientation program for blind students beginning their first term at the university, and a program designed to teach the proper use of crutches to individuals who had suffered minor but temporarily incapacitating leg injuries.

4. Each student was required to spend part of one day in a wheelchair and write about their experiences by focusing on the people barriers and architectural barriers they encountered, how they had tried to overcome these barriers, and what help nondisabled persons could have offered them.

MAJOR HYPOTHESES

The major hypotheses of the study relate to changes in what students can do, know, and feel with respect to interactions with persons with a physical disability:

1. Students will increase the level of human relations skills they can offer a physically disabled person, as measured by the ratings of a taped interview with a physically disabled person.

2. Students will also increase their written level of human relations skills as measured by the rating of their written responses to 15 written problem statements made by a physically disabled client.

3. Students will increase their knowledge about how to distinguish a helpful response from an unhelpful response, as measured by the average deviation of their response ratings from those of experts.

4. Students will increase their knowledge about how best to interact with a person with a physical disability, as measured by the scores on an 18-item multiple choice test.

5. Students will increase their positive feelings about persons with a physical disability, as measured by the ATDP Scale.

SECONDARY HYPOTHESES

The secondary hypotheses relate to specific training issues that can be examined through correlational analyses.

6. The impact of the course on student development will also be reflected on significant posttest correlations between the various course outcome measures. (This hypothesis assumes that students who are affected by the course should grow in all three areas of functioning.)

7. There will be a significant correlation between the student's pre- and posttest scores on each of the five outcome measures. Previous research has

shown that observable measures of student growth can be predicted from the student's initial level of functioning on these observable measures (Anthony, Gormally & Miller 1974; Anthony & Wain 1971; Carkhuff 1969, 1971).

METHOD

Subjects

The group consisted of 24 graduate students in a course in psychosocial aspects of physical disability. Most were rehabilitation counseling students; a few were registered nurses.

Procedures

Each student was pre- and posttested on all 5 outcome measures. The course met 5 times a week, 1 ½ hours per day, for a period of 6 weeks.

Human Relations Skill Ratings

Ratings were made by a trained pair of raters. Rate-rerate and interrater reliabilities were in the .90's.

RESULTS

The first five hypotheses concerning pre-post changes in the course outcome measures were analyzed with the use of the t test for correlated means. With the exception of the ATDP measure, all measures of course work outcome increased significantly ($p < .01$). Correlation data pertinent to hypothesis 6 indicated that five of the ten posttest correlations were significant at the .05 level. In contrast, only one of these correlations was significant at pretesting. Concerning hypothesis 7 there were

significant ($p < .05$) correlations between the students' pre- and posttest scores for each of the outcome measures, with the exception of the written human relations skills measure.

DISCUSSION

The course proved effective in changing four of the five observable outcome criteria it had been designed to affect. The course's nonsignificant impact on the ATDP scores may have been due to a ceiling effect, since, according to the suggested norms of the ATDP, the average pretest student score was at about the 75th percentile and the average posttest score at about the 90th percentile. Even though the results indicated no statistically significant change on the ATDP, it seems safe to assume that the students' post-course attitudes were indeed positive. It must also be pointed out that the present study lacked a control group. Thus the results of the study cannot be regarded as conclusive research evidence of the efficacy of the course.

However, the results do seem to suggest a number of advantages in the restructuring of rehabilitation course work in order to achieve more observable, concrete goals:

1. It gives students a concrete idea of what they are going to get from the course. For example, in the course described in this article students could be told that the goals of the course are to change what they do, know, and feel concerning their interactions with persons with a physical disability. More specifically, they could be told exactly

how changes on each of these dimensions would be assessed.

2. Because observable goals can always be evaluated, course instructors can obtain feedback and make course changes based on how well they are achieving these goals. For example, although nonsignificant changes in the ATDP may have been due to a ceiling effect, it may be that the students' contact with physically disabled persons who served as either guest lecturers or human relations trainers was not of sufficient interpersonal intensity to bring about a change in attitude (Anthony 1969; Yuker, Block & Young 1966). Also, students' final levels of human relations skills were below minimally effective levels (Carkhuff 1969), suggesting the need for additional training on this dimension.

3. In cases where enrollment in a course is restricted, selection can be based in part on the students' pretest scores on the course outcome measure. Numerous training studies, including the present investigation, have found significant correlations between students' pre- and posttest levels of functioning.

4. Observable course goals can facilitate the definition of what constitutes the specific skills and knowledge of the rehabilitation counselor (Anthony 1973a; Anthony, Margules & Collingwood 1974). Each course in rehabilitation counseling must attempt to identify, demonstrate, and evaluate the changes it brings about in the students that take the course. It may be that further growth and development of the field of rehabilitation counseling is,

in large part, a function of the extent to which rehabilitation educators are successful in this endeavor. The practice of rehabilitation counseling must be identified by something more than just degrees and certificates that indicate the successful completion of a certain number of academic credits and field work experiences. That "something more" may be training in a unique combination of physical, intellectual, and emotional skills that are presently duplicated by no other profession. The setting of observable goals for each required course in rehabilitation counseling could be an important first step toward developing the specific skills and knowledge of the rehabilitation counselor.

REFERENCES

Anthony, W. A. The effect of contact on an individual's attitudes toward physical disability. Rehabilitation Counseling Bulletin, 1969, 12:168–170.

Anthony, W. A. Human relations skills and training: Implications for rehabilitation counseling. Rehabilitation Counseling Bulletin, 1973, 16:160–168. (a)

Anthony, W. A. The relationship between human relations skills and an index of psychological adjustment. Journal of Counseling Psychology, 1973, 20:489–490. (b)

Anthony, W. A. Human relations training and rehabilitation counseling: Further implications. Rehabilitation Counseling Bulletin, 1974, 17:171–175.

Anthony, W. A.; Gormally, J. F.; & Miller, H. K. The prediction of human relations training outcome by traditional and nontraditional selection indices. Counselor Education and Supervision, 1974, 14:105–111.

Anthony, W. A.; Margules, A.; & Collingwood, T. R. Rehabilitation counseling: A decisive approach. Journal of Rehabilitation, 1974, 40(3):18–20.

Anthony, W. A., & Wain, H. J. Two methods of selecting prospective helpers. Journal of Counseling Psychology, 1971, 18:155–156.

Carkhuff, R. R. Helping and human relations (Vols. 1 and 2). New York: Holt, Rinehart & Winston, 1969.

Carkhuff, R. R. The development of human resources. New York: Holt, Rinehart & Winston, 1971.

Carkhuff, R. R. The art of helping. Amherst, Mass.: Human Resource Development Press, 1972.

Carkhuff, R. R. How to help yourself: The art of program development. Amherst, Mass.: Human Resource Development Press, 1974.

Yuker, H. E.; Block, J. R.; & Young, J. H. The measurement of attitudes toward disabled persons. Albertson, N.Y.: Human Resources Center, 1966.

36 Rehabilitation Counselor Education and Competency-Based Instruction

Joseph M. Steger

A two year master's degree program with traditional academic instruction supplemented by supervised clinical practice has been the standard for professional rehabilitation counselor education for nearly twenty years (Hall & Warren 1956). The appropriateness of this model has been questioned on a number of grounds (Anthony 1974; Olshansky 1957). Educators and rehabilitation administrators often seem to be in disagreement regarding the types of knowledge and skills which can be expected of a recent graduate, and it has been difficult to provide clear evidence of the effects of graduate education in rehabilitation counseling (Jaques 1974). In part, these difficulties and questions can be attributed to a lack of precisely defined objectives for rehabilitation counselor education programs. Objectives are typically not specific enough to allow evaluation of the extent to which program graduates reflect program objectives or to which program objectives reflect counselor effectiveness. Competency-based, instruction (CBI), with its emphasis on specification of demonstrable knowledge and performance standards, seems to be an attractive curriculum model in this regard. If the challenges of the CBI model are taken seriously and developed carefully, it has the potential to significantly influence curriculum, educational accountability, and even the professional identity of rehabilitation counselors. Certain basic concepts and implications of the CBI approach are highlighted here in an attempt to stimulate interest in overcoming the practical problems facing a careful test of CBI's potential for rehabilitation counselor education.

CENTRAL CONCEPTS OF CBI

The fundamental components of CBI include (a) careful specification of objectives in behavioral terms, (b) explicit focus on performance skills as well as knowledge, (c) selection of instructional methods strictly as means to the specified objectives, (d) criterion referenced assessment of each individual's mastery, and (e) individualization in the selection of objectives and instructional methods. Extensive use of modern instructional technology, use of a systems approach to program development and management, and packaging of instructional materials into modules are typical of CBI but not really essential (Houston & Howsam 1972). Setting goals and specifying behavioral objectives are an essential first step. Methods of developing goals and

Reprinted by permission from the June 1977 *Rehabilitation Counseling Bulletin*, pp. 260–266.

objectives and examples of cognitive, performance, and affective goals have been widely developed in related fields (Hartwig 1975; Horan 1972; Krathwohl, Bloom, & Masia 1964; Lechowicz & Gazda 1975; Mager 1962; Saylor 1976; Winborn, Hinds, & Stewart 1971). The logic of CBI requires more than just specificity, however. It requires that the objective include all the characteristics necessary for at least minimally effective professional functioning. The objectives should be tied rather directly to counselor behavior that benefits clients. Fairness and consistency further require that only those levels of competence that actually are necessary for acceptable professional performance should be mandated, but opportunities for superior students to develop greater than minimal levels of competency should be provided.

Individual responsibility is clearly spelled out in CBI. Once objectives have been set and assessment methods worked out, students must demonstrate the required levels of competence in the specified manner. Dedication, effort, maturity, attractiveness, experience, and educational background are relevant only to the extent that they help an individual develop the specified levels of competence. Competence comes to have a specific, carefully restricted meaning. Lack of competence, in turn, results only from the observation that an individual has not demonstrated a specified level of competence in an appropriate manner as of some date. It is no longer an attribution of undesirable traits or an unfavorable comparison with peers. Strictly speaking, no inferences should be drawn regarding an individual's potential from the observation that some level of competence has not yet been demonstrated.

IMPLICATIONS FOR REHABILITATION COUNSELOR EDUCATION

If these rather simple ideas are taken seriously they imply potentially substantial changes in rehabilitation counselor education. The typical pattern of courses and field experiences makes no sense from the perspective of CBI. Requiring 300 hours of agency experience, for example, may make administrative sense, but does not specify any particular set or levels of competencies. If competency levels are identified and assessed, it is quite certain that some students will have demonstrated attainment of the necessary levels in less than 300 hours and others will take considerably longer than 300 hours. Both efficiency and effectiveness of instruction imply individualization of time and tasks in internship placement. The realities of agency organization and function may make such individualization hard to implement. In addition, the old questions regarding time in the curriculum when field experience should occur, as well as prerequisites and the best means for integration of academic knowledge with performance skill may be expected to arise with renewed urgency (Houston & Howsam 1972; Kennedy 1976).

Assessment poses another set of challenges. Most current educational assessment is organized as courses are organized; that is, rather broad subject areas are identified to fit allotted time and interest. Classroom assessment is typically of unknown reliability and validity. It is basically normative; students are all presented with essentially identical stimuli and their responses are recorded and rank ordered. Since the process is very similar from class to class, the students are ranked with their peers several times. As a result the overall grade point average tends to be a pretty good indicator of students' relative standing. Since CBI emphasizes mastery rather than ranking, tests must be developed with much greater concern for reliability and validity. Separate competencies are assessed in each test so an overall average has no real meaning. Each individual test must adequately reflect the level and nature of the content domain it is expected to assess. Since testing is aimed at the required level of competence rather than the maximum level, moreover, there is no explicit way to recognize superior performance except through recommendations.

Criterion and instructional methods development may be expected to take a substantial time commitment. It is essential that the competence levels identified be acceptable to the profession, accreditation and certification commissions, the college or university, and potential employers of graduates. Moreover, they should eventually be tied in a demonstrable way to counselor behaviors which have been shown to be beneficial to clients. Consultation with all the above groups and testing of criteria in this context are necessary for the development of competence specifications and assessment methods.

Skipping any of these steps threatens the logical basis of the CBI model. Developing or adopting instructional materials is an additional time consuming task. Since not all students will enter a program with identical competencies nor learn at the same rate after entry, management of assessment and instruction is necessarily individualized. Faculty roles may be expected to undergo a shift as the problems of assessment, instructional module development, management, and educational planning with students become more important and traditional classes diminish in relevance. Not all faculty members will find these changes congenial (Jones 1972). In short, transition to a CBI model implies a great deal of faculty effort (Kennedy 1976; Houston & Howsam 1972; Stewart 1972).

POTENTIAL BENEFITS

The costs of implementing CBI appear rapidly once an attempt is made to go from the talking to the operational stage. The benefits are neither immediate nor certain, but do appear to be potentially substantial. Clarity of purpose, program objective, and responsibility resulting from a CBI approach should allow students, educators, and employers to know what they can expect. Students should have a clear understanding of what is required for graduation and what their skills will be. They can expect that there will be at least one effective instructional module for every level of competence they will be expected to show. Employers will know that every graduate who applies for work will have at least the minimum levels of competence necessary for professional functioning, and they will be able to turn their attention to other areas in selection and staff development. Educators will know what each student needs to learn and will have concrete evidence of how well the instructional modules actually work. They will be able to expect at least those employers they have consulted to accept their graduates as appropriately trained. An operational competency-based system would provide a structure for educational accountability and evaluation in which misunderstanding and *ad hominem* arguments should be minimized.

A variety of technical benefits may be expected also. Criteria development should clarify the extent of agreement regarding the components of successful rehabilitation counseling and more clearly indentify the uncertainties. Improvement of assessment methods should be useful for research and certification as well as suggest qualification procedures which could be used to recognize competence developed in other than academic settings. Effective instructional modules may be shared as their assumptions and objectives are made clear. Finally, the explicitness of assumptions being made about effective counselor performance required by CBI and the explicit commitment to tie competence to client benefit should improve the ability of rehabilitation counselor education to be self-correcting.

WHERE DO WE GO FROM HERE?

Since the apparently endless stream of difficult detail involved in establishing a well-grounded competency-based approach is more quickly discouraging than its benefits are encouraging, two outcomes are likely. Persons not convinced of the ultimate payoff may reasonably conclude that CBI is a nice idea which simply is not practical and may drop the effort. This makes sense for persons who are not interested in CBI, but does not clarify anything at all about its potential benefits. A more subtle threat may be posed by those who are committed to trying CBI, but when faced with apparently insurmountable resource limitations make poorly identified compromises and shortcuts. The experience in areas such as behavior modification suggests that unclearly labeled shortcuts may result in language confusion and inexplicable failures. If widespread, this will turn CBI into a fad in which the same old curriculum is presented in a new form but with few real improvements.

Since there are probably few institutions which now have the resources to develop and test a program thoroughly based on the CBI model, some form of collaboration seems imperative. At least two alternatives can be suggested. A variety of resources in the form of general competency-based program models in related fields (Houston & Howsam 1972; Zifferblatt 1972), tested instructional modules (e.g. Anthony, Slowkowski, & Bendix 1976; Danish, D'Angelli, & Brock 1976; Ivey 1974), and individuals who have expertise in the study of rehabilitation counselor effectiveness or in implementation of CBI programs already exist. Literally dozens of articles and books not referenced here provide suggestions, models, and methods. It may be possible to pool resources and divide up some of the tasks remaining. Certainly serious questions may be raised as to how this can be coordinated and integrated, but it may help provide potential components at least. Better results might be achieved if a few centers or consortia with clear orientations to rehabilitation counseling and a commitment to CBI were to be supported sufficiently to develop articulated, internally consistent models for testing and possible adoption. The most interesting results may come from supporting a few programs with distinctly different orientations. While most interest so far seems to be centered around behavioral approaches to counseling that suggest a sort of technician's model (Calia 1974), existential-humanistic approaches may also be developed (Arbuckle 1975).

A number of issues can logically be raised regarding these alternatives. For instance, it is certainly not clear that a complex interactive set of skills, knowledge, and attitudes such as typifies counseling can be developed piece by piece, nor that different people working independently will be able to develop the components of a useable system. It is not certain that all the facets of effective rehabilitation counseling have been conceptually or empirically identified. There are a number of professional and ethical standards which may or may not be expressible in competency terms. Important skills of integration, generalization and innovation may be difficult to recognize appropriately. In an important sense, however, these and related issues can best be answered by the experience of serious, well-supported attempts to de-velop CBI programs in rehabilitation counseling.

The data are not all in on CBI. It does seem to improve clarity and efficiency of instruction in some situations, but integrated programs and evaluations of the extent to which its potential is being realized are rare. In a field committed to evaluation and the development of a scientific foundation, a model with the potential of CBI should become neither institutionalized nor rejected without a substantial effort to test it. Even if all its potential is not achieved, appropriate investigation should at least provide better empirical grounds than now exist for identifying those areas of curriculum that can be improved by CBI.

REFERENCES

Anthony, W. A. Human relations training and rehabilitation counseling: Further implications. Rehabilitation Counseling Bulletin, 1974, 17:171–175.

Anthony, W. A.; Slowkowski, P.; & Bendix, L. Developing the specific skills and knowledge of the rehabilitation counselor. Rehabilitation Counseling Bulletin, 1976, 19 (3):456–462.

Arbuckle, D. S. An existential-humanistic program of counselor education. Counselor Education and Supervision, 1975, 14 (3):168–174.

Calia, V. F. Systematic human relations training: Appraisal and status. Counselor Education and Supervision, 1974, 14:85–94.

Danish, S. J.; D'Angelli, A. R.; & Brock, G. W. An evaluation of helping skills training: Effects on helpers' verbal responses. Journal of Counseling Psychology, 1976, 23:259–266.

Hall, J. H., & Warren, S. L. (Eds.) Rehabilitation counselor preparation. Washington, D. C.: The National Rehabilitation Association and the National Vocational Guidance Association, 1956.

Hartwig, J. E. A competency-based approach to adult counseling and guidance. Counselor Education and Supervision, 1975, 15:12–20.

Horan, J. J. Behavior goals in systematic counselor education. Counselor Education and Supervision, 1972, 11:162–170.

Houston, W. R., & Howsam, R. B. (Eds.) Competency-based teacher education. Chicago: Science Research Associates, 1972.

Ivey, A. E. Microcounseling and media therapy: State of the art. Counselor Education and Supervision, 1974, 13:(3):172–183.

Jaques, M. E. Testimony on behalf of the Council of Rehabilitation Counselor Education given before the Subcommittee on Depts. of Labor and Health, Education and Welfare and Related Agencies of the House Committee on Appropriations. 93rd Congress, 2nd Session, pt. 7. pp. 893–911, 1974.

Jones, H. L. Implementation of programs. *In* Houston, W. R., & Howsam, R. B. (Eds.) Competency based teacher education. Chicago: Science Research Associates, 1972, 102–141.

Kennedy, D. A. Some impressions of competency based training programs. Counselor Education and Supervision, 1976, 15(4):244–250.

Krathwohl, D. R.; Bloom, B. S.; & Masia, B. B. Taxonomy of educational objectives. The classification of educational goals, Handbook II: Affective domain. New York: David McKay, 1964.

Lechowicz, J. S., & Gazda, G. M. Group counseling instruction: Objectives established by experts. Counselor Education and Supervision, 1975, 15:21–27.

Mager, R. Preparing instructional objectives. Palo Alto, California: Fearon, 1962.

Olshansky, S. An evaluation of rehabilitation counselor training. Vocational Guidance Quarterly, 1957, 5:164–167.

Saylor, R. H. Managing competency-based preparation of school counselors. Counselor Education and Supervision 1976, 15:195–199.

Stewart, N. R. Counselor training systems: A figure-ground perspective. Counseling Psychologist, 1972, 3(4):63–66.

Winborn, B.; Hinds, W.; & Stewart, N. Instructional objectives for the professional preparation of counselors. Counselor Education and Supervision, 1971, 10:133–137.

Zifferblatt, S. M. Analysis and design of counselor training systems: An operant and operations research, perspective. Counseling Psychologist, 1972, 3(4):12–31.

37 "Real" Therapy and the Rehabilitation Counseling Student

Robert B. Slaney

For the last three years I have supervised rehabilitation counseling education students, primarily at the master's level, in one of their field placements. During this time, I have increased my understanding of rehabilitation counseling; however, having received my training in a related but different field, counseling psychology, I may retain something of an outsider's perspective. The following are some tentative observations and suggestions that may have relevance for others in the field.

The observation that concerns me here is the frequency with which I have heard students say that they want clients with whom they could do "real" therapy. On inspection, this type of therapy appears to refer to an insight-oriented, reflective style of counseling that places major emphasis on verbal interchange as the element leading to client improvement. Modes of treatment such as vocational counseling, skill training in community living or interview behavior, job placement, and referrals for education or on-the-job training are seen as less interesting and important. This perspective leads logically to a preference for persons with psychological problems who are "amenable to therapy," that is, clients who are articulate about their problems.

Also, there appears to be a belief that a significant and relatively rapid transformation should take place at some level, usually cognitive or affective, through which the client will be restored to previous levels of functioning or raised to higher and better ones. In summary, real therapy is a process that may be somewhat reminiscent of anecdotal reports of religious conversion, through which something fundamental, such as an individual's personality, will be changed.

I consider this belief in rapid personality change to be a myth. Although this myth is not unique to the world of rehabilitation students, there are some aspects of the setting in which I supervise students that help accentuate this myth and make it more readily observable. The setting is a veterans administration hospital inpatient unit where rehabilitation students interact with clinical psychology trainees. Within the setting, however, the training is quite different. The rehabilitation training focuses on basic counseling skills (e.g., empathy and understanding), skills training, vocational counseling and evaluation, and placement; the psychological instruments used are primarily empirical (WAIS, MMPI, SCII) rather than projective. The clinical psy-

Reprinted by permission from the March 1977 *Rehabilitation Counseling Bulletin*, pp. 202–205.

chology training focuses on short-term psychoanalytical therapy and projective testing. Although the rehabilitation students are not formally included in the psychology training, they are aware of it and free to attend lectures and case conferences. It is this clinical psychology training that helps to perpetuate the myth of real therapy by referring to the construct of personality as a stable entity that the therapeutic approach is designed to alter. That there is a paradoxical element in hypothesizing a stability and then attempting to alter it is not stressed. The important point is that the psychology students appear to be engaged in what the rehabilitation students see as real therapy.

An experience related to me by one particularly perceptive student illustrates my point. She had requested projective testing on a patient for whom she had primary responsibility. Even though she was aware of the research on the projectives concerning questionable reliability and validity, she was intrigued by the report. While she had a good knowledge of the person and a solid relationship with him, as well as a carefully reasoned and mutually agreed on plan, she remarked that after seeing the report she felt uncertain. She wondered whether the projectives were revealing the real person and whether the client needed something more fundamental than she was providing. Maybe he needed real therapy.

This feeling is not unique to the particular student described. An interesting contrast to the anecdote is the number of clinical psychology students who have questioned the relevance of what they were doing and expressed the feeling that the rehabilitation goals appeared obtainable and actually made differences in people's lives. What is revealing is that when statements like these have been related to the rehabilitation students, they have been pleased but also surprised.

In trying to convey my perception of this real therapy myth in supervision, I have found it necessary to clarify and support my position. Although more could be listed, I will mention only four points that seem most relevant to the training of rehabilitation counselors.

First, much of the literature on counseling and therapy appears to support the argument that basic and positive changes in people do not occur rapidly as a result of counseling interventions. The conclusion is not that change does not occur but that quick, major improvements are not the typical results of counseling outcome studies. The group study by Lieberman, Yalom, and Miles (1973) supports this point but also suggests that client expectations of dramatic change are correlated with negative experiences.

Second, the dearth of recent, global theorizing on personality, as well as the research on instruments to measure personality, do not inspire confidence in the conclusion that personality as a construct that has stability over time exists or is taken seriously by workers in this area. Rather, the personality literature seems dominated by mini-theories, discussions of traits and states, and interactionism, which includes situational factors as they interact with traits to effect behavior (Carlson 1975, Sechrest 1976).

Third, the experiences of counselors working in the field suggest that changes in counseling are not rapid but usually gradual and time consuming in acquisition, incorporation, and stabilization, and they seldom involve personality change as a goal.

Fourth, assuming it is possible to change an individual's personality, there appears to be a basic difference in the message conveyed by an approach that clearly suggests the client's personality needs to be changed and an approach that suggests the client has assets that need to be utilized more fully. Not only does the latter imply acceptance of the client by the counselor, it also involves a perspective toward clients that focuses on strengths and assets.

IMPLICATIONS

There is a continuing need to have students remain aware of current research, but one must also take into account the tentative conclusions of this research. The sheer number of current and projected studies raises the possibility that the difficult task of synthesis will not be accomplished without direction. Certainly, the conclusions suggested here are simplistic and subject to qualification. It appears more important that the task be attempted rather than any set of conclusions be agreed on. If not, the many existing studies remain separate from each other, sometimes interesting, but predictably forgettable and of questionable use to counselors.

I further suggest that experienced counselors discuss their experiences with student counselors. Although this may occur in practicum settings, it might be arranged before practicum experiences and in an organized way, albeit with some difficulty. Although even the most competent and conscientious counselors have clients who experience setbacks and failures, their case histories do not make exciting and inspiring conversations and are not placed in casebooks or cited in class. With the difficulty in establishing criteria for counselor competence and at least a real or imagined prejudice that sometimes exists among academics toward applied counselors, it may take a very healthy and self-assured counselor to present a realistic picture of rehabilitation counseling. The search for such counselors, however, would be worthwhile.

There are several issues worth raising that may help students think about the myth of real counseling. If one magically had the influence and ability to make whatever personality changes one desired in a client, what changes should be made? Would it be desirable to have such an influence and what would be the implications? Given the present state of our knowledge, what changes are possible? Can we, in fact, alter the hypothesized fundamental structure of the person? On the other hand, can we make statements about future probabilities for this client based on our knowledge? Can we use our knowledge to help clients develop skills that will allow them to capitalize on their assets or minimize their deficits? Or can we help clients place themselves in settings where assets and potential will have a maximum beneficial effect?

I believe that the latter goals are obtainable. They are consistent with the areas of research mentioned, and they are not mythical. The recent work of Goldstein (1973) and associates is a scholarly example of the use of research for establishing realistic and pragmatic goals.

An examination of the myth of real therapy by counselors and students will lead to an increase in the relevance and quality of rehabilitation services and an affirmation of the methods and goals of rehabilitation counseling. In essence, a real therapy appears possible without reference to a myth.

REFERENCES

Carlson, R. Personality. *In* M. R. Rosenzweig and L. W. Porter (Eds.), Annual review of psychology (Vol. 26). Palo Alto, California: Annual Reviews, 1975. Pp. 393–415.

Goldstein, A. P. Structured learning therapy: Towards a psychotherapy for the poor. New York: Academic Press, 1973.

Lieberman, M. A.; Yalom, I. D.; & Miles, M. B. Encounter groups: First facts. New York: Basic Books, 1973.

Sechrest, L. Personality. *In* M. R. Rosenzweig and L. W. Porter (Eds.), Annual review of psychology (Vol. 27). Palo Alto, California: Annual Reviews, 1976. Pp. 1–27.

38 Sexual Rehabilitation of the Spinal Cord Injured

A Program for Counselor Education

Martha Lentz Walker,
Robert P. Clark,
and Horace Sawyer

Research over the past few years has exploded the misconception that with spinal cord injury sexual activity ceases (Krusen, Kottke & Ellwood 1965; Talbot 1971). However, efforts to prepare rehabilitation counselors for counseling the spinal cord injured regarding their sexual functioning have been limited. Articles have been written detailing the information that should be discussed with the spinal cord injured patient, yet there are few available strategies for training the counselor to deal with the sexual rehabilitation of clients (Hohmann 1972; Tomko, Timms & Griffith 1972). This article shows how existing media and medical information can be used in an instructional sequence designed to decrease the avoidance reactions of counselors to discussion of sexual problems. Though the focus of the program is on the cord injured, the concepts (assertions) and procedures would be applicable to any severely handicapping condition.

Avoidance is perhaps a strong term for the behavior of rehabilitation counselors in the past. However, examination of our own sexuality supports Kempton's (1972) thesis that we have been traumatized sexually through the socialization process and have negative feelings toward our bodies and sexual behaviors. Couple this attitude with the fear and disgust many persons feel toward persons with physical problems, and avoidance seems a likely explanation for the lack of education for sexual rehabilitation ("Hostility . . ." 1971; Shearer 1972). Preparation of rehabilitation counselors should include experiences that enable them to discuss with clients any sexual problems that arise as a result of injury, retardation, or a disease process.

NATURE OF INSTRUCTIONAL SEQUENCE

A few pioneers have tried to restructure attitudes toward the sexuality concerns of the physically disabled ("Sex and the Paraplegic" 1972). The two films that are used in this instructional sequence are products of the National Sex Forum (1971) and are increasingly being used in sexuality seminars. Because these workshops and seminars are not widely available to rehabilitation students and personnel, this instructional sequence offers an alternative for counselor education.

Reprinted by permission from the June 1975 *Rehabilitation Counseling Bulletin*, pp. 279–285.

Both films, "Just What Can You Do?" and "Touching," have been used as a basis for discussion with varied populations, including medical students, ministers, and the spinal cord injured and their spouses. Participants in "attitude restructuring" seminars report initial anxiety and discomfort when presented with the visual and verbal stimuli in the film. Thus, using the film brings the issue of sexuality immediately to the forefront.

In this instructional sequence, positive conditions are built into the experience, including a discussion leader who is relaxed, pleasant surroundings, and ample time to "debrief." Participants are bombarded with words and visual cues having heavy sexual loadings, yet the aversive consequences they have learned to expect do not occur. The fearsome situation is neutralized, and future discussion of sexual problems should not result in avoidance behavior.

This instructional sequence has been developed, implemented, and revised over a period of two years with the help of graduate students in rehabilitation counseling and practicing rehabilitation counselors. The students and counselors have provided feedback regarding the structure and sequence in terms of their own learning. In addition, attitude changes in the participating students and counselors were evaluated by the use of a semantic differential, using related concepts. It was administered to the 15 participants before and after the use of the two films. Attitude changes indicated were promising, but the sample size precludes a definitive statement. A majority of participants in such sessions viewed the experience as worthwhile, suggesting that the sequence be included in rehabilitation counselor education.

A limitation of the sequence is the lack of existing media relating to the sexual adjustment of the cord injured female. Such a film is currently in the planning stages by the National Sex Forum. Collateral readings which have served to compensate for this gap include articles by Bors and Comarr (1960), Comarr (1963), Jackson (1972), Robertson and Guttmann (1964), and Romano and Lassiter (1972).

INSTRUCTIONAL MATERIALS AND REFERENCES

The program requires two three-hour sessions, a relaxed and informed discussion leader for every 10 participants, a comfortable setting equipped for 16mm projection, and two films: "Just What Can You Do?" and "Touching." Since the first film evokes less anxiety than "Touching," it is used during the first session.

Initial Session

Objectives
1. Following the initial session, the participants will recognize the importance of counseling for sexual adjustment with the handicapped.
2. At the close of the first session, the participants will identify the feelings and thoughts of the spinal cord injured toward sexual activity.

Introduction   The group leader presents the following assertions, encouraging discussion within the group and illustrations they have to offer.

Assertion 1: Handicapped persons have sexual needs. The group leader can use quotes from handicapped persons to emphasize this:

> ... the natural inference seems to be that the physically handicapped person is also a eunuch, a sexless being undisturbed by even the faintest of primal urges. (Chapman 1970)

Or a doctor's description:

> One day we convened a panel of wheelchair men for some of our residents. These men were in their twenties, and I was amazed to learn that if they had their choice between walking or their normal sexual function, they'd choose sex. ("Sex and the Paraplegic" 1972)

Assertion 2: Sexual functioning may become more important to physically handicapped individuals than it is to "normals." Again, a quote from a person with a handicap may invite discussion:

> Since we have been defeated on the physical level, it is on the physical level and on that alone that we can be wholly reassured. (Shearer 1972)

Or the leader may add the concept here that sexuality is composed of psychic, gonadal, and neuromuscular factors (Talbot 1971). Since the spinal cord injured may have lost the gonadal and neuromuscular factors, the psychic becomes all the more important. Gratification derived from psychological closeness and adequacy gained from sources other than procreation become highly meaningful to the person with a physical handicap.

Assertion 3: Discussions of sexual functioning are rare between professionals and those with physical handicaps. The leader can draw on Kempton's (1972) discussion of how our attitudes toward sexuality are formed, including early training and religious and cultural influences, to identify barriers to discussion. Public attitudes of fear and disgust toward the handicapped are intensified in the area of sexual relationships. The disbelief encountered by a nonhandicapped wife and a handicapped husband ("You have sexual relations with *him*?") is illustrative of the second barrier to discussion. The leader will find Shearer's (1972) article particularly helpful here.

Assertion 4: Openness to discussion of sexual functioning of the physically handicapped is an important competency for a rehabilitation counselor. The leader states that belief in this statement is the basis for these two sessions and prepares participants for viewing the film "Just What Can You Do?" by making the following statements.

"First, the focus here is on the spinal cord injured, but many of the issues raised would be applicable to persons with other physical handicaps (e.g., chronic renal failure, amputation, cerebral palsy).

"Second, this film is a discussion of three wheelchair patients and their mates and one single paraplegic female. Dr. Theodore Cole is the group leader. As you listen, try to identify the feelings of both the injured person and his spouse and their thoughts regarding sexual gratification after injury. What helped?"

The leader should be prepared to clarify some information presented in the film. Involuntary muscle spasm and catheterization are mentioned.

Symington and Fordyce (1965), Smith (1969), and Long (1965) explain these concepts fully. Intercourse, erection, and ejaculation are also specifically discussed in the film. The leader should be acquainted with statistics concerning the sexual functioning of the male spinal cord injured (Comarr 1970; Tomko, Timms & Griffith 1972). Though research is slim on female cord injured, the readings mentioned earlier will prepare the leader minimally for questions regarding female sexual adjustment. At this point, the leader shows the film "Just What Can You Do?" (22 minutes).

Postfilm discussion   After dividing the group into smaller groups (no larger than 10), the leader may launch discussion with the following questions:

What sexual needs were expressed?

What is your reaction to the patient who said, "The able-bodied person who understands is extremely rare"?

Would you agree with the man who said, "Culture accepts your backing out of life if your body is beat up"?

How do you feel now about the sex future of a paraplegic or quadriplegic?

What did they feel was most helpful in retaining their sexual functioning?

A discussion of approximately one hour arising from the questions above or clarifying information for the group should culminate in a summary for the entire group.

Summary   The leader can refer to statements in the film that the prime reasons for sexual inactivity of the wheelchair patient are ignorance of the partners and medical personnel and a

lack of verbal ability. Knowledge and developing alternative behaviors is compensation for loss of mobility. A counselor can provide information as well as practice in learning new behaviors.

The leader may foreshadow the final session by providing the following explanation:

"The final session will deal with explicit sexual expression. 'Just What Can You Do?' involved persons with high verbal ability. 'Touching' has no spoken dialogue and has been used with core injured patients to dispel their hopelessness about their sex future.

"Counseling strategies for providing information and strengthening new behaviors will also be explored in the second session."

Final Session

Objectives

1. Following the film "Touching," participants will discuss explicit sexual behavior in small groups.

2. Following the final session, participants can imagine themselves counseling with the physically handicapped for sexual adjustment.

Introduction   The leader recalls the prior session and the stress placed on the development of new behaviors (e.g., experimentation, verbal skills). The leader then poses the question of how to help low-verbal patients bridge that gap and suggests that "Touching" may serve as a modeling device for the acquisition of new sexual practices. The leader should allow time for any questions or reflections following the initial session but move rapidly into the showing of "Touching" following this orientation:

"Imagine yourself a newly cord injured male patient. Try to stay in this role while viewing the film. This couple has been together for three years. The man has a C-7 cord injury but has some sensation near the anus and the corona."

The leader should be prepared to answer several questions or guide discussion on key issues after the film showing. Value clarification techniques (Simon, Howe & Kirschenbaum 1972) would be helpful in discussing value-laden topics such as: Is sex outside marriage a possibility for the spouse to consider? Is artificial insemination a possibility for an impotent cord injured male and his mate? Is non-orgastic sex gratifying over time?

Information needs that must be met during discussion include some concrete considerations such as frequency of intercourse. Jackson (1972) has written an excellent article giving detailed information on most frequently asked questions. Though the cord injured male is the focus of "Touching," many questions arise regarding the female paraplegic. Comarr (1966) and Romano and Lassiter (1972) discuss menstruation, pregnancy, labor, and contraception thoroughly. Questions about divorce rates among patients with spinal cord injury are also to be anticipated. Comarr (1963) found that divorce after injury was slightly higher than the general population rate, reflecting adjustment problems. However, brides who never knew their husbands as physically intact have fewer adjustment problems. This article is ex-

cellent background reading for other data regarding marriage and divorce among spinal cord injured patients.

Alternate sexual behaviors such as fellatio, cunnilingus, and masturbation are used exclusively throughout "Touching." The leader should be prepared to refer specifically and correctly to these practices by name.

Postfilm discussion After the film "Touching" (14 minutes) has been shown, divide the larger group into smaller discussion groups of no more than 10. The leader should allow participants several moments to settle into their new location and to adjust to this new group. The leader might begin by asking who was successful in staying in the role of the cord injured patient (this is an anxiety reducing device, rarely accomplished). The following questions may be introduced, if they seem relevant to the group:

What feelings are you aware of in yourself now?

Were there any "turn-offs" for you in the film? (Stimulation of the anal region, an area where the male has sensation, is usually highly aversive.)

Were any questions about sexual functioning of the cord injured answered for you?

What questions were raised? (Inadequacy feelings are sometimes expressed here, through doubt as to whether the female was orgastic or was "faking." The sex flush on her breast may be noted here.)

What do you think would be helpful in the sexual rehabilitation of the cord injured? (The leader may introduce the idea of group counseling as described by Romano and Lassiter (1972); use of media such as "Touching"; assertive training for the female partner who must learn to be more active in a sexual relationship (Jakubowski-Spector 1973); and self-modification for the cord injured male who must learn verbal skills (Goldiamond 1973).

The leader should review the four assertions presented in the initial session and ask the participants how they feel about counseling with the physically handicapped for sexual adjustment. A natural follow-up to this instructional model would be the opportunity for each participant to talk with a physically handicapped person about his or her sexual adjustment. Such an experience would strengthen the desired response of informed and relaxed interaction.

It is hoped that these specific references and the tested sequence will enable others who are concerned about the delivery of sexual rehabilitation services to initiate such instruction and modify this outline to meet their needs.

REFERENCES

Bors, E., & Comarr, A. E. Neurological disturbances of sexual function with special reference to 529 patients with spinal cord injury. Neurological Survey, 1960, 50:191–222.

Chapman, J. Sexual potential of the handicapped. Active Handicapped, 1970, 1: 30–31.

Comarr, A. E. Observations in menstruation and pregnancy among female spinal cord injury patients. Paraplegia, 166, 3: 263–272.

Comarr, A. E. Marriage and divorce among patients with spinal cord injury. Journal of Indian Medical Profession, 1963, 9: 4181–4186.

Comarr, A. E. Sexual functions among patients with spinal cord injury. Urologica Internationalis, 1970, 25:134–168.

Goldiamond, I. A diary of self-modification. Psychology Today, November 1973, 7:95–102.

Hohmann, G. Considerations in management of psychosexual readjustment in the cord-injured male. Rehabilitation Psychology, 1972, 19:50–58.

Hostility to the handicapped. America, 20 March 1971, p. 287.

Jackson, R. W. Sexual rehabilitation after cord injury. Paraplegia, 1972, 10:50–55.

Jakubowski-Spector, P. Facilitating the growth of women through assertive training. Counseling Psychologist, 1973, 4:75–86.

Kempton, W. Guidelines for planning a training course on the subject of human sexuality and the retarded. Philadelphia: Planned Parenthood of Southeastern Pennsylvania, 1972.

Krusen, L.; Kottke, B.; & Ellwood, O. Handbook of physical medicine and rehabilitation. Philadelphia: W. B. Saunders, 1965.

Long, C. Congenital and traumatic lesions of the spinal cord. In L. Krusen, B. Kottke, and O. Ellwood (Eds.), Handbook of physical medicine and rehabilitation. Philadelphia: W. B. Saunders, 1965. Pp. 559–571.

National Sex Forum (Producer). Touching. San Francisco: Multimedia Resource Center, 1971. (Film)

National Sex Forum (Producer). Just what can you do? San Francisco: Multimedia Resource Center, 1971. (Film)

Robertson, S., & Guttmann, L. The paraplegic patient and pregnancy and labour. Neurological Survey, 1964, 53:381–387.

Romano, M. D., & Lassiter, R. E. Sexual counseling with the spinal-cord injured. Archives of Physical Medicine, 1972, 53:568–572.

Sex and the paraplegic. Medical World News, 14 January 1972, pp. 37–38.

Shearer, A. A right to love. Unpublished manuscript, 1972. (Available from The Spastics Society, London.)

Simon, S.; Howe, L.; & Kirschenbaum, H. Values clarification. New York: Hart, 1972.

Smith, D. General urology. Los Altos, Calif.: Lange, 1969.

Symington, M. D., & Fordyce, W. Changing concepts in the management of traumatic paraplegia. GP, 1965, 22:141–155.

Talbot, J. S. Psychosocial aspects of sexuality in spinal cord injury. Paraplegia, 1972, 9:37–39.

Tomko, M. A.; Timms, R. J.; & Griffith, E. R. Sexual adjustment counseling with the spinal-cord-injured male. Journal of Applied Rehabilitation Counseling, 1972, 3:167–172.

39 Continuing Education and Rehabilitation of the Severely Disabled

Dwight R. Kauppi

Although continuing education has always been important, the recent legislated emphasis on working with the severely disabled has highlighted the significance of continued education for the rehabilitation counselor. Rehabilitation of severely disabled persons requires several kinds of knowledge and skill, which can be gained in a variety of ways following employment. This article discusses some of the reasons for continuing education and suggests some of the ways in which it will facilitate rehabilitating severely disabled persons.

WHY CONTINUING EDUCATION?

Continuing education is thought of as any educational experience that occurs after the completion of preservice education and entrance into a job or profession. Continuing education is offered in many forms, including formal courses in universities, workshops, seminars, retreats, inservice training meetings, the informal staff training meetings at bag lunches in local offices, and the self-directed individual study that most professionals pursue by reading books and journals.

Continuing education is gaining greater importance in rehabilitation counseling and in other professions because of increasing obsolescence created by new knowledge, information, research, and techniques now being reported at an ever-increasing rate (Dubin 1972). The preservice education of the rehabilitation counselor becomes quickly outdated. Another complicating problem in a field that is still developing standards is the number of professionals who have entered practice with different educational backgrounds. These practitioners need an opportunity to develop basic skills while employed as counselors. One effort that has stimulated continuing education is the development of certification (McAlees & Schumacher 1974). As certification requirements mandate certain knowledge and competencies, practitioners seeking certification will require education to gain those requirements. Eventually, rehabilitation counseling will require some kind of certification maintenance, which may involve periodic reexaminations and participation in approved continuing education courses.

Another reason for the growing need for continuing education is the difficulty of meeting all projected professional needs in a brief graduate degree program. As the tasks and tools of the rehabilitation counselor have grown more complex, preparation for what-

---

Reprinted by permission from the June 1976 *Rehabilitation Counseling Bulletin*, pp. 587–596.

ever might be required has become increasingly difficult, thus frustrating educational institutions, students, and employers. Jones (1975) has pointed out that one of the benefits of increased continuing education requirements might be greater flexibility in graduate school curriculums.

Many of the needs for continuing education have existed for a long time. To meet these needs, the field of rehabilitation counseling has always had a substantial component of continuing education, which has included short courses, institutes, films, research and training centers, and other resources (CEPR 2, 1975).

Although a variety of training resources have been available, continuing education has not been uniformly applied. In the Studies in Continuing Education for Rehabilitation Counselors (SCERC), a survey of the inservice training participation of 345 state agency counselors from three midwestern states found that about a third of the counselors had no training involvement during the preceding year, whereas another third had more than five separate training experiences during that time (Miller & Roberts 1971a). Moreover, there was no apparent agreement among the agencies on the rationale for an inservice training program.

A further analysis of some of the SCERC data found differences among states in the topics and formats of training and in the amount of training conducted (Dickerson & Roberts 1973). It was concluded that inservice training goals needed to be clarified and a larger segment of the population reached, if the training needs of the counselors were to be met. The SCERC project

experimented with several ways of delivering continuing education programs and developed training materials that are still in use (Miller & Roberts 1971b). Some of the SCERC data suggested that those counselors who received inservice training perceived it as helpful. Richardson and Obermann (1972) found that only 6 percent of the 282 counselors responding said their inservice training was "rarely" helpful in performing their job, whereas 65.5 percent said it was "frequently," "generally," or "almost always" helpful.

Browning and McGovern (1974) have also noted the thousands of programs conducted since the 1956 passage of Public Law 83-565, which provided grants to support training. They collected data to assess the opinions and practices of training personnel regarding the technology of rehabilitation short-term training. Their list included 199 persons and agencies responsible for training, of which 86 completed and returned the questionnaire. The results suggested that rehabilitation short-term training technology represented only a small portion of the training technology available and that implementation of the technology and more effective program evaluation would serve as a major means of improving program quality and effectiveness.

Wilson (1974) has reported a similar diversity of inservice training practices among all the rehabilitation agencies in a large city. He collected data from all client-serving employees of 28 agencies, a 50 percent random sample of all agencies in the Buffalo, New York, area. Most respondents reported some kind of inservice training experience, and their response to training was uniform across disciplines. He found that the content of training was related to job titles and duties but not to prior experience and education. The most frequent complaint about training events was bad planning and execution.

Apparently, much training is being conducted, and administrators, counselors, and other rehabilitation personnel view training as worthwhile. However, there is a lack of the planning, coordinating, and evaluating needed to assure that the completed training is efficiently and effectively used.

A recent, important development has been the establishment in 1974 of the Regional Rehabilitation Continuing Education Program (RRCEP) by the Rehabilitation Services Administration (RRCEP Directors 1975). The RRCEP's mission is to coordinate and to create continuing education resources that meet the needs of public and private rehabilitation agencies in the United States. The RRCEPs have developed a variety of programs in response to regional needs. Their work falls into the following four major areas: (a) technical assistance in post-employment training program development, (b) development of continuing education packages or modules, (c) delivery of continuing education programs, and (d) coordination of continuing educaton resources.

Although no two regions are alike, some similarities exist among RRCEPs. All have assisted agency staff development personnel in the assessment and evaluation of training needs and resources, and all have offered training to trainers. Where gaps in avail-able content materials have been noted, they have assembled or created packages. All RRCEPs have conducted training on a variety of topics, and they try to coordinate training within their regions and among each other through several communication methods. Although it is too soon for a thorough evaluation, the RRCEPs represent a new, planned approach to the efficient provision of continuing education.

The problems involved in working with the severely disabled clearly illustrate the rehabilitation counselor's need for continuing education. Although the severely disabled have always been a concern of the rehabilitation counselor, recent legislation has mandated a refocusing of the state agencies on their work with the severely disabled (Randolph 1975). The rehabilitation process for the severely disabled illustrates the accelerating rate of knowledge through which highly specialized centers are solving rehabilitation problems only recently thought to be unsolvable. Revolutions in other fields have created revolutions in work with severe disability. For example, the miniaturization of electronic components now allows complex servo-control mechanisms to be used to control artificial appliances (Allen 1974). A counselor who was unaware of the latest practical techniques for any given disability might be depriving a client of a potentially successful experience.

WHAT TYPE OF EDUCATION IS NEEDED?

What kinds of education does the rehabilitation counselor need in working with the severely disabled? Etiology, natural history, and probable outcomes are important areas that should be known in relation to the disability; they should be thoroughly understood, along with any special vocabulary needed. The counselor should know the usual kinds of treatment and their expense and duration, along with likely results, options, and complications. In this way, the counselor will be able to time interventions optimally and provide realistic support for the client and family. The counselor should also know which members of the rehabilitation team are involved in working with a particular disability and the contribution each makes to the rehabilitation of the client.

The counselor should know which special adaptive devices and techniques are available. The difference such knowledge might make to the severely disabled can be dramatic, as in the potential of the development of a talking calculator ("A Breakthrough for the Blind" 1975). Through the combination of audio chips and other electronic circuits, calculators that give audio responses to every key press and that provide the answer to computations are commercially available. A technique that provides audio readout for any electronic unit that gives digital readout has also been developed. These innovations will allow persons who are blind to consider employment in a wide variety of engineering, technical, and electronic jobs formerly considered closed to them because of their inability to use calculators and meters.

Working with the severely disabled does not only require continuing education for attaining knowledge of other fields. Specialized techniques of

rehabilitation counseling may need to be assimilated. A crucial example might be the activity of job placement. Here, as in other domains, severe disability results in a severe reduction of options. A counselor without a knowledge of all the options might too readily conclude that job placement is impossible, and a counselor without the skills needed to provide effective placement might conclude that placement was not part of the role of the counselor.

Specialized techniques that help the counselor do placement include adaptations of specific jobs to specific disabilities, adaptations of job environments to specific disabilities, methods of job development, and the location or creation of jobs that can be done in the home. Basic techniques in job placement, job development, and job-seeking skills training are not necessarily known by every rehabilitation counselor, and therefore must often be taught (Housman & Smith 1975). Relevant laws, such as second injury legislation and fair employment legislation, can be important tools for the counselor (Thoben 1975).

In addition to all the tangible knowledge about medical, rehabilitation, and vocational aspects of severe disability, the counselor should know about its psycho-social effects and the types of interaction involved (Wright 1975). People differ with regard to personal resources and coping styles used to meet the various crises presented by severe disability. Counselors should be aware of the personal, family, and social problems likely to be faced and the mechanisms of coping that are used. In this way, they can be better able to judge when problems are being repressed, when defenses are inadequate, and when help and intervention are needed.

In the psycho-social area, technical advances can be important to the counselor, as new thinking and methods increase the options available to the severely disabled person. For example, techniques for developing a satisfying sex life are now available for severely disabled persons who formerly had to suppress or to ignore their sexual feelings. If rehabilitation counselors are to play a meaningful role in the total rehabilitation of the severely disabled person, they must know what can be done, and they must feel comfortable in discussing sexual problems with clients. Continuing education programs are available both to help counselors get the basic information they need and to deal with the affective aspects of this sensitive topic (Walker, Clark & Sawyer 1975).

Counselors cannot always be successful in their efforts to be empathic and understanding. The experience of severe disability is not close enough to average developmental norms to be sensed unless it is shared. Many counselors have found it enlightening to simulate disability in an experimental way by living the life of a severely disabled person, sometimes under the guidance of severely disabled persons. One program that utilizes simulated disability is conducted at the Institute for Independent Living (Leach 1975). It is important to remember that individuals differ and that not all severely disabled clients respond to a severe disability with the same feelings as those of a particular counselor simulating the experience. However, this limi-

tation should not prevent counselors from trying to explore their reactions and attitudes toward the experience of severe disability. Counselors' attitudes are of great importance, since counselors make decisions about accepting or rejecting clients, guide rehabilitation programs, and communicate with clients and families. In working to remove barriers or in providing further opportunities for rehabilitation for severely disabled clients, counselors may also need to serve as advocates with other professionals or the community. The decision to advocate is a difficult one, since it frequently means that the counselor must go against prevailing attitudes. Counselors always have the easy option of deciding that rehabilitation is impossible because the disability is too severe and the resources too meager. Their decisions depend not only on the knowledge they possess but also on their attitude toward working with severely disabled, whatever the facts in the case may be.

Counselors sometimes complain that knowing what the optimum rehabilitation program might be (one usually conducted in a metropolitan, university-connected, well-financed, medical rehabilitation center) is of no value to them in their day-to-day rehabilitation work, where the best may be inaccessible to many of their clients. Such an attitude is certainly understandable, but it is probably a misguided one. Knowing that more can be done under other circumstances is the only way to know that what is being done is not the best; dissatisfaction with what is done is a prerequisite for change. Counselors can influence the community to develop better rehabilitation services if they know and talk about what can be done and what is not done.

HOW CAN
EDUCATION TAKE PLACE?

With such extensive training and education necessary to work with the severely disabled, what kinds of options are there for ensuring that the counselor will have the necessary information, skill, and attitudinal perspective to work with such clients?

One system used in several places is the establishment of single disability centers, where the counselor can specialize in working with one type or class of severe disabilities. This allows the counseling staff to develop expertise regarding the speciality; indeed, it is at such centers that many of the advancements in rehabilitation and rehabilitation counseling have been made. Similarly, some offices assign specialized caseloads, allowing particular counselors to spend more time working with them and learning about them. In most settings, counselors do not usually have the option of such specialization. The typical rehabilitation counselor carries a general caseload and needs to know how to work with a variety of severe disabilities.

The essential base for working with disabled persons is a thorough knowledge of the rehabilitation process and of the necessary basics in counseling, including psycho-social and medical aspects of disability, vocational psychology, and the other topics that make up the core curriculum of rehabilitation counselor training. In the rush to obtain specialized training, the need for these basic rehabilitation counseling skills is often forgotten. Even if these skills are acquired in the best graduate training program, some of them will be outdated in a few years. Therefore, most counselors need to update their training through some kind of continuing education with the severely disabled, which may take many forms.

Much of the training in working with the severely disabled originates in centers specializing in the rehabilitation of particular types of disabilities, and relevant information is disseminated in various ways. Research and other reports are published in the professional literature; special publications are produced to share knowledge of new techniques with the practitioner; regular or irregular short courses are developed and conducted; and internships may be offered to allow intensive study. The training content developed by the special centers is often adapted and used in a wide variety of formal and informal training packages at local office, state, and regional levels. In addition, much of the work of specialized centers and projects has been included in recent efforts to increase the effectiveness of research utilization. Several special techniques have been used, including the establishment of a research utilization specialist in the state vocational rehabilitation office (Glaser & Backer 1975), visiting consultants (Butler 1975), regional research utilization laboratories (Soloff et al. 1975), and planned interpersonal informational exchanges (Kunce & Hartley 1975).

Although there is much to be learned and many ways to learn it, the fact that continuing education apparently is not uniformly or efficiently distributed has caused a problem. Unless the pattern changes, not all counselors will be well prepared to work with severely disabled clients. To bring about greater coordination, several issues need to be confronted. First, the knowledge and procedures used in working with severely disabled clients need clearer delineation. This will require not just informed speculation but a careful functional analysis. When counselors' current status on the same functional dimensions are assessed, training needs can be specified. When needs are known, resources can be made available and coordinated.

The locus and level of coordination are other issues. Few agencies have the resources to do the necessary training, need analysis, and staff development programming totally independently. Resources and responsibilities need to be shared among agencies. In order to work together, agencies must agree that their problems are similar enough to justify merged efforts, and they must exchange some of their autonomy to increase efficiency. Whether this coordination is best done at an interagency, regional, or national level cannot be determined without examining specific training problems. It is certain, however, that much more coordination, cooperation, and sharing of resources would be possible. Rehabilitation agencies are more alike than they are different, especially in the training needed for working with severely disabled persons.

Amidst all the regional and national concern for training, the individual counselor should not be forgot-

ten. The fact that some counselors get a good deal of training while others get none might have to do with differing reward systems. If continuing education is to reach all counselors, methods need to be found for making training more rewarding. It is important to use teaching methods that are not boring and to make sure that the counselor sees the relevance of the content. Some agencies base merit raises on participation in training. Several kinds of recognition may be suitable, such as certificates, continuing education units, letters in the personnel file, or simply personal recognition of effort by the supervisor. Successful and efficient continuing education will depend on finding ways of making the experience rewarding to all participants.

The most difficult issue in continuing education is likely to be evaluation. The first problem involves settling and specifying the general goals of continuing education and the goals of particular teaching units. In addition, it may be difficult to find a means of assessing the degree to which the goals are met. But unless evaluation efforts are seriously made, training cannot be improved.

Another aspect of training that is often forgotten is the interplay between agency operating procedure and the training of counselors. Agency administrators frequently seem to see continuing education as a means of solving problems without modifying agency procedures. They think that counselors will come back from their special training and be able to place more severely disabled persons, while the agency operations themselves remain the same. In fact, there is an interplay between the counselors' development and the changes in which they and the agency go about their business. Thus, counselors who learn to do new things will seek an agency that provides the opportunity to do so.

SUMMARY AND RECOMMENDATIONS

Severe disability presents problems of limited options, which may cause the counselors, as well as the clients, to succumb. To help clients find feasible options, counselors need to know about the disability, the rehabilitation process, the contributions of the team, and their own role. Counselors must have the skills necessary for fulfilling their role, including knowledge about the recent advancements in the medical and psycho-social aspects of disability and the latest in adaptive devices and techniques. In addition, some counselors may need training or retraining in the basics of rehabilitation counseling applied to working with the severely disabled.

One purpose of continuing education in rehabilitation of the severely disabled is to change the counselor's attitude. Counselors may be too ready to give up on total rehabilitation as a goal with severely disabled if they themselves are not convinced of its possibility. They will not be motivated to work with or to advocate for severely disabled clients, if they cannot see the possibility of success. Positive attitudes and positive motivation can come from learning what can be done and the way to do it; skill leads to confidence, and confidence to motivation.

Learning experiences may range from independent study of written materials to supervised practice in a workshop. Resources include the RRCEPs, research and training centers, and the many specialized disability centers and facilities. Continuing education is the responsibility of the individual rehabilitation counselor and of the agency training personnel and administrators. Planning is essential. There are many resources that can be coordinated to meet the needs of individual counselors and their agencies. Some agencies have developed individual continuing education plans for each employee, in which the strengths and needs of the individual are summarized, with short- and long-range plans for building the worker's skill by appropriate training. Such a plan could be devised by individual counselors for their own use.

As efforts to rehabilitate severely disabled persons grow, training needs will become more evident, and various training resources will attempt to meet them. The specialized centers and research and training centers will be important resources, as will the RRCEPs. As always, the key will be the individual counselor's demand for increased competence in meeting the challenges of changing rehabilitation.

REFERENCES

Allen, J. R. Technology advances the frontiers of rehabilitation. Journal of Rehabilitation, 1974, 40:15–21.

A breakthrough for the blind. Program for the Handicapped, November 1975, 26–27.

Browning, P., & McGovern, K. Technology of rehabilitation short-term training.

Rehabilitation Counseling Bulletin, 1974, 18:117–122.

Butler, A. Visiting consultant program for research utilization. Rehabilitation Counseling Bulletin, 1975, 19:405–415.

CEPR 2, Training resources directory. Buffalo, N.Y.: State University of New York, 1975.

Dickerson, L., & Roberts, R. Inservice training of rehabilitation counselors in state agencies. Rehabilitation Counseling Bulletin, 1973, 17:22–28.

Dubin, S. S. Obsolescence or lifelong education: A choice for the professional. American Psychologist, 1972, 27:486–498.

Glaser, E., & Backer, T. Evaluating the research utilization specialist. Rehabilitation Counseling Bulletin, 1975, 19:387–395.

Housman, R., & Smith, D. Placement for persons with severe physical disabilities. Rehabilitation Counseling Bulletin, 1975, 18:245–252.

Jones, N. F. Continuing education: A new challenge for psychology. American Psychologist, 1975, 30:842–847.

Kunce, J. T., & Hartley, L. B. Planned interpersonal informational exchanges: The RULE project. Rehabilitation Counseling Bulletin, 1975, 19:443–446.

Leach, P. Personal Communication, December 19, 1975.

McAlees, D. C., & Schumacher, B. Toward a new professionalism: Certification and accreditation. Rehabilitation Counseling Bulletin, 1975, 18(3):160–165.

Miller, L., & Roberts. R. Understanding the work milieu and personnel in developing continuing education for rehabilitation counselors, Report No. 2, University of Iowa, CERC Project, 1971. (a)

Miller, L., & Roberts, R. Rehabilitation counselor change associated with experimental continuing education programs, Report No. 3, University of Iowa, SCERC Project, 1971. (b)

Obermann, C. E. A history of vocational rehabilitation in America. Minneapolis, Minn.: T. S. Denison, 1965.

Randolph, A. The Rehabilitation Act of 1973: Implementation and implications, Rehabilitation Counseling Bulletin, 1975, 18:200–204.

Richardson, B., & Obermann, C. E. Inservice training and supervision: Meeting the new demand. Rehabilitation Counseling Bulletin, 1972, 16:46–55.

RRCEP Directors. RRCEP Directors discuss continuing education. Journal of Rehabilitation, 1975, 41:23–47.

Soloff, A.; Goldston, L. J.; Pollack, R. A.; & White, B. Running a research utilization laboratory. Rehabilitation Counseling Bulletin, 1975, 19:416–424.

Thoben, P. J. Civil rights and employment of the severely handicapped. Rehabilitation Counseling Bulletin, 1975, 18:240–244

Walker, M. L.; Clark, R. P.; & Sawyer, H. Sexual rehabilitation of the spinal cord injured: A program for counselor education. Rehabilitation Counseling Bulletin, 1975, 18:279–285.

Wilson, F. An investigation of the nature and correlates of in-service training for various manpower groups. Unpublished doctoral dissertation. State University of New York at Buffalo, 1974.

Wright, B. A. Social-psychological leads to enhance rehabilitation effectiveness. Rehabilitation Counseling Bulletin, 1975, 18:214–223.

AUTHOR INDEX

SUBJECT INDEX

April 28, 2010

To Janet

after reading my book you will understand my mission to never forget and never "let happen again the worst genocide of mankind"

Clara Knopfler

I Am Still Here

My Mother's Voice

CLARA KNOPFLER

Bloomington, IN   Milton Keynes, UK

AuthorHouse™
1663 Liberty Drive, Suite 200
Bloomington, IN 47403
www.authorhouse.com
Phone: 1-800-839-8640

AuthorHouse™ UK Ltd.
500 Avebury Boulevard
Central Milton Keynes, MK9 2BE
www.authorhouse.co.uk
Phone: 08001974150

First published by AuthorHouse 8/30/2007

ISBN: 978-1-4259-9113-5 (sc)

*Printed in the United States of America
Bloomington, Indiana*

This book is printed on acid-free paper.